Research Methods in Psychology
A Practical Introduction

Research Methods in Psychology
A Practical Introduction

Ronald A. McQueen
and
Christina Knussen

Prentice Hall Europe

London New York Toronto Sydney Tokyo
Singapore Madrid Mexico City Munich Paris

First published 1999 by
Prentice Hall Europe
Campus 400, Maylands Avenue
Hemel Hempstead
Hertfordshire, HP2 7EZ
A division of
Simon & Schuster International Group

Typeset in 10/12pt Stone Serif
by T&A Typesetting Services, Rochdale

Printed and bound in Great Britain
by Redwood Books, Wiltshire

Library of Congress Cataloging-in-Publication Data

McQueen, R. A.
    Research methods in psychology: a practical introduction / R. A.
McQueen and Christina Knussen.
        p.   cm.
    Includes bibliographical references and index.
    ISBN 0-13-899238-X (alk. paper)
    1. Psychology–Research–Methodology.   I. Knussen, Christina.
    II. Title.
    BF76.5.M39   1999
150'.7'2–dc21   98-31834
                                                                      CIP

British Library Cataloguing in Publication Data

A catalogue record for this book is available from
the British Library

ISBN 0-13-899238-X

1 2 3 4 5 03 02 01 00 99

Contents

Preface

For the vast majority of undergraduate students, the prospect of designing and carrying out a research project fills them with a certain unease, if not concern – a problem made worse by the fact that most current psychology and social science degrees now contain a compulsory component, of which research methodology plays a central role – which means they have to do it!

Part of the difficulty for students is a conceptual one – many people are simply unsure as to the precise nature and scope of research methods. For those with a grasp of the topic though, there is often little relief, due to the almost certain likelihood that somewhere along the line statistics will rear their ugly head. Add the general fear of numbers to the insecurity about research methods overall, and we have a surefire recipe for student angst.

While no one would ever try to make the claim that methodology and the statistical procedures which serve it are easy, there is no reason why the subject should be either intimidating or inaccessible. Regrettably, though, this is often the case since a great deal of what is currently written on research methods – and much of this is of an extremely high quality – is more suitable for teachers, academics and researchers, people who usually have considerable experience and a keen interest in the material. Often, however, this same material can prove too much for many students who lack experience, are mathematically weak, or for whom the topic of methodology is a requirement rather than an interest.

With these points in mind, and with the intention of offering a practical guide to designing, carrying through and indeed surviving a research project, the following textbook has been written. It is a book for students, based on many years of teaching statistics and methodology, and incorporating the experience of having supervised countless empirical projects, at introductory, honours and postgraduate level. It has been written with an understanding of, and sensitivity, to the concerns and misgivings of the majority of undergraduates, and in the hope that the study of research methods, and all that goes with it, will become not only an accessible activity, but a rewarding one also.

Acknowledgements

The authors would like to thank Alan Tuohy for his advice and encouragement during the formative stages of this book; Sharon Campbell and May Donaldson, our undergraduate reviewers for providing the student perspective, and those colleagues whose comments and suggestions have made all of this possible. In particular, many thanks to the following people for help on earlier drafts and especially for their comments on the qualitative elements: Margaret Flynn, Terry Mayes, Rosemary McIntyre, George Newbigging, Stephen Nicholson, Fiona Quinn, Tricia Sloper and Fred Yule.

We would also like to thank the group of anonymous reviewers who contributed immensely to our interpretation of research methods – in almost every instance their suggestions and corrections constituted an improvement to the text. To all of the above, we offer our thanks.

Introduction

The aim of writing this book is to provide, not only an introduction, but also a practical guide, to the planning, implementation and presentation of research. While the entry level and style of the material makes it accessible to any student of psychology, statistics and behavioural studies, irrespective of their degree level, the text is directed primarily at undergraduate students embarking, perhaps for the first time, on the treacherous course of designing and carrying out a major piece of empirical research.

Structurally, the book follows the accepted procedure for the conduct of any study, from the initial selection of a topic to the preparation of a final report. For the novice, this structure will in itself serve as a guide, leading from the conceptual processes involved in the development of ideas through all the intermediate stages of design, methodology and analysis, and offering real practical help whenever possible. For the more advanced student, each chapter can be regarded as an independent or modular unit, offering in-depth treatment of a particular topic, e.g., for the student already involved in the design of a questionnaire, there is a section on ethical considerations; for students at an earlier stage, there are sections covering decisions on whether or not to use closed or open-ended items. For those at the very beginnings of an experimental study there is help on distinguishing between independent groups and repeated measures – and other notorious design matters; and for students at the end of the data gathering stage, an introduction to analytical techniques is offered.

Fundamental to the entire book, however, is a sympathetic understanding of the student's approach to research methods. Several years of dealing with sobbing undergraduates have gone into the design of this text and an appreciation of the real difficulties experienced by many students is expressed at the beginning of each chapter, when a selection of typical cries for help are presented. It is our hope that, as far as it is humanly possible, these cries for help have not gone unanswered!

The structure of this book

This text is divided into a number of chapters, presented in the conventional sequence of activities which comprise a research project, such that even a student lacking a background in research methods, and without so much as an idea where to begin, can progress from the most basic of decision levels to the competent handling of data.

Each chapter deals with a specific topic and, although reference will be made to other sections, chapters can be viewed as stand-alone units. In addition to topic headings, an outline of the contents is offered prior to the main body of the text, and there is a review of contents at the end.

At the beginning of each new chapter, there is a series of comments, typical of the average student's perception of an issue, and reflecting commonly expressed queries:

'How do I start?'
'Where do I get numbers from?'
'What's the difference between a variable and a condition?'
'What questions should I ask?'
'Am I looking at differences or relationships?'
'Should I be writing any of this down?'

Far from an attempt at flippancy, the inclusion of such – albeit often humorous – statements is an attempt to say that we understand, and that we will do our best to resolve these issues in the text.

Where a statistical content is relevant, examples have utilised SPSS (Version 6 and upwards, applicable to both PC and Macintosh users) for both analysis and presentation. In all such cases, full explanations of procedures used, commands and hints have been offered – after all, the book is designed to provide a complete introduction, offering everything you need to get started.

What it will not do is provide mathematical proofs or detailed calculations involving formulae, and there are four reasons for taking this approach:

1. This is not a statistics textbook, rather it is a general introduction to the much broader field of research methodology. The inclusion of complex calculations would detract from, and might possibly impede, the attainment of its stated purpose.

2. There are currently many dedicated statistical texts available to students and it would be impossible here to more than scratch the surface of what is done so competently elsewhere. Consequently, and this will strike the reader almost immediately, there are hardly any numbers in this book, something which ought to allay one or two fears at least. Where appropriate, however, reference is made to a number of accessible statistical sources, and these should be consulted for a deeper under-standing of the material which is offered here only in introductory form. Indeed, it is hoped that many readers, wishing to more fully explore the concepts presented here, will actively pursue their interests in this way, since it is often only through the processes of computation that particular procedures can be fully understood.

3. With developments in software and the wide availability of computers, both at home and within colleges and universities, it is rare nowadays for

any student to attempt manual calculations of, for instance, t-tests, ANOVAs or correlations. (Fear not – these terms will be fully explained elsewhere). It is far more important that students understand the concepts of any analysis they undertake, recognising not just what a particular statistical test is doing, but also how and when to use it.

4. The actual experience of most undergraduates at the moment – and this is likely to be the future pattern – involves the interpretation of statistical outputs far more than actual calculations. To this end, we have concentrated on discussing various designs, the respective outputs available in SPSS, and how to make sense of them.

How to use this book

There are two ways in which this book can be used, depending on your own particular needs, your background and your experience in designing and carrying out a piece of psychological research.

For those of you new to research methodology, or to those just about to embark on your first psychology exercise or project, and who haven't a clue where to begin, the various chapters are laid out in the logical sequence of events, ideas and procedures which form the structure of all studies.

As a newcomer you need merely start at the beginning, at Chapter 1, where routes and suggestions are offered in terms of exploring theories, coming up with ideas and using the literature.

Once the idea for a workable research study has developed, the next part in the logical sequence will take you into the area of design: how a study might be carried out, what problems are likely to emerge and how to deal with them. As with all the major elements of the text, each chapter is subdivided into sections, dealing with discrete issues, and you may wish to merely dip in to particular topics, concentrating on those specific sections which are of interest. You will also find, within each chapter, various illustrative boxes, in which examples are given showing elements of the most common types of study available to undergraduates, e.g., in the formulation stages discussed in Chapter 1, you may decide on an area which is essentially empirical in nature; some of you may opt for a topic best explored via survey techniques, while others will be considering dealing with issues of a more qualitative nature. The function of the boxes is to offer real-life – and sometimes not so real – examples reflecting the content of each chapter and showing how the various issues might be dealt with in practical terms.

The other way to use this book is to selectively review those chapters or sections which meet your own particular needs at the time. This approach will probably be of most use to the more advanced student: you probably already have a research topic to explore, but don't know how best to design your study; you might have chosen a sample, but could use some guidance on how best to word questionnaire items; or you might even have gathered all your data and now need help in choosing the best analytical test.

For those of you in this position, the various sections are clearly labelled, both within the text and as an overview to each chapter, and sufficiently free-standing to answer most of your specific questions.

A note on style

An emerging issue within the psychology profession concerns the use of the term 'subjects' to describe those who take part in behavioural research. A growing number of researchers and academics feel that the expression is too impersonal, lacking in dignity and in some respects derogatory for those individuals who willingly give of their own time to participate in research. Indeed the British Psychological Society (1997)[1] has recently argued that the term be replaced with 'participants'; 'respondents'; 'individuals'; 'students'; 'children'. On the other hand, others feel that 'subjects' has been used quite dispassionately for many years merely as an identifier of the role taken by any given individual in a study, and to distinguish them from 'experimenters', 'observers', 'facilitators' and 'researchers'. In no respect does the use of such terminology imply anything other than a descriptor of the part played in a study. It is the latter view which has been adopted in this textbook, although the reader should be aware that the debate continues.

In reading this textbook it will become apparent that the authors have chosen to illustrate many of the ideas and concepts through the medium of humour. This is a deliberate ploy since we believe that complex and potentially intimidating material can often be 'defused' in this manner. This style of course will not be to everybody's taste but it should be pointed out that the approach is not intended to diminish or trivialise but is a serious attempt to introduce complex ideas in an accessible manner. Indeed, for every humorous anecdote there is usually a more sober example to act as a balance.

How to start

Option 1

If you've never tried to design an experiment or explore a research topic before, start at the beginning of Chapter 1 and simply read on.

Option 2

Alternatively, a summarised review of this process is shown in flowchart form, and some of you might prefer to think about researching a topic in this manner before looking at the more detailed sections on each issue. The flowchart also offers an at-a-glance view of what this chapter of the book is all about, and you can expect to find similar charts at the beginning of each of the major elements of the book.

Option 3

If you think you know what you're doing, but you have specific problems or questions, choose from the Contents section and you will find most of your queries answered.

The authors would like to thank SPSS Inc. for providing permission to reproduce screen-shots and output generated from SPSS software. Please note that SPSS is a registered trademark, and the product names are the trademarks of SPSS Inc. Material reproduced from SPSS 6.1.1 (Macintosh) [Macintosh is a trademark of Apple Computer, Inc. Registered in the US and other countries]; SPSS 6.0.1 (PC); SPSS 8.0 (PC). Reproduced with permission of SPSS Inc.

We would also like to thank the American Psychological Association for its advice and information on the PsycINFO® range of institutional products and services.

The authors are on the staff of the Psychology department at Glasgow Caledonian University, where they have taught research methods for a number of years.

[1] The Psychologist, 10, (7), p. 293.

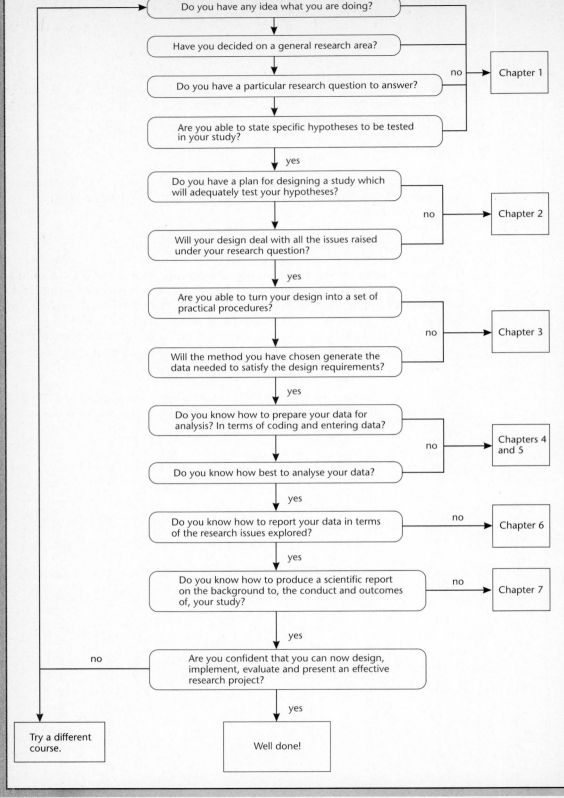

Notes

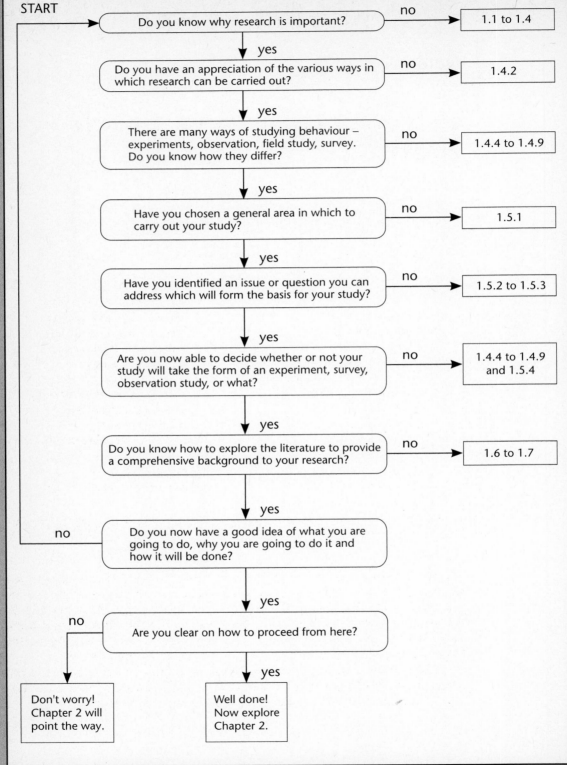

Flow Chart 1

START

Do you know why research is important? — no → 1.1 to 1.4

yes

Do you have an appreciation of the various ways in which research can be carried out? — no → 1.4.2

yes

There are many ways of studying behaviour – experiments, observation, field study, survey. Do you know how they differ? — no → 1.4.4 to 1.4.9

yes

Have you chosen a general area in which to carry out your study? — no → 1.5.1

yes

Have you identified an issue or question you can address which will form the basis for your study? — no → 1.5.2 to 1.5.3

yes

Are you now able to decide whether or not your study will take the form of an experiment, survey, observation study, or what? — no → 1.4.4 to 1.4.9 and 1.5.4

yes

Do you know how to explore the literature to provide a comprehensive background to your research? — no → 1.6 to 1.7

yes

no — Do you now have a good idea of what you are going to do, why you are going to do it and how it will be done?

yes

no — Are you clear on how to proceed from here?

yes

Don't worry! Chapter 2 will point the way.

Well done! Now explore Chapter 2.

CHAPTER 1

Introduction to research methods

'I have to do this research project but don't know where to start.'

'I have this idea, but don't know how to turn it into a study.'

Overview

- 📁 Psychology: definition
- 📁 Psychology: aims
- 📁 Psychology: scope
- 📁 Research and scientific method
  - 📂 the nature of research
  - 📂 scientific method
  - 📂 hypotheses
  - 📂 experimentation
  - 📂 observation
  - 📂 field studies
  - 📂 case studies
  - 📂 surveys
  - 📂 questionnaire-based research
- 📁 Beginning a research project
  - 📂 choosing a research area
  - 📂 the research question
  - 📂 proposing a testable hypothesis
  - 📂 deciding on a type of study
- 📁 Reviewing the literature
- 📁 Evaluating research
- 📁 The structure of a research project
- 📁 Review
- 📁 Explanation of terms
- 📁 Recommended reading

Chapter 1 introduces the concept of scientific research, discusses why it is important and examines the various approaches which can be taken. Specific guidelines are offered on how to commence a research project, exploring the background to a topic, conducting information searches and making initial decisions on the type of study to be carried out. For beginning project students, this chapter represents the starting point of the process.

The flowchart can be used to guide you to sections of particular interest. Alternatively, if the entire process of conducting a research project is new to you, you might prefer to work through each section in order.

1.1 Psychology: definition

Psychology is a relatively young discipline, not really arriving as a fully recognised sphere of interest until the early 1900s. Of course the work of people like Freud, James and Adler had been well publicised before this, but their approach to the study of the mind had been largely introspective, and primarily philosophical in nature. Even the apparently more rigorous approaches of people like Mesmer on hypnotism, or Galton on reaction times, lacked a proper understanding of their subject, or an appropriate scientific methodology to allow them to study it successfully. However, by the turn of the century, as individuals from backgrounds ranging from medicine to engineering, or working in areas as diverse as industry and education, began to recognise a shared interest in human behaviour, the discipline of psychology was born.

Today, a generally held definition of psychology is **the scientific study of human behaviour**, although this definition has to be extremely loosely applied, since psychologists are not just concerned with behaviour, but also with internal processes like thinking, judging and feeling. To further complicate issues, there are some instances in which the subjects in a **study** will be animal rather than human – occasionally there are practical or ethical reasons for using a non-human sample although the ultimate objective is usually to apply findings to human behaviour. And even here, this is a generalisation since there exists a respectable body of research whose sole aim is an understanding of animal behaviour in its own right.

1.2 Psychology: aims

The major aim of studying people is to increase our understanding about why we behave in the ways that we do. This is merely a reflection of other forms of scientific endeavour and is an expression of a general human curiosity about the world we live in. But there is more to psychology than mere understanding – like all other sciences, an evolution of understanding is part of the promotion of change, or intervention, for the attainment of some form of improvement in our environment. Fusion research for instance looks beyond an explanation of matter at atomic levels towards the possibility of a cheap energy source in the future; medical research has as its ultimate aim longevity and the elimination of disease. Similarly, psychology aims to apply an understanding of behaviour to an overall improvement in the human condition.

In this applied mode, psychology has met with mixed success. Certainly in the clinical sphere, huge advances have been made in the treatment of mental disorders, yet there are still many areas of mental functioning which remain barely understood. Likewise, in the occupational setting, developments in testing have dramatically increased the likelihood that the right people will be hired for the right jobs, but there is still disagreement as to what makes an effective leader, or whether or not personality measures actually predict success. There is an additional problem here and it is an ethical one: as with all forms of investigation, it is possible to abuse the findings of psychological research, to use them, not for betterment, but for exploitation and manipulation. The most appalling example can be found in the application of nuclear research to the weapons industry. But one might wonder whether it is any less exploitative for advertisers to use an understanding of human behaviour to persuade people to buy products which they do not need. This is an issue to which we will return later in the section on ethics.

1.3   Psychology: scope

Since the early days when psychology was seen as a loose collection of interests, limited by the methods available to its researchers, the field has witnessed unparalleled growth – growth reflected in its popularity as an undergraduate topic and by the sheer scope of the subject. Psychologists today find themselves concerned with learning, cognition, social behaviour, developmental processes, work, consumerism, language, abnormality, emotion and many other spheres of knowledge, too numerous to recount. Yet this should not surprise us since any discipline purporting to be interested in people will inevitably find itself concerned with virtually every single aspect of human endeavour. What links all these diverse threads of interest, however, is the way in which psychology approaches its subject, the unifying set of techniques, ethics and philosophy which comprise its methodology.

1.4   Research and scientific method

1.4.1   *The nature of research*

All scientists have their own particular view of the purpose of research, but essentially research is carried out in order to describe, explain and predict, with each of these reflecting a progressively sophisticated function. At its simplest level, research on any subject aims to describe a phenomenon or a process which has previously been inaccessible or only vaguely understood. For example, sleep, once an immeasurable and unfathomable activity (sometimes regarded merely as the absence of wakefulness) can now be readily described as a complex altered state of consciousness involving several stages or cycles, each associated with differing levels of brain activity. More interestingly, it is now possible to attempt to explain what is actually going on during these processes, and why they occur – at least, up to a point (more of this later). And finally, if these sleep processes have been accurately described, and if our explanations are indeed correct, we are now in a position to go for the big one: to make predictions, i.e., we can now suggest what will happen if we deprive subjects of sleep for a specific length of time, or what the effects on behaviour would be if particular sleep cycles were interrupted. Each of these activities – describing, explaining and predicting – represent the essential functions of research and are the goals of all researchers. But how are these goals achieved?

1.4.2   *Scientific method*

In order to understand a phenomenon, there are a number of things we can do. We can take an armchair, introspective approach and simply think about the world, applying our own past experience and self-knowledge. Much of what we believe to be true in life is based on this very approach – intuition, feelings or beliefs about the way things contribute to a large part of how we perceive the world and, as a rough and ready rule-of-thumb guide to life, it's not a bad approach: the superstitious belief that walking under a ladder will give us bad luck will at least prevent the pot of paint falling on top of us – or even the painter; the fear of flying many of us experience will prevent us becoming victims of an air disaster and our almost reflexive sense of danger in the presence of multi-legged creepy crawlies might prevent a fatal bite from the Australian funnel-web spider. However, reliance on such a scheme for negotiating life is by no means foolproof and can, in some cases, lead to a complete misconception of 'the way things are'. The gambler who, on observing a run of ten reds on the roulette wheel, places his entire savings on black (because it *must* be black's turn) is likely to leave the casino minus his shirt because his intuitive view of the probability of events is flawed. Like many people, the gambler has assumed that consecutive runs of the wheel are connected and that the laws of chance must eventually balance out. Similarly, the parent who, on observing two sunny weekends in a row, plans an outdoor children's party for the third, is inviting disaster. (The authors, showing a marked disregard for the British climate, can attest to this.)

Closer scrutiny of the flying example will also show the limitations of the intuitive approach since, in comparison to road travel, flying remains one of the safest modes of transport. And as for our poor arachnaphobic, unless he lives in Australia, that particular denizen is unlikely to be a problem, while most of the other species of wrigglers and scuttlers actually serve a useful function.

The point of all of the above is that the usual way we approach the world is flawed, subjective and judgmental. It may get us by, on a day-to-day basis, but it's not an approach designed accurately to describe, explain or predict. To be able to do this, we need a more rigorous, systematic and scientific approach to life. Which is precisely what the first scientists felt.

Science really only takes off where intuition stops; many of our ideas about gambling, flying spiders and the rest may well be true, but until they can be proved they remain at the level of heuristics, unsupported beliefs or even superstition. Science takes the next step and attempts to find this proof, using a methodology which has evolved over many years.

The starting point of scientific research is theory, and theory is simply a general set of beliefs about the way the universe, or a part of it, operates – nothing more or less than those very intuitions, rule-of-thumb heuristics and general beliefs discussed above. Theories can be vague, ill-defined and personal (I have this theory about why the dog does that...!) or they can be concise, well-structured and supported by a large body of evidence (as in behavioural learning theories). Either way, theories provide the descriptive and explanatory functions of research introduced at the beginning of this chapter. The major difference between theory and intuition, however, is that, while intuition is usually based on belief, feelings or even faith, theory is a much more systematic thing – any researcher attempting to develop a theory is constantly asking the questions: Does this describe...? Does this theory explain...? Consequently, a theory demands more thought and more enquiry than any heuristic: a theory will be based on observations, experience and the experiences of others; it will represent a balance of perceptions and information and it will be held up as presenting a better view of the world than possible alternatives. However, by far the most important aspect of a theory is that if it is correct, if it provides an accurate description of the world, then it will predict events which have not yet occurred.

1.4.3   *Hypotheses*

Psychological theories are always general views or propositions about people, representing the best descriptions and explanations we can come up with. We may have arrived at them through observing people, through thinking about our own behaviour, or through discussions with others who share our interest in the human condition. However, such theories will never develop beyond the level of being just one of many possible explanations, unless we can produce evidence to suggest that our theory is actually better than all the rest.

This is where the predictability issue comes in. If a particular theory represents an accurate description and explanation of events, it ought to predict what will occur or how people will behave in specific instances. Consider a theory of learning: if we believed that learning occurred simply by associating one event with another (a general theory) then we should be able to make a prediction, or **an hypothesis** about what would happen in a particular learning situation. Assume we were able to find a dog noted for its uncontrollable drooling at the sight of food: if our theory of learning held true, then presenting some other stimulus (say, the sound of a bell) every time the animal was offered food would eventually lead to an association between the two events (food and the bell). Ultimately the dog would salivate to the sound of the bell only. If an experiment along these lines were tried, and the prediction borne out, then we would have evidence in support of our more general view of behaviour. The more our predictions come true and the more hypotheses we can accept, the stronger our theory becomes. If our hypotheses are rejected, or our predictions produce contradictory results, then our theory weakens.

One important point to note here is that while it's all very well to propose hypotheses based on a general theory, unless the predictions which form a part of these hypotheses can be tested, then the theory will never develop. The theory that man evolved, not naturally from early mammals, but as a result of alien intervention and genetic engineering is all very well, yet unless we can come up with a way to test this view, the theory will remain forever at the level of idle speculation. The hypothesis that examining the DNA of Jurassic rodents would show up this tampering is simply untestable. (See 1.5.3 for further discussion on hypotheses.)

1.4.4   *Experimentation*

So far, the scientific process has been presented as a systematic development from general theories to more specific hypotheses. The next step is to consider how best to test these hypotheses. There are several options available to the researcher – surveys can be carried out, questionnaires compiled, observations made – the choice depending on a number of elements, such as the type of subjects being used, the context in which the research is being carried out, ethical issues and practical problems. However, the approach most often associated with psychology is that of experimentation, and this will be our starting point.

The very term, experiment, implies control; experimenters control all aspects of the environment in which a study is carried out (as far as this is possible). They determine the nature of the subjects taking part in their study; they decide on all tasks and activities which will form part of the experiment and control the sequence in which events are experienced. But why would such a high level of control be required?

At the risk of sounding obvious, human behaviour is extremely complex. Any single human act can be linked to and influenced by a multitude of factors, all of which are tangled up in such a way that it is often impossible to identify cause and effect relationships. A researcher studying decision making would find the mix of possible influences daunting – motivation would obviously play a part: we often choose things which will satisfy needs within us (a need to be loved, a need to be successful, etc.); learning too is important, since much of what we do is habitual in nature; and then there is perception, with different people seeing issues and problems in different ways. Gender too will be an issue, since males and females will have been shaped by their upbringing to have different preferences, while personality factors may lead inward-looking introverts rarely to select the same options as the more outgoing extravert.

Just think of your own decision to study psychology as a subject – all of the above factors would have played some part in your decision, as would attitudes towards the course, aspirations, availability and what your friends did. Clearly, if asked why you chose to do this subject, once you started to really think about it you would be surprised by the number and variety of contributory factors. This is why researchers, wishing to study such a complex process, may well choose to do so under laboratory conditions: here they can determine the type of decision to be made, control the environment in which the process occurs and restrict the many sources of variation among their subjects. Only then does it become possible to isolate and manipulate specific factors and record their impact on behaviour.

Occasionally some classes of behaviour are deemed too complex to be studied adequately even under the most rigorous of experimental conditions and in those instances, some researchers have resorted to using different, and much less complex, species. A great deal of what we now understand about learned behaviour has developed from studies on rats, pigeons and, in Pavlov's case, dogs – the rationale being that although the end product represents a universal phenomenon, in lesser species learning is easier to isolate and manipulate.

While experimentation is often seen as the backbone of any science, within a behavioural science like psychology, it is not without its critics. True, the method reduces the number of confounding, interrelated and sometimes downright nuisance factors which might interfere with an object of a study, yet in achieving this it is possible to argue that the essential nature of human behaviour has been lost. While there are undoubtedly some aspects of the individual which can only be studied under controlled laboratory conditions – functions of the brain, memory, the senses, to mention but a few – much of what we do as part of our day-to-day lives is a product of many interacting, interfering and contradicting factors. A laboratory experiment may well be able to tease out pure, uncontaminated cause and effect relationships, but often at a cost: consider that most experimental subjects are not 'real' people but (with apologies to our readership) college or university undergraduates. This group is not typical of the population at large: students are bright, motivated, young and, generally speaking, happy to volunteer to participate in an endless cycle of mindless experiments dreamed up by their professors and peers. Add this bias to experimental tasks created for their simplicity and ease of measurement, and all in a clinical environment free from outside contaminants, and you have – artificiality. In some cases experimentation can refine behaviour to such a point where all relevance to real life has been lost and it becomes impossible, or at least pointless, to try and generalise from experimental findings to the real world. A big enough problem when dealing with humans, but what do you do when your subjects are rats?

This issue is known, not surprisingly, as the **generalisation problem**, describing the sometimes problematic process of applying observations from one situation to another in which conditions might be quite different and for which the original findings might no longer be relevant. However, it also reflects a conflict between two methodological positions, or philosophies: that between reductive analytic approaches and an holistic perspective.

The classic, traditional method for studying just about anything can be described as adopting a reductive analytic model. This is a straightforward scientific approach whereby a given issue is reduced to its various components and the element of particular interest is then analysed. The examples of experimentation above reflected this view. In the early days of medical investigation, if you wanted to know how the brain worked, you got hold of a brain (discarding the rest of the body) and commenced an examination. This is largely why people still talk about the brain as 'grey matter' – dead brains, lacking a continuous blood supply, are grey. They are also, of course, dead, making it difficult to apply findings to the fully functioning, living organ. Similarly, nuclear research into the properties of electrons would have reduced atomic particles to their constituent parts, isolated the element of interest, and subjected it to analysis.

As an approach to investigation the reductive analytic method has merit. By removing a key component from its environment or context, you remove the possibility of contamination by other things. A good example here relates to early studies on leadership in which leadership situations – military, political and business – were reduced to their constituent components (which would include subordinates, type of task and other contextual factors), the leader isolated and then analysed in terms of his or her personality or behavioural styles (see Box 1.1).

The feeling was that leaders are constantly interacting with other elements of a situation, and variables like time constraints, task characteristics and type of subordinates will invariably reflect on how the leader behaves. It was argued that these other factors would fudge, obscure or contaminate the very leadership characteristics which were the focus of interest. As we have observed, however, these very 'contaminating' factors are what provide the essence of this behaviour in real life, and the activity of attempting to reduce an essentially social process to its components serves only to dilute and obscure that process. For this reason many early studies failed properly to describe and explain the actual interactions involved. In much the same way as Fatherhood can only be understood by looking at how fathers behave

Box 1.1 A typical reductive analytic approach

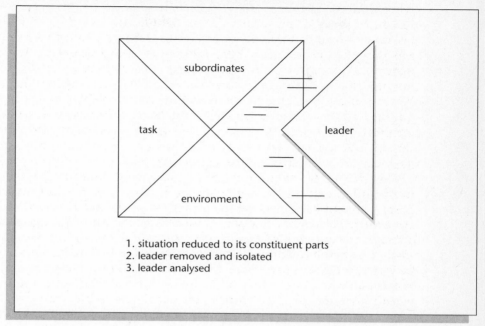

subordinates

task

leader

environment

1. situation reduced to its constituent parts
2. leader removed and isolated
3. leader analysed

within the family, so a true picture of leadership could not emerge until leaders were viewed within the context of specific followers and particular tasks.

This alternative, holistic view argues that any process which, in its normal functioning, interacts with other processes, can only really be understood when viewed in its context; the whole situation has to be considered, and not just its parts. Taking this particular view largely (though not completely) precludes the experimental approach. If we wish to study behaviour in its natural context, using real people, doing real things, then we have to adopt a different strategy, one in which the researcher does not become directly involved, does not manipulate and does not control. In this scenario the researcher becomes an observer, rather than an experimenter.

1.4.5 Observation

Observations can vary in nature from the kind of casual observations from which we notice, in an unplanned way, certain salient things about our environment, through the kind of naturalistic or ethographic observations in which animals are studied in their natural habitats simply to see what they do, to a systematic form of observation in which the researcher has a predetermined scheme relating to particular types of behaviours and structured methods for recording information (see Box 1.2).

This approach to the study of behaviour is truly holistic, in a way in which experimentation can never be. Subjects observed in their 'natural habitat' tend to produce more typical behaviours, a major implication of which is that findings of observational research can usually be generalised quite validly to other similar situations. Experimentation, as we pointed out, can produce findings which, because of the artificiality of the experimental set-up (subjects, task, context), can be difficult to generalise to real life. Quite simply, the further our research setting is from real life, the greater the likelihood that findings will be untypical.

However, before we go overboard in our praise of this method, it has to be recognised that, just as with experimentation, the factors which make observation so valuable a research tool also represent its major drawbacks. Observing behaviour in natural surroundings, without manipulation or attempts to control other factors, means that what we see will be a product of many interactions. Consequently, identifying cause and effect relationships will sometimes be impossible, because several contributory causes will be tangled up with one another. To further complicate the issue, it is not strictly true to claim that an observation approach allows people to behave naturally; often, when we become aware that we are being watched, our behaviour changes. Consider the common experience of passing a high street shop window and suddenly seeing yourself on a television monitor: almost without thinking, the stomach is sucked in, the shoulders pressed back and our normal slouching shamble replaced by a graceful stride. Or think of the student whose performance on a statistical problem improves dramatically when the tutor peers over their shoulder. Or the student's hapless neighbour, who falls to pieces in the same situation. There are many examples of this phenomenon, known variously as a 'mere presence effect', a 'social

Box 1.2   Some observations on observation

1. 'I noticed a funny thing in the bank today . . .' (the casual observer)

2. 'Good Lord! Look at that!' (the ethographer)

3. 'During a trial of twenty interactions, the number of eye-contacts between bank tellers and customers increased by 40 per cent when interactions were opposite sexed, compared to an average of 5 contacts per minute for same-sexed subjects.' (the systematic observer)

facilitation/inhibition effect', an 'observer' or 'experimenter' effect, and, in some situations, a Hawthorne effect, a name taken from an early series of industrial studies in which the impact of observers on work behaviour was noted. Whatever term is used to describe the effect, they all serve to demonstrate the same thing: the known presence of an observer invariably affects the behaviour of the observed in one way or another.

There is one final point to be made here, and it is an important one. Observation is, by its very nature, a human, judgemental activity in which we note when a behaviour occurs, and classify such behaviour, usually according to some kind of scheme. In planned, psychological research, we normally have a clearly defined set of behaviours in which we are interested, plus a logical plan for recording and coding what we see (see Box 1.2: Some observations on observation). However, because we are human, and since most of our everyday observations are coloured by a variety of factors – social, political, sexual, cognitive, motivational and so on, it is actually quite difficult to guarantee that what we apparently observe is actually what is happening. Consider the observation of a glance from one individual to another. If we are attempting to describe what has happened, how do we decide if the glance was casual, intimate, hostile, curious, friendly, aggressive, questioning, contemptuous, or whatever – or even if the 'glance' itself actually took place? We rely on experience, we seek other cues: e.g., was the glance accompanied by a smile? a frown? a raised eyebrow? We might even make a guess. In short, most forms of observation involve judgement of one kind or another and, as all psychology undergraduates quickly learn, human judgement is not something which can be wholly trusted (see Box 1.3).

It is important to point out, however, that many of the problems with observation methods can be dealt with: some through rigorous advance planning, and some through sophisticated statistical techniques which can effectively control for the influence of intervening factors, in an after-the-fact manner. Chapter 2, which deals with how studies are designed, will explore these matters more fully.

Box 1.3   The truth is in the eyes of the beholder

This was a triumph of skill over strength, of confidence over complacency, in which the opposing team was outmatched, outplayed and outperformed. There is no doubt that the best team won. (fan of the winning team)

This was an example of the worst excesses of football today, in which the winning team hacked its way to victory on the back of foul play and a blatantly partisan attitude from the referee. We were robbed! (fan of the losing team)

1.4.6   *Field studies*

It is obvious that the two normal methods of researching into human behaviour are not without their problems: an experiment usually has all the advantages of controlling for interfering factors at the expense of realism, whereas observation studies show the reverse – lots of realism, but no controls. There is however another approach which, potentially, possesses the advantages of both, while minimising the disadvantages – field research.

A field study involves subjects behaving in their natural surroundings, but with the researcher actively manipulating aspects of the environment and noting the outcome. This can be in a covert manner, in which confederates are used and unobtrusive observations taken, as in studies on pedestrians violating the red man 'don't walk' signs at street crossings in response to the behaviour of a model, or it can resemble a conventional, controlled experiment in which a group of production workers operate under a new type of supervisory regime and their output compared with that of an identical group, working under a standard management scheme. This kind of unobtrusive approach offers the researcher an alternative to experimentation and observation which goes some way towards handling the difficulties with the previous two methods. Field research though is not without its own set of drawbacks:

1. One of the guiding principles of psychological research is that subjects participate willingly, and under informed consent: i.e., they are aware of what is being done and, given that awareness, have agreed to participate. Furthermore, it is an accepted standard now that subjects have the right to withdraw from any research, without prejudice and at their own volition. There is also an expectation that subjects' rights on confidentiality and anonymity will be secured. However, in the kind of unobtrusive observation study common to much social research, subjects are usually unaware that their environment has been manipulated, nor do they know that their responses are being recorded, or even videoed. Consequently they are not willing participants in the study, they have not had an opportunity to give informed consent and, arguably, their rights to anonymity and confidentiality have been violated. This is an important ethical issue, which will be more fully explored elsewhere.

2. Where the research is more overt in nature, involving for example manipulation within a hospital, school or factory, various forms of experimenter effect will come into play, possibly interfering with the aim of the study.

3. Any research involving changes or manipulations within an organisation runs the risk of interfering with and undermining normal organisational processes, practices and procedures. Consequently, unless a study can guarantee minimal disruption, or unless there is a strong rationale for the

study, it is unlikely that such research would be permitted. Most organisations now support their own ethics committees, whose purpose is to safeguard their employees, patients and relevant individuals. Such committees nowadays are unlikely to approve research which is disruptive, unscientific or unethical.

1.4.7 *Case studies*

Most of the above discussions on the methods available to the psychological researcher involve experimentation with, or observations of, large numbers of subjects. This is based on the view that the more people for whom a prediction holds true, or across which observations are consistent, then the more likely we are to accept an hypothesis and provide evidence for a theory. However, there are certain situations in which it might not be possible to conduct research in the conventional way: we may only have access to a few subjects, or the event we are interested in may be so unusual that there are only one or two subjects to study – consider trying to investigate coping behaviour of mothers with sextuplets, or the memory problems of people suffering accidental brain damage, and you'll get the idea. In situations like this, a case study approach is often the only option available to the researcher – an attempt to gather information on an individual from as many sources as possible.

Case study data are usually highly descriptive, and may take the form of interview notes, observations, video material; they can comprise introspections, narrative and psychometric measurements – in fact, anything at all which can offer an insight into an individual might be used. The approach rarely involves experimentation in the usual sense of the word, but may involve observation of behavioural change over a period of time as a result of a particular form of, say, drug treatment or therapy. Not surprisingly, the case study approach has been most closely associated with the clinical sphere, but it needn't be, since any instance of novelty or limited subject numbers will lend itself to this technique: studies on the experiences of astronauts, of people who have encountered near-death phenomena or, indeed, of the mother with the large family, would naturally suggest this type of in-depth approach.

The beginnings of an investigation, or the exploration of a new area, might also benefit from the extremely detailed analysis of just one single subject – indeed, modern psychoanalysis is built on the personal introspections of the early theorists like Freud and the detailed case notes on individual patients. As a way of initially exploring issues, of gathering rich, descriptive data and providing the first steps in hypotheses generation, the case study approach is ideal.

As with all previous methods of research, the case study is not without its own problems. All the disadvantages of observer biases discussed earlier will also come to bear on the single subject case: an observer may well attend selectively to the information presented to him, may overvalue some events at the expense of others and may even be guilty of a form of motivated perception, if the aim of the study is to promote a favoured belief or theory. The subjects themselves, if relying on memory or introspection to provide descriptions of experiences and emotions, may fall victim to the many factors which influence our recall for past events. Not to mention the tendency, present in us all, to modify our view of the world and our role in it to play down anything which might show us in a poor light, or to modify our behaviour in terms of what we believe to be the researcher's expectations – a particular problem with the case study approach since the intensive nature of the relationship between the participants allows the subjects to study the experimenter even as they themselves are being studied.

There is a final problem here, already encountered during our brief discussion on experimentation: the generalisation problem. There are many reasons why it is sometimes difficult to expand findings from a study involving a sample to the population as a whole. We have already encountered some of these, and they include problems like the artificiality of an experimental situation, or the inability to control for interfering factors in an observation study. In the case study though, there is the added problem that there is only one subject, and it would be very difficult to make an argument for generalising observations on an individual to society as a whole. However, this is not necessarily an issue, since the purpose of many case studies is not to find out something about people in general, but about the individual in particular who is the object of the case. And where a broader perspective is the aim, a case study would be used only to provide a first, tentative hypothesis about human behaviour, which would be the starting point of a larger piece of research. For a fuller review of these issues, Chapter 6 offers an extensive introduction to qualitative techniques.

1.4.8   *Surveys*

A method of data collection which, in comparison to the other techniques available, is only sparsely used by psychological researchers, is the survey. Either as a kind of structured interview or in its more common printed, self-report format, surveys aim to generate primarily descriptive information. Consequently, the other stated functions of psychological research, those of explanation and prediction, tend to be inaccessible by this method, which is why the survey is not a commonly used instrument for many psychologists. For other researchers in the broader sphere of the social sciences however, or for those psychologists whose area of interest is social behaviour, the survey remains a primary instrument of research. From the massive government census which attempts to describe the state of the nation in 10-yearly snapshots, through the ubiquitous market research interviews occurring on every street corner, to the frenetic political polling which takes place in the lead-up to every election, surveys provide huge quantities of descriptive information. For the psychologist, however, concerned with hypotheses and theory, the quality of survey information is often too limited (proportion of the population who intend to vote conservative at the next election; what percentage of income is spent on leisure pursuits; how many households own a microwave, etc.), although there are statistical techniques which allow certain inferences to be made with such data. The main contribution of the survey tradition to psychological research is not so much in the type of data it generates, but in the rigours of its approach to data gathering. Sampling techniques, methods for dealing with bias in our subjects, ways of ensuring that a sample accurately reflects the population as a whole, all owe much of their development to the simple survey, and provide an important foundation for developments in the next, and last methodology to be discussed – questionnaire research.

1.4.9 Questionnaire-based research

A great deal of contemporary psychological research is carried out via questionnaire – not the simple, descriptive device of survey research, but a sophisticated test instrument which can contain items on attitudes, perceptions, thoughts, feelings and behaviour. Furthermore, when combined with other established instruments such as personality measures, stress instruments, measures of self-esteem or any of a large number of psychometric tests which have been developed over the years – many of which are in themselves a form of questionnaire – we have at our disposal an extremely powerful technique for not just describing, but also explaining, and predicting. A well-constructed questionnaire-based study can demonstrate relationships, explore differences and test hypotheses; in some respects it acts as an amalgam of observational and experimental approaches, with responses to questions serving as observations across a wide range of subjects. Moreover, if the right kind of information is sought, real cause and effect relationships can be examined, allowing for similar kinds of controls to be exercised as those used in classical experimentation – always remembering of course that what is being measured is not what people actually do, but what they *say* they do, a proviso which must always be borne in mind when interpreting questionnaire data.

An added advantage of the questionnaire however, is that, like the survey, it is a potentially quick, cheap and straightforward method of obtaining information: large numbers of questionnaires can be administered simultaneously and, if items are correctly constructed, data can be readily collated using various kinds of scoring keys devised by the researcher. Moreover, since

Box 1.4   A simple sample example

> Unbelievably, 95 per cent of our sample, representing the population at large, strongly agreed with the statement that the police in this country would benefit from increased powers of arrest, detention and personal exemption from prosecution. (questionnaires administered to a random sample of 200 subjects, outside Scotland Yard, London)

they require little in the way of facilities (laboratory space, computers, instrumentation, technical support) they are among the most readily implemented of research designs, and hence a favourite of undergraduate students everywhere. There is however a danger in assuming that because questionnaire-based studies appear easy, cheap and straightforward to implement, then they are in some way better than other approaches; some researchers would even go as far as to claim that, because of the nature of this method, it is almost impossible to obtain useful information of any sort (remember, questionnaires invite people to make judgements, state views and recall events, among other things, inviting the possibility of bias in all its forms). Other potential problems can arise as a result of the process of handing out questionnaires: as with surveys, unless the sample filling in our forms truly represents the group or population we are interested in, any results will be seriously flawed and unrepresentative (see Box 1.4).

And finally, returning to the earlier comment about the apparent simplicity of the questionnaire, it is useful to remember that, in this kind of research, you get what you ask for – no more, no less. The skill of asking the right questions and in the right way is an exacting one, and will be discussed in greater detail in the section on questionnaire design. (Chapter 3, 3.4).

1.5   Beginning a research project

1.5.1   *Choosing a research area*

This is where it starts: as an undergraduate student of psychology or another of the behavioural sciences, you are now preparing to design and implement a study – either on your own or as part of a group – and the first question to be dealt with is: where do I begin?

The starting point is normally the selection of a research area: Should the study be on the general topic of social psychology? Should it be on developmental issues? Or occupational? Forensic or what? How do you choose?

The simple answer is probably to begin with a general area which is of interest – one particular module in your course of study may appeal to you more than others and you might decide to conduct a study in this field, or there might be a contemporary issue which suggests a study to you: at the time of writing, current media topics are bullying in schools, attitudes towards the police and the problems of AIDS sufferers. Any one of these issues would represent an interesting and fruitful research area, and scanning the newspapers remains a consistent source of research topics for the student of human behaviour, providing the student's natural desire to tackle the great issues of life can be tempered by practical considerations. Personal observation is another potential source of research: you may have noted something about the way human interactions change inside a lift, or how people sometimes appear happier on sunny days than on rainy ones. Or perhaps a particular textbook has stimulated an interest in an issue (even reading this passage might have drawn you to the idea of looking at bullying in schools), or a recent article in a psychological or scientific journal might point to a new area of research. Even your poor, overworked tutors can be a useful source of mental stimulation: most university staff have their own pet research fields, and all of us are suckers for even a modest display of interest from students – it is only too easy to wheedle research ideas from academics who will be more than pleased to talk about what concerns them.

There is a special situation which, for some, offers a potential short-cut to research ideas, and it involves access to special subject groups: many students, for matters of conscience, or for financial reasons, find themselves involved with subject groups outside the normal student population – some work part time in offices, some do weekends for burger chains, while others offer up their spare time to help out in nursery groups or as volunteer carers. In such instances, access to particular groups might in itself offer a source of rich ideas – in addition to solving the perennial problem of finding subjects. Where such opportunities are available, they should be considered as extremely useful sources of inspiration, providing the ethical implications of doing so are understood; the step from convenience to exploitation is a short one... (see Box 1.5).

Box 1.5   Where the ideas come from

contemporary issues – press, media, societal, health
personal observations/theories
academic interests
journal articles
staff expertise
access to subject groups

Most students will readily settle on an area of interest from any one or a combination of the sources outlined above, but for anyone who still has difficulty choosing a topic, the simplest solution is to try a few of the approaches mentioned and generate a list of general topics. The next stage is to take each topic in turn and decide whether or not there is a specific aspect of this issue which is of interest – this becomes the research question.

1.5.2 | The research question

The research question acts as a kind of anchor for a study: it identifies the area in which the research is being carried out, it clearly defines the aim of the research and, very often, it also indicates any sub-issues which might be involved in the study. In many instances it will also dictate the nature of the study – be it experimental, observation or case-based.

For these reasons, considerable thought should go into formulating the research question. Get it right and it acts as a continuous reminder of what a particular study is all about and provides a guide through all the subsequent stages of design, implementation and data analysis. Get it wrong and you will flounder. A common problem with undergraduate projects arises when students approach the data analysis part of a study with no clear idea of what kind of analysis they should be doing, and why. Some of this can be attributable to a generalised fear of statistics within the student population, but much of it will also be due to having lost sight of the research question, or having a question which is too vague and fails to provide sufficient direction.

Generally speaking, the research question provides a statement of the overall aims of a piece of research and indicates, in broad terms, what you are trying to do. This is different from the previous exercise of selecting a topic area in which to carry out your research, a distinction which, unfortunately, is a continuous source of annoyance to undergraduates everywhere. Choosing a topic is, as it appears, merely the selection of which field you wish to work in: clinical, educational, social, or whatever. Constructing a research question, however, requires that you select a quite specific issue from within this topic area. For instance, you might be interested in the general, medical issue of recovery time following major heart surgery, having noted that such recovery is an extremely variable thing. This interest might subsequently resolve into the research question of 'What factors contribute to variation in post-operative recovery times', thus providing a starting point for the subsequent study, and a reminder of what it was all about. Such a research question identifies the area in which you will be working and also provides the important statement of what you are trying to do. However, the research question at this stage is still a relatively general thing. It requires refinement or qualification, so the next stage in the process is to turn our rather general question into something more specific – what precisely is it about post-operative recovery which we wish to investigate?

1.5.3   *Proposing a testable hypothesis*

The research question gives us our starting point, but before we can begin our study, we need to home in on something more specific: we need to refine our research question. Developing our medical example from the previous section, we now need to qualify the issue of what factors contribute to variation in recovery times. To assist this refinement, we may review previous research in the area, consult colleagues or refer to personal observations, coming up with a number of more specific questions, such as: Is personality related to recovery time, or self-image, or neuroticism? And are there other factors involved – do women recover more speedily from surgery than men? Do post-operative counselling schemes reduce recovery times? Does the kind of operation have an impact? Or the particular hospital in which the operation is carried out? All these are logical extensions of the original question, the difference being that they now offer something specific which can be tested – they offer the basis for experimental hypotheses (see Box 1.6).

1.5.4   *Deciding on a type of study*

We have already indicated that there are a number of ways to research an issue: we can design a laboratory experiment, we can conduct surveys, we can set up an observation study, and so on. The choice of which approach to take will involve a number of factors: do we want to study behaviour as it occurs in its natural habitat, without any kind of external interference or manipulation? Or do we want to control certain factors and study behaviour

Box 1.6   From the general to the specific

1. I'm interested in physical and psychological responses to traumatic surgical procedures (or what happens to people after operations). The general topic.

2. What factors contribute to variation in post-operative recovery times? The research question.

3. The mean recovery time (days) for Type A patients from a surgical procedure will be significantly longer than the mean recovery time from identical procedures (days) for Type B patients. The hypothesis.

in a more rigid environment? In most cases, the research area and the research question will point to a particular type of study, in others, practical or ethical issues will play a part. For an undergraduate study, a particular department might not have the technical staff or equipment to support certain projects, where others might be rich in audio-visual suites and observation chambers. For some studies ample numbers of subjects might be available, making a questionnaire-based project attractive, while for others, access to subjects may be so limited as to necessitate a case study approach. Whichever approach is chosen, however, they all require the same adherence to the principles governing scientific research: the study should be systematic, professionally conducted and with due respect for the rights of the individual.

1.6   Reviewing the literature

A fundamental part of any study is a thorough knowledge of the area in which the research is to be carried out and a familiarity with other research on the same or related topics. Without this information we would never know that our brilliant, ingenious project had actually been published two years previously, or that the paper on which we are basing our own work had been subsequently refuted by the original authors. Moreover, the essential, reasoned justification for our work would be impossible unless we were able to provide a balanced review of previous research in the area. And to be able to do this we must read, and read widely.

In some cases this might involve tracking down back copies of newspapers – some research is based on contemporary issues, with relevant material available through library sources, either as hard copy (i.e., originals), on microfilm or, where facilities permit, on a computerised system. Unfortunately, many students – and even highly qualified researchers – often ignore the rich reservoir of material available through the popular media; after all, television and newspapers provide an expression of society's concerns and obsessions and anyone hoping to explore a contemporary social issue, like attitudes towards AIDS, the police or the provision of care in the community, could do worse than review a few back copies of their local and national newspaper.

Textbooks, providing they are recent publications, also provide a useful source of background information, although it is in the nature of textbooks that the material covered is, of necessity, general in nature. However, they can offer useful reviews of topics of interest, in addition to providing sources of more specific reading in their reference sections – including details of key articles on which much contemporary research will have been based. It is worth remembering though that textbooks provide *secondary data* – they present, summarise and often interpret original, or *primary* work and it is not always the case that such interpretations fully reflect the intentions of original authors.

For many students of psychology, however, scientific journals will provide their main source of background and reference material, and in a burgeoning science like psychology, the sheer number and variety of journals is both intimidating and satisfying. Journals are regular publications (sometimes monthly, quarterly or annually) closely attached to particular scientific domains and comprising a collection of articles, reports and research papers reflecting current work in particular fields. The studies described and the reports presented offer information on current research which are about as up to date as it is possible to get. Moreover, before any material is accepted for inclusion in a journal, it is subjected to a process of peer review, in which other researchers and academics have the opportunity to (anonymously) comment, evaluate and offer suggestions for improvement. Consequently, for anyone wishing to explore a particular issue in any detail, journals will represent a key source of primary information. Typical contents of a journal issue might be an editorial, commenting on any particular trends or themes represented in the particular issue, a number of research reports on a variety of topics within the discipline and possibly a book review or two.

For established researchers, keeping track of relevant research in their own area is usually quite straightforward – by and large they will subscribe to a relatively small range of journals, reflecting personal interest and providing a locus for their own publications. For the undergraduate, however, perhaps embarking on their first major study, the wealth of sources and information available to them can be quite overwhelming. A cursory glance through any library catalogue of academic publications will turn up some 200 references to psychological research, presenting a hopeless task for the uninitiated. Fortunately, information management (librarianship, for the ignorant) has evolved to the point that even the greenest of undergraduates can negotiate the wealth of information available to them to find what they want. Most psychologically relevant material is regularly catalogued and entered into what are termed psychological abstracts – as the name suggests, this is a listing of the abstracts, or summaries of various pieces of research, and they provide a brief but concise review of what a study was about and what the findings were (see Box 1.7). Psychological abstracts (PA) are produced by the PsycINFO® department of the American Psychological Association (APA). It is a monthly printed index of journal articles, books and book chapters. Issues are organised by topic and contain author, subject and book title indexes. Annual author and subject indexes are also published to make searching easier.

For the computer literate, however, most university libraries now offer electronic search facilities which serve similar, if not superior, functions. One of the products of PsycINFO®, referred to above, is the CD-ROM database PsycLIT®. This is a (substantial) subset of the main PsycINFO® database and

Box 1.7   An abstract

Title:
HIV/AIDS and health care workers: Contact with patients and attitudes towards them.

Abstract
Data on the range of variables associated with contact with patients with HIV/AIDS and attitudes towards them were collected from 174 Scottish health care workers. Measures of attitudes and contact (overall, social and physical) were derived from the scales devised by Pleck et al. (1988). The measure of overall contact was not significantly related to attitudes, but those with predominantly social contact with patients with HIV/AIDS had more positive attitudes towards them. This relationship was moderated by occupational characteristics, and concern about working with people of unknown HIV status and neuroticism. With all of these variables controlled, including social contact, those who had not received in-service training relating to HIV/AIDS had more negative attitudes. The results are discussed with regard to the measurement of social contact with patients, salient beliefs, the occupational characteristics associated with attitudes, and in-service education. (from Knussen, C. and Niven, C.A. (In Press). HIV/AIDS and health careworkers: contact with patients and attitudes towards them. Pyschology and Health, Nov 98.) Reprinted with the permission of the authors and Harwood Academic Publishers.

it covers journal articles, books and book chapters, all updated quarterly. Access is normally via a networked personal computer or a library information system. By entering a few key terms a full listing of relevant abstracts can be displayed on screen, although care should be exercised in the selection of search terms – an unwary user who simply requests a search for any journal article with the word 'attitudes' in the title would spend weeks sifting through the mountain of returns. Selecting 'attitudes and police' on the other hand would generate a relatively small and much more specific selection of articles (see Box 1.8).

Other common sources of electronically-stored information are MEDLINE, which offers an index of international articles from medical and biomedical journals, ASSIA – Applied Social Science Index and Abstracts, which is concerned primarily with health and social services publications, and BIDS – Bath Information and Data Services. This latter service is now available through most academic libraries and provides access to a vast data store owned by the Institute for Scientific Information and through which access can be obtained to more than 7,500 journals world-wide. The search process is similar to that used for CD-ROM-based materials, except that the medium is the world-wide Internet, reflecting a trend which is likely to continue.

Box 1.8　A typical response to a CD-ROM search

Search: TYPE A AND SUCCESS
　6 of 6
AN: 1996-04764-003
DT: Journal-Article
TI: The stress of managerial and professional women: Is the price too high?
AU: Beatty,-Carol-A.
AF: Queen's U, Kingston, ON, Canada
SO: Journal-of-Organizational-Behavior. 1996 May; Vol 17(3): 233-251
JN: Journal-of-Organizational-Behavior
IS: 0894-3796
PY: 1996
LA: English
AB: Explores aspects of the relationship between career and emotional health and well-being for a group of highly successful career women. 193 Canadian professional and managerial women (aged mid-30s to late 40s) responded to a survey measuring organizational stressors, spousal support, work-family conflict, social support, Type A behavior, anxiety, and depression. Results indicate successful professional women did not exhibit higher levels of anxiety, depression and hostility, nor did these outcomes increase for women in higher level executive positions. Negative outcome measures were not higher for women with children, nor did work stress and work-family conflict interact to produce more negative health outcomes. The findings are consistent with the R. A. Karasek and T. Theorell model (1990) in which strain is hypothesized to be lower under conditions of high control rather than under conditions of low control. ((c) 1997 APA/PsycINFO, all rights reserved)
KP: career level and marital and parenthood status, emotional health and well being, highly successful professional and managerial females, Canada
DE: *Human-Females; *Middle-Level-Managers; *Top-Level-Managers; *Occupational-Success; *Well-Being
DE: Adulthood-; Marital-Status; Parenthood-Status
CC: 3640-Management-and-Management-Training; 3640; 36
AG: Adulthood; Thirties; Middle-Age
PO: Human; Female
LO: Canada
PT: Empirical-Study
SF: References
UD: 199701
JC: 2223
The above extract represents the standard output from a CD-ROM search of the PsycLIT® database. In this case, the information supplied is in response to one researcher's interest in the relationship between the Type A personality typology and career success. The key words chosen for the search were 'Type A' and 'Success', and the record produced can be explained as follows:

1. Six articles were found containing both key words, and the present outline relates to the last of these (6 of 6).

2. TI gives the title of the article.
3. AU cites the authors.
4. IN states the institution in which the research was located, or in which the authors work.
5. JN is the journal in which the article appeared, giving all the relevant details including page numbers.
6. IS is the unique International Standard number which identifies all printed material and is used as part of an international library catalogue system.
7. LA refers to the language in which the paper is written – in this case, English.
8. PY identifies the publication year.
9. AB identifies the text which follows as the abstract of the research as it appears on the original article.

The remaining abbreviations can be explained via an option available to the user.

Reprinted with the permission of the American Psychological Association, publisher of the PsycINFO® and PsycLIT® Databases (Copyright 1887–1998 by the American Psychological Association). All rights reserved. For more information contact psycinfo@apa.org.

In the event that our study is based on one specific piece of published research – perhaps the aim is to develop an idea, or explore a novel aspect of previous work – then our starting point would be the Science or the Social Science Citation Index. This particular index focuses on individual studies, and identifies any subsequent research which has cited the original. It is a useful method for following particular trends in a research area and it is also now available through the BIDS data service.

For those keen to review research in progress, but not necessarily published, the Internet now offers direct links to individuals in university departments all over the country; while still at an embryonic level, information pages are appearing every day, outlining interests, publications and ongoing work. It is conceivable that, within a relatively short time, surfing the net will provide the most direct route to current psychological research.

1.7 Evaluating research

Much of the foregoing has emphasised the need to read widely around a topic before embarking on the design of a specific study. However, simply consuming journals and textbooks in an effort to amass information is, in itself, not enough; when we read and consider the work of others, we need to do so critically, adopting a questioning, and sometimes downright suspicious, perspective. The importance of this stance is obvious when one considers that, for the purposes of research, we are not merely trying to find out more about an issue, we are also looking for flaws in a theory, limitations in the way a study has been carried out, or possible sources of development. After all, it could well be that the very limitations of an early study provide us with the impetus for our own work, yet we would never have identified those limitations had our approach not been critical.

Asking questions while reviewing the work of others is a skill most undergraduates are expected to acquire as they progress through a degree course – the trick is in knowing what questions to ask. In the field of psychological research, this process is possibly more straightforward than in other areas, due to the manner in which research is carried out. Earlier sections of this chapter emphasised the logical, systematic and scientific nature of psychology, and because the study of human behaviour now tends to follow an established structure, our questioning can follow similar systematic guidelines.

The first object of doubt in consideration of any study will be the literature review and background information cited in support of the research. We would want to know if the review seemed broad enough to provide thorough and balanced coverage of an issue:

1. Are there any aspects of the research issue which, in your view, seem to have been overlooked, or not fully considered?
2. Does the review provide a sound basis for the research question being explored?
3. Do hypotheses follow logically from what has gone before?

If, at any time while reading a rationale for research, we find ourselves saying: 'Yes, but what about...?' this could indicate a weakness or limitation.

If a review is broad in coverage, the research issue clearly stated and rationally justified, and the hypotheses logical extensions of what has gone before, the next area of concern is the design of the study. When we read this section, we are evaluating the plan drawn up by the researcher to examine the hypotheses. What we should be asking ourselves is:

1. Does this seem like a good way of exploring the issue?
2. Will all the considerations raised as being relevant to the research question be covered with this particular approach?
3. Does it seem practical to research an issue in this way?
4. Are there any ethical problems with this approach?
5. Is there a better way to do this?

Once again, if we find ourselves saying, 'Yes, but what about...?' then there may be some problem with the design.

If a researcher's plan or intentions for a study seem acceptable, the next thing we want to know is how well the plan was executed. Some studies, for instance, require many subjects, yet obtaining volunteers in large numbers is not always possible. Our judgement here would have to be whether or not failure to obtain sufficient subjects, or subjects of the right type, detracts from the study in any way. Generally speaking, close scrutiny of research procedure might highlight difficulties experienced by the researcher, or deviations from the original design which might lead us to question whether or not the research issue has actually been addressed.

When it comes to considering the results of a research study, many undergraduates find themselves bemused, if not intimidated, by the information presented to them. In part, this is due to the relative statistical unsophistication common among early students and, while this is a facility which will develop as the individual matures, there are always some research designs which rely on complex analytical procedures inaccessible to most students. There is also the possibility that a researcher, due to his own statistical limitations or (and this is thankfully rare) in an attempt to deliberately mislead, may present results which are ambiguous or incomplete. Either way, it is sometimes difficult for the student to make a judgement on the validity of research findings from consideration of the results. However, there are some guidelines which can be applied:

1. Are the results clearly presented – do tables and figures offer a clear indication of what happened?
2. Is it made clear that the hypotheses have been supported or refuted?
3. Do the results appear to address the issues raised during the literature review?
4. Do the analyses seem appropriate?
5. Do the data suggest some other form of analysis which has been overlooked?

Posing these questions will at least go some way towards evaluating the quality of research, yet this section of a published study will always be problematic since rarely will actual data be available to the reader. In most cases, if readers wish to look at actual scores or measurements, or even the precise calculations and computer outputs on which analyses are based, they must contact the researcher in question with a special request to look more closely at the data. Most undergraduates, reviewing literature for their own research, will be unlikely to gain access to primary data in this way.

The final discussion section of a published study is often the most interesting, for it is here that the authors can explore their results in greater detail, consider the way in which they conducted themselves and, generally speaking, review the whole issue on which the study was based. The kind of questioning we should be considering here might take the following form:

1. Have the authors effectively considered and explained the results, making it clear what the outcome of the study was?
2. Did any unexpected findings emerge and were the authors able to explain these in light of the research question originally posed?
3. Were the authors able to relate the findings to the research question?
4. If the study failed to support the hypotheses, are the authors' explanations convincing?
5. Have the authors recognised and discussed any limitations in their work?
6. If the authors have speculated about their research findings, does this speculation seem justified?
7. Does the study overall add anything to our understanding of the original issue?

All of the above examples merely represent typical questions which the student might ask of a piece of psychological research – the list is not exhaustive, and not all of these issues will be relevant to every study. The point though is that we should get into the habit of approaching published material from a critical point of view, an approach which will not only offer us an improved understanding of other people's work, but which might make us more professional in our own. After all, anything which we ourselves might someday publish will be viewed from precisely this critical perspective.

1.8 The structure of a research project

By now, if you have read the preceding sections, you will have a good idea of how a research project is carried out. This final section presents an outline of the main steps:

1. Selection of a field in which to carry out a study.
2. Carrying out a literature review on the topic.
3. Statement of a research question (what is the study trying to do).
4. Providing a rationale for the research question.
5. Refining your rationale into a number of specific, and testable hypotheses.
6. Designing and planning an appropriate way of testing your hypotheses.
7. Implementing your plan and gathering data (carrying out the study).
8. Analysing your data and presenting the results of the study.
9. Discussing your data, reappraising the research question in the light of your findings and considering the entire rationale, conduct and theoretical basis for your study.

`1.9`   Review

This chapter has attempted to provide an overview of psychological research, explaining the reasons for carrying out such research, and providing a general guide to the various processes and limitations of the many different approaches which can be taken to the study of human behaviour. The chapters which follow take a more detailed look at the design and conduct of research.

`1.10`   Explanation of terms

Case study   An intensive and detailed study of a very small number of subjects – and sometimes only one – usually over a period of time. The case study is a common qualitative approach.

Experiment   A procedure for gathering data which involves an experimenter manipulating key aspects of a study, such as the way in which subjects are assigned to groups, the experiences they encounter and the way in which measures are taken.

Field study   A procedure for gathering data in which the researcher manipulates key factors within a natural setting.

Generalisation problem   A common difficulty in research in which the findings of a study might not be typical of, or generalisable to, the world at large.

Hypothesis   A specific prediction about some aspect of the universe, based on the more general beliefs which comprise a theory, e.g., 'There will be a significant difference in the mean performance scores of a group of male and female subjects tested on a choice-dilemma problem solving task.'

Observation study   A procedure for gathering data in which the researcher does not manipulate key elements of a study, but instead observes behaviour as it occurs naturally.

Project   An undertaking (for the purposes of this textbook) whereby a study is devised and carried out as part of a formal undergraduate course. Such an undertaking is usually assessable.

Research   A process of investigating, scrutinising or studying an issue, usually conducted according to a set of predetermined guidelines and procedures.

Research area   The general area of interest in which the research is carried out, e.g., cognitive, developmental, occupational.

Research question   A general issue within an area of interest which provides the basis for a study, e.g., 'Are there sex differences in certain elements of cognitive functioning?' Sometimes referred to as the research issue.

Study A planned investigation of a specified topic or issue involving a systematic process of reading, exploration, experimentation and research.

Scientific method A set of established procedures for the conduct of research, common to all disciplines. These are the procedures referred to in **Research** above.

Theory A general set of beliefs about some aspect of the universe which may or may not be supported by evidence, e.g., 'Women are superior to men in most aspects of cognitive functioning.'

1.11 Recommended reading

Coolican, H. (1996). *Introduction to Research Methods and Statistics in Psychology.* London: Hodder & Stoughton.

Dracup, C. (1995). Hypothesis testing – what it really is. *The Psychologist*, **8**, 359–362.

Horn, R. (1996). Negotiating research access to organisations. *The Psychologist*, **9**, 551–554.

Lindsay, G. and Colley, A. (1995). Ethical dilemmas of members of the society. *The Psychologist*, **8**, 448–453.

Morgan, M. (1996). Qualitative research: A Package deal? *The Psychologist*, **9**, 31–32.

Robson, C. (1993). *Real World Research.* Oxford: Blackwell.

Stevenson, C. and Cooper, N. (1997). Qualitative and quantitative research. *The Psychologist*, **10**, 159–160.

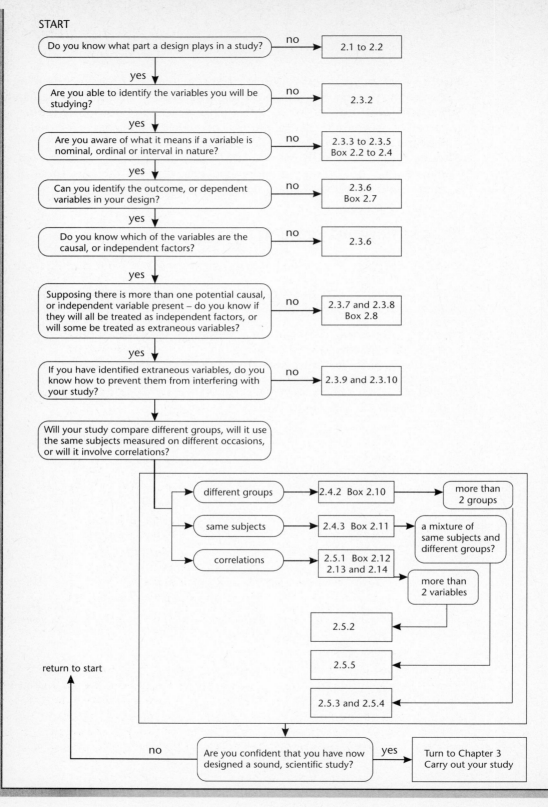

Flow Chart 2

START

Do you know what part a design plays in a study? — no → 2.1 to 2.2

yes ↓

Are you able to identify the variables you will be studying? — no → 2.3.2

yes ↓

Are you aware of what it means if a variable is nominal, ordinal or interval in nature? — no → 2.3.3 to 2.3.5 Box 2.2 to 2.4

yes ↓

Can you identify the outcome, or dependent variables in your design? — no → 2.3.6 Box 2.7

yes ↓

Do you know which of the variables are the causal, or independent factors? — no → 2.3.6

yes ↓

Supposing there is more than one potential causal, or independent variable present – do you know if they will all be treated as independent factors, or will some be treated as extraneous variables? — no → 2.3.7 and 2.3.8 Box 2.8

yes ↓

If you have identified extraneous variables, do you know how to prevent them from interfering with your study? — no → 2.3.9 and 2.3.10

↓

Will your study compare different groups, will it use the same subjects measured on different occasions, or will it involve correlations?

different groups → 2.4.2 Box 2.10 → more than 2 groups

same subjects → 2.4.3 Box 2.11 → a mixture of same subjects and different groups?

correlations → 2.5.1 Box 2.12 2.13 and 2.14 → more than 2 variables

2.5.2

2.5.5

2.5.3 and 2.5.4

return to start

no — Are you confident that you have now designed a sound, scientific study? — yes → Turn to Chapter 3 Carry out your study

2

Designing a study

'What's a condition?'

'How do I tell an independent variable from a dependent one?'

'What on earth is a repeated measures factorial design with double-blind controls?'

Chapter 2 considers the ways in which a study can be planned, or designed, identifying the different ways in which research is carried out and illustrating some of the things which can go wrong. It covers the essential characteristics of good research design, explains the terminology and offers examples of the various design options with discussion on the advantages and disadvantages of each. For students who have already identified a research issue to investigate, and who have gone as far as proposing hypotheses to test, this section represents the next stage in the research process: how to plan a systematic, scientific and ethical study which will effectively explore the research issue under investigation and test the specific hypotheses proposed.

If you have specific questions on designing a study, please consult the flowchart. Alternatively, beginning with Section 2.1, the entire process is explained in a logical sequence.

2.1   The purpose of a design

The logical sequence of activities common to most studies usually begins with the preliminary statement of a research question, followed by a literature review, a research rationale and the statement of hypotheses. This represents the first, preparatory stage of a research project and reflects the general coverage of the previous chapter. However, up to this point all we have is a kind of proposal for what would be a good piece of research, and why. The next stage is to develop a plan for actually setting up a study which will, in the first instance, test the stated hypotheses, and in the second, address the broader issues raised by the research question. In a printed report or scientific article, such a plan or scheme is actually called the **Design**.

At its most general, a design is a plan, a sketch of how to carry out a study. Knowing the research question which forms the basis for our study and having offered a number of specific predictions (hypotheses) about what we expect to find, we are merely trying to come up with an appropriate strategy for testing these predictions and exploring the issue. Put simply, we are saying to ourselves: 'I know what I want to find out, what's the best way of doing it?' More specifically, we want to come up with a practical plan, one which is ethical, scientific and, above all, foolproof. The last thing we want is to carry out a brilliant piece of research and then have some busybody point out to us that we forgot some obvious factor which negates our findings. Aside from being extremely irritating, we will also have wasted time – our own and our subjects' – in what has become a pointless exercise. To avoid this then, our design must be comprehensive and well thought-out – like everything else in life, from decorating a bedroom to coming to grips with human learning, the quality of the finished piece of work is a function of the preparation. Box 2.1 suggests some consequences of a lack of foresight.

2.2   Some common design problems

For many undergraduates, this part of a study often presents major problems, some of which are due to conceptual difficulties with the terminology – the differences between dependent and independent variables for instance are

Box 2.1   Designs, and how to look like an idiot

> '. . . no useful findings can be reported due to subjects' universal inability to follow even the simplest of experimental instructions.'
>
> '. . . the survey was abandoned following receipt of only two postal questionnaires from a possible sample of 300.'
>
> '. . . the favourable response of the sample to proposed increased national funding of psychological research had to be disregarded on discovery that, inadvertently, all subjects were delegates at the annual BPS conference.'

often confused in student reports. Another problem with the design section is a temporal one, the time at which it is actually considered. Typically, the majority of student projects follow the sequence: a research idea, hypotheses, some general thoughts on how to carry out the study, the study itself, analysis and the write-up. Often, it is only at this point that any real thought is given to the design characteristics of the study and students are left wrestling with the problem of which of the variables was the independent one? Or was this a between-subjects or within-subjects design? To make matters worse, the experiment, survey or questionnaire study has already been completed – the student knows what happened – producing an irresistible temptation to offer no more than a summary of the procedure. Add this to the frequent discovery that many people actually don't know what the differences are between a design and a procedure, and it is hardly surprising that this section of an experimental report is often the least satisfactory. The next section will attempt to address these problems.

2.3   The nature of research design

2.3.1   *The principles and language of design*

Remember that the whole point of a design is to plan a study which will effectively explore an issue, answer a question or test an hypothesis. To do this successfully we need to be able to identify a number of things: we need to know what we are going to measure, we need to know whom we are going to measure and we need to know what can go wrong. Most importantly we need to know these things before we start our study – or, at least, try and anticipate them. A vague and badly worked out set of football game tactics will end in a shambles and inevitable defeat. A sound game plan on the other hand, with everyone knowing exactly what they are supposed to be doing, stands a much better chance of succeeding. Things can still go wrong of course – we are dealing with people after all, and the same is true of experimental plans – even the best thought-out designs can end in disaster, but at least this will be less often than in the case of no design at all. The next section begins our consideration of the key components of a good experimental plan, and introduces the sometimes complex language of design.

2.3.2   *Variables and levels of measurement*

If you have no background in research whatsoever, and if this represents your first encounter with the subject, then it is possible that even the notion of a variable may be obscure. Put simply, a variable is the most general of all terms to describe absolutely anything in the universe which can change (or vary). The rainfall in Scotland is a variable; age is a variable; different groups to which we belong are variables and a score on a personality test is also a variable. More significantly, anything which can vary can also be measured, an important point when it comes to assessing the outcome of a study.

In research the aim is usually to demonstrate that one thing causes or influences another thing, or that something is related to something else. For instance, we might want to show that practice produces an improvement in the performance of some experimental task, that belonging to one group as opposed to another determines success in solving a problem, that people's mood varies depending on which day of the week it is. All of these things are variables – aspects of our world which can vary, or change, and they represent the tools of the researcher; being able to prove that one variable changes due to the influence of some other factor is, by and large, the whole point of the research process.

The observant reader might have noticed something odd in the above explanation, concerning the nature of the variables used as examples. Undoubtedly factors like group membership, days of the week and performance are all variables – they can change. But each of these factors is clearly different from the others in some significant way: the time taken to perform a task, or the number of errors made is somehow different from whether or not it is a Monday or a Tuesday. And both of these in turn, are also different from the variable which identifies whether or not subjects belonged to the Male group as opposed to the Female group. They are all certainly variables, but each is a different kind of variable. Understanding these differences is a relatively straightforward matter and requires merely that we look more closely at the composition of a variable, considering its components, the relationship between them and the way in which it can be measured. The next three sections demonstrate this process.

2.3.3 | *Levels of measurement: nominal or category variables*

Most aspects of our universe can be measured in more than one way, with the choice of particular method a function both of the nature of what is being measured and of the researcher's judgement and preference. Measuring a subject's age, for instance, can be a precise thing, in which age is expressed in years, months and weeks, reflecting the true character of this particular variable. Alternatively, age can be expressed in terms of a particular category into which it falls (16 to 25; 26 to 35, etc.) or merely as an order of relative magnitude (old, middle-aged, young). Each of these measurement systems varies descriptively, in terms of precision, and also in terms of what can be done with the information. The existence of different measurement systems though can be problematic, and a common source of anxiety among undergraduates is how best to measure the various components of a study. However, historically, this problem has not been confined to undergraduate students alone.

In 1941 the experimental psychologist S.S.Stevens presented a classification of measurement scales before the International Congress for the Unity of Science, a classification which emerged from a number of years of intensive research within the scientific community in general, and in the field of psychophysics in particular. Debate over the most effective systems for measuring aspects of signal detection (sound, loudness, pitch, etc.) ultimately led Stevens to propose four different measurement scales, varying in level of precision. The scales were **nominal**, **ordinal**, **interval** and **ratio** and they represent the classifications which are now in common usage throughout psychology today. The first of these types of measure is discussed below.

Much of what occurs in our universe can be explained in terms of the group or category to which particular events belong, and this represents one of the simplest ways in which things can vary. The gender variable in the previous section for example is a category variable, in so far as the components, or elements which make up the variable, are categories. In this instance, there are only two categories, but we can readily identify other category variables which contain more components – astrological sign comprises twelve categories, whereas some personality typologies are made up of up to 16 elements.

An important consideration here concerns the relationships between the various components of category variables, relationships which are purely qualitative as opposed to quantitative. This means that being in one particular category simply makes you different (in a qualitative sense) from other categories; there is no implication of such differences being quantifiable in any way and the categories exist in name only, with the names simply supplying descriptive characteristics of each category. Hence the frequently used term nominal variable. Returning to the sex variable, the terms Male and Female describe the characteristics of subjects in each category, but make no suggestion of any intermediate, quantifiable steps between the two. They are merely different. Moreover, to suggest that the male category is in some way better that the female category would be totally inappropriate (not to mention a danger to the health of one of the authors) for this kind of variable.

In terms of research, nominal variables are used most frequently as grouping variables, allowing subjects to be observed or compared on the basis of belonging to one group or another. Comparing males with females on some measurable aspect of behaviour is a common design element, while other studies might involve such variables as personality type, ethnic group, regional location or even the random assignment to experimental groups A, B or C.

An often encountered source of nominal variables is in survey and market research, in which the information being sought from subjects is in terms of which particular response category they would choose for a given variable. A marketer for example might be interested in people's preferences for breakfast cereal, or a political researcher might be trying to measure attitudes towards a referendum issue (possibly using a questionnaire item such as: **Do you support a referendum on a single European currency?**). Here, the nominal variable of food preference might have four categories – cornflakes, bran, muesli and kippers, while the attitudinal issue of support for a referendum, might only have two – YES and NO.

Using the language of research design, all such variables are category or nominal variables, although the more accurate terminology would be nominally-scaled category variables, since the components which comprise them are measured on a nominal scale (see Box 2.2).

2.3.4 | *Ordinally scaled variables.*

The previous section described the basic structure of category variables, i.e., in which the various components of a variable merely represent differences among categories. Such differences are purely nominal (in name alone) and imply nothing quantitative about the relationships among them. As such, they are often frowned upon by more numerically-oriented researchers, which is both unfair and unjustified since, as has already been intimated, category variables and nominal scaling provide the foundations of a great deal of survey and questionnaire research. However, the use of category variables does not preclude the possibility of quantitative relationships among the components of a variable, as the following will illustrate.

Previously, the grouping of events into categories (e.g., subjects or responses on a survey item) has been expressed merely in terms of qualitative differences among them. It is however possible, in the categorisation of variable components, to imply a quantitative relationship. Hence, subjects in

Box 2.2   How category or nominal variables are used

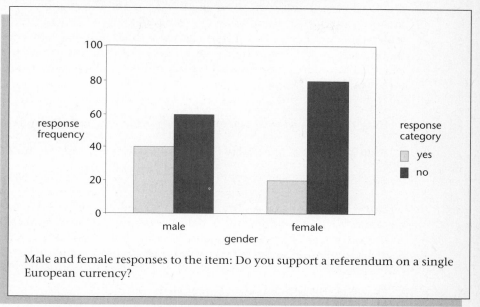

Male and female responses to the item: Do you support a referendum on a single European currency?

Group A might differ from subjects in Group B, not just by being different, but in terms of the direction these differences take. If, instead of subdividing a variable into nominal categories (groups A, B C), we use the categories of Best, Next Best and Worst, we have altered the variable from a nominal one to an ordinal one. It can still be classed as a category variable, but now there is a quantitative element in the relationship among the components. It is important to be aware however that the relationships among the elements of an ordinal variable can only take the form **greater than** or **less than**. There is no implication of how much greater or less and, while being able to place categories in some sort of order is a useful development in the measurability of our universe, it only goes a little way towards numerical sophistication. There are however a number of statistical procedures available for the analysis of data which are in an ordinal format and, consequently, some researchers prefer to work more with ordinal than nominal variables. The use of ordinal categories however is not simply a matter of individual preference – sound practical or statistical reasons will always determine the nature of the variables to be used in a study.

Typically, ordinally-scaled variables are found in cases where subjects are assigned categories or groups on the basis of some kind of ranking or order effect (Most Extravert; Moderately Extravert; least Extravert; or a researcher's estimate of High Income; Moderate Income; Low Income), or in which responses and behaviour are themselves ranked. Asking subjects to rank breakfast cereals in order of preference, as opposed to merely selecting their favourite one (as in the previous, nominal example) will produce ordinally-scaled data (see Box 2.3). Similarly, when a study requires subjects to respond to a questionnaire item which offers a range of options, these can often take the form of ordered categories. A typical item on behavioural research surveys might take the form:

How likely are you to travel to Europe via the channel tunnel?

Highly likely   **Likely**   **Unlikely**   **Highly unlikely**

In this instance the response categories are not only different from one another, but provide a specific order of response. An individual choosing one of the categories is placing himself on an imaginary behavioural continuum, and can therefore be described as more likely than some or less likely than

Box 2.3   Using ordinally-scaled categories

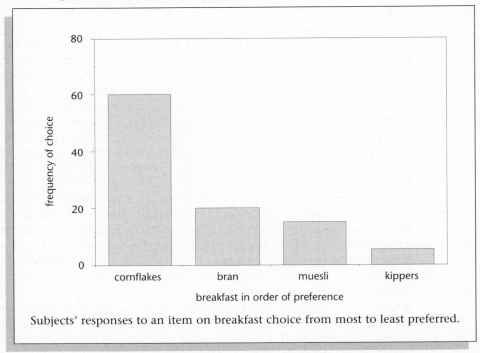

Subjects' responses to an item on breakfast choice from most to least preferred.

others to produce the stated behaviour. What cannot be ascertained of course is just how much more likely one category is than another. It is the classic school grade problem most of us have experienced at some time – if all we know is that Carol was first in Arithmetic and Jonathon second, we actually have very little information on the relationship between the two pupils, other than the order in which they performed on the test. Lacking would be any information on the magnitude of this relationship, which would considerably enrich our understanding of what actually occurred. Consider how much more useful it would be to know that Carol's mark was 85 and Jonathon's 84, or that Carol scored 85 and Jonathon only 40. In both examples we have a far greater understanding of the relationship between the two pupils than if all we knew was that one scored better than the other. This is the problem with all ordinal variables.

2.3.5 | Interval- and ratio-scaled variables

This final type of variable incorporates the most sophisticated form of scale, and is often the most preferred by statisticians, due to the amount of information provided. Here, the components of the variable are not discrete categories, nor are they categories which are related according to some ranking system. In fact, the elements which comprise this type of variable are not really categories at all, but rather a range of values which differ from one another in some systematic way. By way of example, if performance on some experimental task were to be measured under conditions of varying temperature, then both variables in this study would be interval-scaled. Temperature is represented by a range of values but more importantly the difference (interval) between one temperature and another is the same as the difference between any other two temperatures (i.e., the interval between 14° and 15° represents the same change as the difference between 26° and 27°).

Likewise, if performance on the task can be measured by speed of response, or number of errors, again these variables comprise a range of values, each of which differs by the same amount from the next. The difference between interval and ratio measures concerns the existence of a true zero point – interval scales may well have an arbitrary zero point, as does temperature, but this is not the same as a true zero, or starting point for the scale. (The temperature scale ranges from plus to minus.) A variable like age on the other hand, or response rate, has a true zero point which reflects the beginning of the scale; all of these examples are interval, but only the latter two cases are ratio. Box 2.4 illustrates the measurement of an interval-scaled variable, and note how this is depicted in a different manner from the previous nominal and ordinal examples (as in Boxes 2.2 and 2.3).

The advantage which interval (and ratio) scaled variables have over other forms of measurement lies in their susceptibility to statistical analysis. Most

Box 2.4   Interval-scaled variables

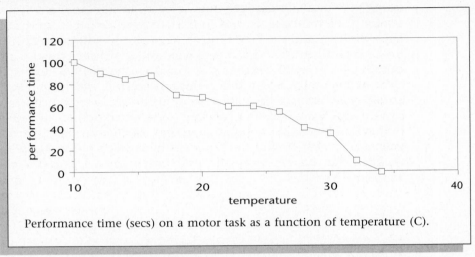

Performance time (secs) on a motor task as a function of temperature (C).

research relies on statistical procedures to support hypotheses, validate theories and answer research questions and while both nominal and ordinal variables have their own procedures, many researchers feel that only when data are available in at least interval format can useful analysis begin. (Note, this is not a position with which the authors agree but we nonetheless recognise the levels of sophistication possible with interval-scaled variables.) The calculation of averages, measures of spread and other valuable statistics are only possible with interval-scaled variables, allowing an impressive range of analytical techniques to be used.

2.3.6 | *Dependent variables*

The starting point for designing a study is to identify what it is we are trying to measure. To some this might seem an odd thing to say – surely it will be obvious what the study is about, and what measures are to be taken, but it wouldn't be the first time that an undergraduate student has asked in hushed and somewhat embarrassed tones what it is they are supposed to be measuring. The simplest way to deal with this is to return to the research question posed at the outset. For example, the issue of whether or not females possess a social gene absent in males suggests immediately that we are trying to measure some aspect of social behaviour. If we believe that some psychology tuition methods are superior to others, then we are interested in measuring academic performance, and so on. Looking at the hypotheses we proposed following from the literature review will tell us even more explicitly what the study is trying to achieve (and if it doesn't, then our hypotheses are flawed). In the social gene example for instance, an hypothesis might be that social behaviour in pre-school children will demonstrate marked differences between males and females. This allows us to be more specific about what we are measuring: some aspect of behaviour, as measured by an appropriate observational instrument, using young children as subjects. These aspects of behaviour which we are trying to measure are the dependent variables; they represent the aim of the study and they provide the quantitative material which allows us to answer the research question. They are termed dependent because they are believed to be caused by (dependent upon) other factors – some naturally occurring and some the result of the researcher's manipulation. In the case of the social gene idea, the proposition is that social behaviour is dependent upon (caused by) a sex-linked gene; in the tuition example, we are trying to demonstrate that pass grades are dependent upon particular tuition methods. Remember, when in doubt, always return to the research issue and hypotheses – what questions are you asking and what are you predicting. It is a relatively short step towards identifying what *outcomes* could be measured in answer to these questions, and it is this step which identifies the dependent variables. (In fact, occasionally the dependent variable is also termed the **outcome variable**, another piece of jargon which might actually help if the point is still not clear.)

Sometimes, the outcome of a study can be measured in more than one way, allowing for the possibility of two or more dependent variables. Consider the example of a study in which performance on some experimental task is to be the dependent variable (dependent on some factor such as training, experience, attention or some other eventuality). In such cases a straightforward and readily available measure is usually taken as an indication of performance, such as the time, in seconds, to carry out the task. However, other measures will also be possible – the number of errors made during performance of the task, for instance. One might expect that one measure would serve to reinforce the other, which would in itself be a useful finding – the more experienced a subject is, the shorter is the time to complete the task, and the fewer errors made An alternative outcome, however, might be that while the time taken to perform a task remains constant, irrespective of experience, the number of errors produced would decline. An experienced cyclist, for instance, might take the same time to cycle from point A to point B as would a novice, but he would run over fewer frogs. Had this study been carried out using only the one dependent variable, the relationship between experience and performance would not have been demonstrated. Using more than one dependent variable, however, demonstrates that a relationship does exist, although it is not always apparent. Box 2.5 illustrates the point.

Box 2.5   Two dependent variables

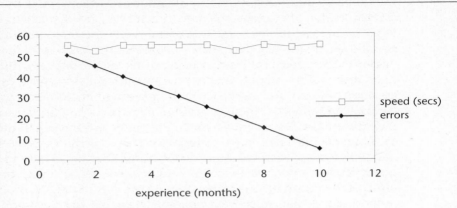

The relationship between two dependent (outcome) variables.

The above figure demonstrates a paradoxical effect in which an independent factor can give rise to two very different outcomes. If we were to measure performance on a perceptual task, such as proof-reading, we might well find that experience has little effect on the speed of performance: it takes experienced proof-readers just as long to scan a set length of text as novices. However, were we to look at a different measure, such as the number of errors made, we might well observe a decline with experience. Alternatively, reverting to our cycling example, experience might not relate to speed of performance, but might well be related to a decline in error rate (the number of frogs run over).

On a final note, it will be observed that both these variables (speed and errors) are interval-scaled variables. It is of course possible for dependent variables to comprise any of the variable types outlined in the previous sections.

2.3.7 | Independent variables

The previous section identified the dependent variable as an essential component in any study, that aspect of behaviour which changes, and whose change can be measured as a consequence of the influence of some other factor. That other factor, the aspect of behaviour which is (assumed to be) responsible for changes in a dependent variable, is termed the **independent variable**.

It is called independent because any changes to or variation within this variable are not dependent upon, or influenced by, any other factor in the study. Manipulation of this variable is under the control of the researchers – it is they who assign subjects to groups and select the comparisons to be made. Consequently, this variable can be regarded as relatively independent of any other factor (except of course the judgement of the researchers who make the initial decision on which variables to include in a study).

The relationship between these two kinds of variable is assumed to be a cause and effect one, with changes in an independent variable producing some kind of corresponding change in the dependent one. In fact, the general aim of most research is to demonstrate that such a relationship actually exists. Do reaction time scores decline as the measured amounts of alcohol ingested by subjects increases (i.e., are changes in reaction times (dependent variable) caused by changes in alcohol consumption (independent variable); are scholastic grades (dependent variable) a function of the sex of the individual (independent variable)? These are all examples of attempts to point to relationships between the two different kinds of variable, a process which underlies the majority of psychological research.

We have already seen that a study need not involve just one dependent variable, and the same is true of independent variables. Certainly, a common design for a research project – especially at undergraduate level – attempts to relate one independent variable to one dependent variable. This makes for simplicity, both in the conduct of a study and subsequently at the analysis stage, where statistical procedures for this kind of experimental set-up are relatively straightforward. However, as we are continually reminded by experience, people are complex and it is rare that any piece of behaviour would be influenced by only one factor. The notion of multicausality of behaviour implies that for anything humans can do, there will be a variety of causes.

The implications for research are that, in the design of any study, a number of independent variables are likely to be at work in the determination of some dependent or outcome variable, and it is here that an important decision must be made by the researcher: do we concentrate on one single factor which we believe is the key causal variable, and in so doing, somehow eliminate or minimise the impact of all the other factors, or do we attempt to include all the important variables and examine their combined effects on the dependent variable?

The solution to this dilemma is never easy and provides one of the trickiest challenges for the researcher, not to mention the overall quality of the research itself. Get it wrong and opt for the single independent variable design and you risk ignoring or minimising key causal factors. Alternatively, combining several independent variables might serve only to dilute the effects of a single, key factor.

Ultimately these risks have to be borne by the individual, but they can be minimised; knowing the research area in detail and building on a thorough literature review of the particular issues being explored in a study, will allow a pretty good guess as to the likely relationships between independent and dependent variables. After all, the process whereby hypotheses are proposed requires the researcher to have made a number of judgements about cause and effect from the early stages, helping to at least reduce the chances of choosing the wrong option.

The issues involved in minimising the effects of other factors are discussed in the next section, but for the moment we will take a closer look at the case of more than one independent variable.

Returning to our earlier example in which we examined performance on some experimental task, let us assume that the literature implied that not only would experience be a factor, but that there might be sex differences also. It would of course be possible to carry out two separate studies, one in which performance was measured as a function of the subjects' experience, and a second in which males and females were compared. This though would be clumsy and time consuming. More important, by treating both factors separately we are ignoring the possibility that they act in combination to influence performance, and we might miss any interaction which exists between the two. Box 2.6 illustrates the point, demonstrating that, while increasing experience does result in a decline in errors for female subjects, this relationship falls down with males, who demonstrate a dramatic increase in errors with experience. Why this should be the authors have no idea – this is merely an unfortunate example proposed for illustration purposes. Pity about the frogs, all the same.

Box 2.6   Interacting independent variables

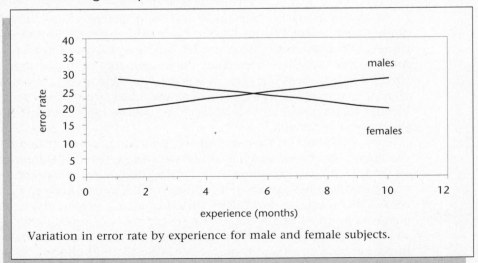

Variation in error rate by experience for male and female subjects.

There is one final point worth mentioning before we leave our consideration of independent variables – recall that Section 2.3.3 identified a number of different types of variable, differentiated in terms of structure and composition (nominal, ordinal and interval). Just as it is possible to have dependent variables measured on each of the scales, so we can have nominal-, ordinal- and interval-scaled independent variables. In the frog-squishing example we have become stuck with, there are two types of independent variable at work: Sex, which is a nominally-scaled variable, comprising the two categories of Male and Female, and Experience, which is an interval-scaled variable. Quite simply, independent variables can take any of the forms, and can further be mixed in any combination. As a further complication, most independent variables can also be dependent variables (although not usually in the same experiment). Consider a study trying to demonstrate that stress proneness (as measured by some form of stress questionnaire) might be caused, or at least influenced by, personality type, with the driving, competitive Type A individuals suffering more continual pressure than their more laid-back, Type B counterparts. Here, stress-proneness is the dependent variable. In another study, however, a researcher might be interested in the relationship between stress-proneness and performance on a complex, problem solving task. In this instance, stress-proneness has become an independent variable.

In short, there is a case for arguing that there are no independent or dependent variables in the universe, only variables. It is how we perceive and use them that makes the difference.

2.3.8 Extraneous variables

While it is the aim of most studies to demonstrate a relationship between an independent and a dependent variable, there will be instances in which this anticipated relationship will fail to materialise. One obvious reason for this is that there is no relationship between the variables and that our study was based on an inappropriate premise. (Consider an investigation trying to equate the hours of exercise taken by individuals in a week to their performance in an examination. We would be very surprised to find any relationship between the two variables.) Another possible explanation however is that there is a relationship between the variables under investigation, but a relationship which has been obscured, or interfered with, by some other, unanticipated factor – an extraneous variable.

Extraneous variables are so called because they lie outside the planned structure of a study – either ignored, on the assumption that their influence on some dependent variable will be minimal, unanticipated by the researcher, or acting as a nuisance factor which interferes with the planned purpose of a study. They are, in effect, all the other independent variables

Box 2.7 Types of variable

The following show examples of various hypothetical studies. Independent and dependent variables are identified for each example, as are the variable types, in terms of levels of measurement.

1. Males and Females will perform differently in a social situation.

Independent variable	**Dependent variable**
Gender	Social behaviour, as measured by the number of interactions observed between subjects
Nominally-scaled variable	Interval-scaled variable
Categories: 2	

Male   Female

2. Different personality types will exhibit differing levels of stress as measured by a stress event questionnaire.

Independent variable	**Dependent variable**
Personality type	Numerical scores on a stress questionnaire
Nominally-scaled variable	Interval-scaled variable
Categories : 2	
Type A Type B	

3. General health (as measured by the number of visits to a GP in a year) will be determined by Social Class.

Independent variable	**Dependent variable**
Social Class	Number of GP visits
Ordinally-scaled variable	Interval-scaled variable
Categories : 5	
1. Professional; 2. Managerial; 3. Skilled; 4. Semi-skilled; 5. Unskilled	

4. Ranking in a psychology test will be related to the height of individual students.

Independent variable	**Dependent variable**
Height	Test ranking
Ordinally-scaled variable	Ordinally-scaled variable
Categories : 5	Categories : n
1.Tall; 2.Above average; 3.Average; 4.Below average; 5.Short	1st.; 2nd.; 3rd.; ......nth.

5. The number of frogs run over by cyclists will be related to their cycling experience.

Independent variable	**Dependent variable**
Number of months experience	Number of squashed frogs in a given period
Interval-scaled variable	Interval-scaled variable

which comprise the multi-causal nature of human behaviour and their effects have to be anticipated as far as possible.

The previous section raised the problem in terms of what can be done with all these variables through the use of more than one independent variable; if the researcher believes that change in some outcome is determined by a combination of, or interaction between, two independent variables, then these variables become a part of the research design itself. However, if the aim of a study is to concentrate on the influence of one key variable on its own – even though it is recognised that other factors will be at work – then all other possible causal factors are seen, not as contributory elements, but as irritations whose effects have to be minimised. By treating these factors not as independent variables in their own right, but as extraneous elements in a study which have to be somehow eliminated, the impact of the key independent variable (or variables) can be examined.

The issue ultimately resolves into a matter of perception. In any given situation a large number of variables will always be present; whether or not we choose to treat them as independent or extraneous variables, however, depends on how we view the outcomes we are ultimately interested in. If we believe a particular dependent variable changes as a function of several factors, and we want to explore the relative importance of these factors, either in combination or by way of interactions, then we are treating our causal factors as independent variables. If, on the other hand, we want to determine the precise influence of only one factor on a dependent variable, then all the other influencing factors have to be treated as extraneous variables. To adapt the concluding statement made at the end of the section on independent variables, there are no independent, dependent or extraneous variables in the universe, only variables. It is what we do with them that makes the difference. How extraneous variables are dealt with is considered in the next section.

2.3.9 Controls

The procedure whereby the influence of extraneous variables on some dependent measure is minimised or removed is termed control. In a study relating some personality measure (independent variable) to an index of stress (dependent variable), if the researcher felt that the likely influence of a subject's sex had to be minimised in the study, then we say that the gender effects would be controlled for.

There are a number of ways in which extraneous variables can be dealt with, although since the main source of such influences has to do with characteristics of the subjects themselves (age, gender, education, personality, etc.), the commonest way to deal with them is to control the way in which individuals are assigned to groups. In the above example, relating personality types to stress, if we felt that males were inherently more stress-prone than

Box 2.8   Independent or extraneous?

Recovery times following major heart surgery are known to vary considerably
from one individual to another. The major factors which contribute to this
variability have been identified as post-operative exercise; the sex of the patient;
the fitness level of the patient prior to surgery; certain 'medical' factors, such as
length of time under anaesthetic; certain personality variables, such as Type A
versus Type B; and even the particular health authority under which the
operation was carried out.

If a researcher were interested in determining the relative impacts of these
factors on post-operative recovery times, then all of these variables would be
treated as independent.

Independent	**Extraneous**	**Dependent**
exercise	none	recovery times
personality		
prior fitness		
gender		
medical		
health authority		

If the researcher felt that most of these factors were relevant in determining
variability in recovery rates, but regarded the health authority under which the
operation was carried out as irrelevant (but still having a possible influence),
then all the variables with the exception of the health authority would be
treated as independent variables. The authority would be regarded as an
extraneous variable whose effects would have to be minimised.

Independent	**Extraneous**	**Dependent**
exercise	health authority	recovery times
personality		
prior fitness		
gender		
medical		

A third version of this study might reflect a specific interest in the role of
different personality types on the speed of post-operative recovery. In this
scenario, although all the variables would be recognised as being important, the
major interest is in the role of the psychological factor. Consequently all the
other factors are viewed as extraneous.

Independent	**Extraneous**	**Dependent**
personality	exercise	recovery times
	health authority	
	prior fitness	
	gender	
	medical	

females anyway, this sex-linked effect could well obscure the personality factor we are interested in. A simple control is to ensure that the sex composition of one group (Type A personality, for example) *matched* the sex composition of the other (Type B personality). More simply, we ensure there are the same number of males as females in each group. This would serve to minimise the influence of the particular extraneous variable, or at least ensure that its effects were similar in both groups.

This process of matching subject characteristics can be extended to most extraneous factors: subjects can be matched on the basis of age, education, personality, shoe size and, in fact, almost any variable which might be regarded as extraneous to a research design. Unfortunately, the process of matching tends to prove costly in terms of sample sizes – if the only factor we wanted to match subjects for was, for instance, gender, then there is little problem: there are lots of men and women around. However, using the example cited in Box 2.8, if we tried to find even just two groups of subjects, all of whom were matched on the variables of gender, prior fitness, medical factors, health authority and, more than likely, age and specific type of operation, then it is extremely unlikely that we would have more than a handful of subjects to compare in each exercise condition. This then is the problem with using matching procedures to control for extraneous variables: if we attempt to take into account the multitude of ways in which people differ, we find that there will be very few who actually share the same nature, background and psychological composition, certainly too few for any kind of valid study. In reality, however, most researchers accept the impossibility of eliminating all sources of variability, opting for what they believe will be the main nuisance factors for their particular study. Taking this approach of course allows for the possibility of key influencing factors being overlooked but then, research into human behaviour can never be perfect and it would not be the first time that an otherwise sound study has been undermined by the influence of an unexpected extraneous variable.

2.3.10 *A special case – the double-blind control*

There is a particular kind of control which is worth mentioning, not because it is special, or different in some way from other kinds of procedures – after all, there are only variables and it is up to us what we do with them – but because the procedure puts the role of the researcher into perspective. From much of the foregoing discussion on variables, it would be easy to get the impression that most of the problems with extraneous effects are to be found in the experimental subjects used for a study: their biases, personal characteristics and limitations seem to be continually interfering with the research process and it is the lot of the overworked but brilliant researcher to deal effectively with all these problems. This view however is somewhat

Box 2.9   Let's eat

Imagine a study in which it is believed that there is an easy route to learning; eating this textbook (no doubt seasoned with a little salt and garlic) will lead to an increased understanding of research methods unattainable by any other study method.

In a simple study, two groups are used, one ingesting the textbook and one studying in the usual manner (attending lectures, etc.). At an end of semester test you find that the eating group outperform the other; smugly we claim that we have proved our hypothesis and prepare to sell our new training method to the world, prior to retiring to a South Sea island.

Unfortunately, before we can buy our tickets, a slightly better researcher than ourselves points out a crucial flaw in our findings – all the people in the textbook-eating group were female, while all the people in the conventional group were male. It is possible that the females would have outperformed the males in any case and this could be the explanation for their success, not the experimental treatment. In short, our attempt to demonstrate a relationship between study technique and academic performance was interrupted by something we hadn't accounted for – a nuisance, or extraneous variable.

Upset by this discovery we postpone early retirement and decide to repeat the experiment under more rigorous conditions – again we obtain two groups but this time we ensure there are the same numbers of males and females in each, hence controlling for a possible sex effect. Again the textbook-eating group proves superior and, unable to supress a smile, we present our results to our critic.

Regrettably this person is a better researcher and points out that, although we've taken sex differences into account, it so happens that all the subjects in the eating condition were introverts, while the other group comprised mainly extraverts and the performance differences could well be attributable to these differences in personality type.

Depressed now, we accept that there was indeed another nuisance variable we forgot about and once again we repeat the experiment. This time we ensure both groups contain similar distributions of males, females, extraverts and introverts. Once more we find a performance difference between the groups and await the comments of our critic with trepidation, if not anticipation.

Congratulating us on our attempts at rigour, our critic does however point out that all the subjects in the textbook-eating group were born under the star sign of Sagittarius, whereas the other group comprised mainly Scorpios. Incensed, we retire from experimental life and take up writing textbooks instead.

The alternative to matching subjects is simply to assign individuals to groups in a random fashion. Certainly, doing things this way allows for the possibility of some kind of bias to develop (there may be more males in one group than another, or a group may be unusual in the number of introverts present), but if subject numbers are kept high enough, the influence of one or two unusual subjects will be minimised.

Ultimately the decision whether or not to match or randomly assign subjects is a matter of judgement. If the researcher is convinced that there will be one or two key variables which must be controlled for, then matching will provide the best solution. Where there is no single major extraneous variable which would dramatically affect the outcome of a study, or where subject numbers are likely to be small, randomisation is probably the answer.

demeaning of our subjects, and presents ourselves in a positive light which is more in the mind of the researcher than in reality. Of course, we as researchers are just as flawed, possessing the same quirks and foibles as our subjects – we are all people after all – and because of this, the possibility exists that limitations within a study may be due to factors within ourselves just as much as within our subjects. Moreover, since any given study is likely to concern an hypothesis we will have developed ourselves, we are likely to have a keen interest in its outcome.

In recognition of this and to control for a peculiar kind of experimenter effect, the double-blind control has evolved, a technique which achieved a certain amount of fame in the explosion in drug trials of the 1960s, but which has its place in any situation in which some factor within the experimenter might influence an outcome.

Visualise a study in which a new 'smart' drug is to be tested on human subjects. The drug is believed to improve learning and problem-solving ability and subjects have been selected to participate in an appropriate drug trial. Of course, if only one group of subjects were used, and they knew they were taking an intellect-enhancing substance, the expectation associated with this knowledge would in itself produce an improved performance on some task, hence masking a possible real drug effect.

The normal method of dealing with this is to use a second group to whom a placebo has been administered (i.e., a neutral substance), and with none of the subjects knowing which has been given the real drug. Subjects are blind to the experimental manipulation in what is usually termed a **single-blind design**. However, the fact that the researchers know which is the real drug group might lead them to inadvertently inform subjects of the fact (through non-verbal cues), or to allow their expectations to influence the recording of results. To control for this effect, the researchers also must be blind to the experimental manipulation. Hence the term, **double-blind control**, with neither subject nor researcher being aware of the precise manipulation.

2.4 Design elements in research

2.4.1 *Experimental design introduced*

In Chapter 1 psychology was discussed in terms of describing, explaining and predicting behaviour. The methods available to us for doing this are surveys, observation and questionnaire-based studies and experiments. Moreover, the power of these methods progresses in the sequence shown – with surveys being most useful for descriptive purposes and experiments the preferred procedure for making predictions. Observation and questionnaire-based research fall somewhere in between: they can both be applied successfully to the description of behaviour but they can also, depending on the nature of the research, be used to predict.

The distinction among the various methods can be understood by considering the purpose of experimentation and the processes which underlie the technique. Essentially, experiments are carried out to demonstrate a relationship between an independent variable and a dependent one. This can, of course, be done using any of the techniques available to us – surveys, although primarily a source of descriptive information might, potentially, be used to examine different kinds of response as a function of group membership (problems in childhood development could be related to social class, regional location, ethnic group, or whatever). Observation too allows us to record variations in behaviour as a function of many factors (for example, we could observe the number and frequency of social interactions in situations where the social distance among individuals varies). Questionnaires can also be used for the more sophisticated purposes of explaining and predicting: we might predict, for instance, that subjects who score highly on a measure of internal locus of control will gain a low score on a measure of psychological well-being. And finally, experiments can be carried out in which subjects are assigned to groups, manipulations carried out, extraneous variables controlled for and outcomes measured.

The difference, and what makes one technique more useful for predictive purposes than others, is the amount of control the researcher has over what happens in the study and how much scope there is for manipulation of the variables involved. In an experiment it is the researcher who determines group membership, who chooses tasks and determines what outcomes are to be measured. And, most importantly, the experimenter has the opportunity to control for a wide range of intervening variables. Under such circumstances, and because of the degree of control exercised by the researcher, any apparent relationships between dependent and independent variables are likely to be real and causal in nature. With the other techniques the opportunities for such strict controls, while still present, are nonetheless much reduced. The subsequent sections describe the ways in which such experimental studies can be structured.

2.4.2 | Between-subjects designs (independent groups designs)

The most basic kind of experimental design involves two groups being compared on some outcome measure. Typically, one group receives one kind of experimental procedure (a treatment), and the second group, a different kind. Often, one of these groups actually experiences no kind of experimental manipulation whatsoever, so as to serve as a comparison with the treatment group. This comparison group is then termed the **control group**, with the group receiving the treatment being known as the **experimental group**.

The assumption is that if both groups were similar on some measurable characteristic prior to the experiment, yet demonstrated differences after the experiment, then the change must have been due to the experimental treatment.

In the language of experimental design, the different groups which are being compared represent the different categories of an independent variable: they could be the male and female components of a gender variable, they could be the experienced versus inexperienced categories of the skill variable in the cycling example or they could be the non-treatment (control) group and treatment (experimental) groups of our textbook eating study. Other frequently used terms for the components of an independent variable are **conditions** (the gender variable comprises two conditions – male and female) and **levels** (there were two levels of skill – experienced and inexperienced).

The big problem with this approach is to be found in the underlying assumption that the two groups are essentially similar at the outset. This is a considerable assumption, considering the many ways in which people differ and it is highly likely that, if any two groups of subjects were drawn at random from the population at large, there would be substantial differences on a number of important psychological characteristics among the subjects. Yet, this process of random assignment to groups is the commonest way of setting up an experiment. However, although the problem of individual differences is well understood by most researchers, the general expectation is that, providing group sizes are large enough, individual differences will become at least diluted, if not totally balanced. This does, however, require fairly large samples and in situations where numbers are likely to be small, randomisation might produce unexpected group differences.

These issues have been raised earlier, in the sections looking at extraneous variables and controls (Sections 2.3.8 and 2.3.9), and, just as then, a possible solution to the individual differences problem is **matching**.

When subject numbers are limited, or where one or two extraneous variables are identified as having possible confounding effects on a measured experimental outcome, the process of matching subjects in the two comparison groups can be used. This would have the effect of deliberately balancing the groups on key factors, which otherwise would act like independent variables in their own right. Generally speaking, the process of balancing groups is highly desirable, since it should serve to minimise the effects of individual differences. In practical terms, however, random assignment is often preferred because of its simplicity and many undergraduates adopt this approach. Moreover, matching can become counter productive if matches are sought on too many factors – the more potential sources of variation are controlled for, the fewer subjects will meet our requirements, until group sizes become so small as to make any kind of experimental comparison unviable (see Box 2.10).

Box 2.10 A perfect match

Two sets of identical twins were divided into a control group and an experimental group, with each group containing one half of the sets of twins. By way of manipulation, the experimental group was subjected to a television viewing diet of Australian soaps, exclusively, for the duration of one week, while the experimental group was free to pursue its normal and varied viewing habits for the same time period. At the end of the experimental trial, both groups were assessed on intellectual functioning, using a standard questionnaire. The results are shown.

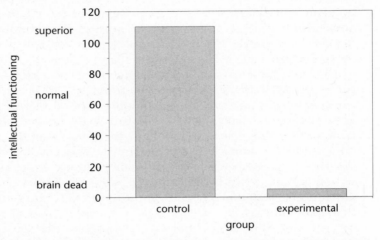

Differences in a measure of intellectual functioning between the control group and the experimental group.

Clearly, because the subjects were drawn from sets of identical twins, there is no possibility of arguing that the observed differences in the outcome variable could be attributed to gender, age effects, initial differences in intellectual functioning, or any other significant variable. The results then can only be explained by the treatment received by the experimental group and not the control group, hence confirming the fears of parents everywhere.

2.4.3 Within-subjects designs (dependent groups designs; repeated-measures designs)

The major alternative to the independent groups design is the within-subjects design. Here, each subject experiences each condition of an independent variable, with measurements of some outcome taken on each occasion. As in the between-subjects situation, comparisons are still made between the conditions, the difference being that now, the same subjects appear in each group or level. In a memory study, for example, a group of subjects might be required to recall lists of common nouns under different conditions of interference; during the interval between initial learning of one particular list and recall, subjects might experience a passive activity, such as watching television. In a repetition, the same subjects learn a different (but similar to the first in terms of difficulty) set of common nouns with a more active, problem-solving activity taking place between initial learning and recall. Subjects would then be compared on their recall under each of the conditions. Comparisons are not being made between different sets of subjects, but within the same subjects across different conditions.

The major advantage in using this particular design, and one of the reasons many researchers opt for the approach whenever possible, is that it almost entirely eliminates the problems of individual variability which represent the main drawback of between-group designs. Recall that, when different subjects comprise the different categories of an independent variable, any observed differences on a corresponding dependent variable, while possibly due to the experimental factor under investigation, could equally be due to different people being in each group. Even if variation in an outcome measure is not directly caused by variation among subjects, such individual differences will often interfere with the direct relationship between independent and dependent variables.

In the memory example above, had we chosen a conventional between-groups design, with one group of subjects in the passive condition and a different group in the active one, any observed differences in recall could have been caused by unpredicted or uncontrolled differences between the subjects themselves. If this were considered a danger, we would have had to resort to either randomisation with a large number of subjects, or the complicated process of matching subjects on key characteristics. None of this is necessary when within-subjects designs are used since individual differences have been effectively eliminated.

A further advantage of the within-subjects approach is that subject numbers are much reduced – even the most basic of between-subjects experiments requires a minimum of two groups, whereas a similar study using the within-subjects procedure needs only one. The same individuals are used for each condition, making the approach especially useful in situations where there are only a few available subjects. (Recall the problems associated with brain-damaged patients.) In undergraduate research, where competition for a limited subject pool is often fierce, the need for smaller subject numbers might be a distinct advantage, although this must be balanced against the fact that subjects may well be exposed to a more lengthy procedure involving repeated measures.

In addition to the above positive arguments for using repeated measures designs, there are some instances in which no other method is feasible – **longitudinal** research for instance, in which a number of variables expected to change over time are measured, depends upon using the same subjects. The alternative **cross-sectional** approach, which uses different groups of subjects of different ages, while more immediate, will most likely exhibit huge variability due, not simply to individual differences, but also to the widely different age groups used. Comparing a group of 20-year-olds with a group of 60-year-olds goes beyond mere age differences, incorporating considerable changes in culture, society and experience which will have a huge impact on almost any imaginable variable. A longitudinal approach, using repeated measures, can follow the changes and developments taking place within the same group over a number of years – today's 40-year-old subject is the same 20-year-old we observed 20 years ago.

Other situations in which the within-subjects design is to be preferred are those in which the relationships between an independent and a dependent variable are believed to be real, consistent but very slight. Under such circumstances a between groups design with all its attendant sources of subject variability would probably completely obscure such effects.

By and large, many between-groups studies can be redesigned to take advantage of the within-subjects approach, reducing the need for large subject pools and controlling for a good deal of undesirable variability. A major exception is when the independent variable providing the basis for comparison in a study is of the subject profile variety. These are characteristics like age, gender and personality type – key descriptive aspects of a person which place them into some mutually exclusive category. With the variable of gender, a given subject can only ever be either male or female, and with the exception of one or two remarkable cases, it is impossible to conceive of a study in which some measure is repeated once subjects have changed from one sex to the other. (Studying certain rare species of frog might allow this!) Consequently, when independent variables take this form the only possible design is between groups. Within-subjects designs are really only possible when the independent variables take the form of either treatment or temporal differences.

Despite the generally positive regard many researchers have for the within-subjects approach to experimentation, the procedure is not without its own problems. The main drawback is the simple fact that *it is* the same subjects who experience all the conditions within a variable, allowing for the very real possibility that experience of one treatment will influence measurements on another. The most obvious **repetition effect** is a practice phenomenon: if, in our textbook eating example (Box 2.9), the same subjects were used in a Before and After design (i.e., subjects are tested in the no-treatment condition, and then retested after consumption of the book) it is likely that an improvement in test performance might be partially due to the subjects simply getting better at the task. If it is the case that exposure to repeated treatments, irrespective of order, results in a generalised practice effect, there is little the researcher can do, other than resort to a between-groups design, swapping the practice problem for the individual differences problem. As ever, the choice as to which design will be the most appropriate comes down to a matter of judgement on the part of the researcher, and a decision as to which effect will prove the more serious.

Repetition effects which are more difficult to deal with are those which are unpredictable: experience of one treatment might improve performance in another condition, as in a practice effect, but not in a third; or prior experiences might inhibit performance at a later stage. Furthermore, the order in which treatments are experienced might also produce differing effects. The solution to this problem is to manipulate the order in which subjects experience the different conditions, such that while one subject might be presented with treatments in the order A,B,C, another subject would undergo the treatments in the order B,A,C, and so on. This process, known as **counterbalancing**, serves to reduce the influence of any one particular repetition effect by restricting the number of subjects to whom it would apply, and by compensating for any effects by subjects who experience a different effect.

There are various ways in which counterbalancing can be achieved. The most complete and effective method is termed, not surprisingly, complete counterbalancing. Here, every possible order of treatments is presented to subjects repetitively until every subject has experienced all combinations. While this is the most effective method for dealing with a mixture of known and unknown repetition effects – the effect of any one order effect is balanced against every other order – there is an obvious drawback. The more conditions there are in an independent variable, the more combinations of different orders are possible and, as the number of conditions increase, so the counterbalancing procedure becomes rapidly impractical, not to mention exhausting for your subjects. Box 2.11 illustrates the problem.

One way round this is to opt for a partial, or incomplete, counterbalancing procedure in which the number of combination treatments is reduced, while at the same time trying to ensure that repetition effects are minimised. Unlike the complete counterbalancing procedure, each subject encounters each treatment only once, but in a different order from the next subject, and so on. An obvious advantage of this approach is that, in an experiment involving a number of conditions, there is a good chance that the experimenter will still be alive at the end of it (death by old age or following a revolt by subjects is minimised). The disadvantage is that any interaction effects between individual subjects and order of treatment presentation cannot be controlled for. Needless to say, this process is potentially complex and there are several models for producing an effective counterbalancing design, most of which go beyond the introductory nature of this book. Moreover, few undergraduate

Box 2.11 A question of balance

When experimental subjects experience a series of conditions, with measurements being taken on each repetition, the order in which they encounter each condition can have an effect on performance. This is more than a practice or repetition effect, but a more complicated order, or experiential effect. To control for this, we can vary the order in which different subjects experience each condition; if we allow for all possible ways in which the order of presentation can vary this will balance out the effects of any particular permutation. However, this can lead to a new problem, as shown below:

Consider two studies investigating the recall of lists of common nouns under different conditions of learning. In the first study, two conditions are present, one in which subjects attempt to memorise a word list by rote, and the other in which they are required to make use of a mnemonic technique, such as considering each word on the list in terms of what it rhymes with. The following design is implemented:
1. A completely counterbalanced within-subjects design with two treatments, A (rote) and B (rhyme), on an independent variable (learning approach). Subjects experience repetitions of experimental treatments as shown.

Permutation 1	A, B
Permutation 2	B, A

In a more complex study, a third approach to learning word lists is introduced, one in which subjects are asked to consider the meaning of each word. The design now:
2. A completely counterbalanced within-subjects design with three treatments, A (rote), B (rhyme) and C (meaning), on an independent variable (learning approach).

Permutation 1	A, B, C
Permutation 2	B, A, C
Permutation 3	C, A, B
Permutation 4	C, B, A
Permutation 5	A, C, B
Permutation 6	B, C, A

Clearly, things are getting out of hand – even with only three conditions, which is far from excessive, we require six different treatment presentations to counterbalance all possible order effects. Just one more learming condition (e.g., another mnemonic system) and our experiment would require 24 separate presentations to allow for all permutations. With five conditions our experiment becomes so cumbersome as to be almost impractical. (Five conditions would require 120 different presentations to cover all the possible order combinations – the enthusiastic reader may wish to try working out all the different permutations, but it is easier taking our word for it). In addition to which, the demands on subject time, patience and co-operation will quickly become intolerable. The only solution, when faced with this kind of prospect, is to accept one of the methods of partial, or incomplete counterbalancing, or, alternatively, to consider the possibility of changing to a between-subjects design.

studies will have either the time or resources to operate at this level of complexity with possibly the majority of supervisors steering their protégés towards something more economical. However, in the event that your own work *is* more complex than a basic two treatment, or even three condition repeated measures design, we recommend Shaughnessy and Zechmeister (1985), who offer a most acceptable discussion on advanced counter-balancing techniques.

2.5 Developments in research design

2.5.1 *Correlational designs*

All of the foregoing discussion has emphasised the conventional orientation to experimental design – one in which the objective of a study is to explore the relationship between an independent variable and a dependent one. This relationship is usually evaluated in terms of some observed difference in a dependent measure, caused or influenced by one experimental condition or treatment as opposed to another. Moreover, such differences are invariably expressed in terms of an appropriate statistical measure, such as an average, or **mean** (extensive discussion on statistics appears later in this book) – such that we might state that the average number of errors made by novice cyclists was 45, but by experienced cyclists, only 15. Alternatively, we might present the results of a repeated-measures study as the mean score at Time 1 = 15; the mean score at Time 2 = 45.

A further characteristic of this kind of research design is that the independent variables are usually nominal or category variables: in the between-subjects examples, differences between subjects were in terms of the group or category to which they belonged; the within-subjects examples regarded subjects being measured successively over differing treatment or time categories. Returning to Box 2.7 however, you will observe that one kind of independent–dependent relationship involved a causal factor which is of the continuous, interval-scaled variety. Thus, rather than having a number of discrete categories to act as our predictor, we have instead a series of measures, observations or scores on some kind of scale. Equating irritability scores to variations in temperature would be one such example; number of errors on an experimental task as a function of the number of practice hours would be another.

This type of design, in which both the independent and the outcome variables are interval-scaled, is called a correlational design. In some respects the method can be regarded as an extension of the previous approaches: the range of values on the independent variable could, at a stretch, be regarded as a many category nominal variable; alternatively, some researchers and statisticians would regard the category-analysis type of design as a special case of the correlation method. This is not a common interpretation though and correlational approaches are sufficiently different from others that they have both their own procedures and statistical analyses.

Correlational designs are concerned with change: specifically, a study using the approach is interested in the type of change, and how much change occurs in some outcome variable, as a result of variation in a predictor, causal or independent variable. Box 2.12 illustrates this.

In the above example, the relationship between the two variables is of a particular kind – as one variable changes, the other variable changes in the same direction (as temperature increases, the number of reported road rage incidents also increases). In such cases we state that a **positive correlation** exists between the two variables. Moreover, in this example, because for each unit increase in temperature there is an almost proportional increase in rage rates, we can claim that there is a strong correlation between the variables. A similar illustration appears in Box 2.13, in which a hypothetical relationship between the amount of time people spend studying and exam marks is shown. Amazingly, there appears to be a strong positive correlation between these two variables, which might come as something of a surprise to many students.

Box 2.12 Taking the heat out of correlation

Following growing speculation concerning the relationship between incidents of road rage and variations in temperature, a researcher notes the frequency of reported traffic incidents under this category over a given time interval, and records the temperature at each observation. The data obtained are shown below:

Temperature values and associated road rage rates

Observation	Temperature °C	No. of road rage incidents
1	11	1
2	11	3
3	13	4
4	15	4
5	18	6
6	19	8
7	22	11
8	25	15
9	31	13
10	34	20

The table indicates the key characteristic of a correlation study – each observation comprises two measures, one on an independent variable, and the other its corresponding dependent value. Here, it is noted that, on the first observation, when the temperature is 11°, one incident of road rage occurred. On the second observation, temperature was again 11°, but this time, three incidents are noted. When a temperature of 13° occurred, there were 4 incidents, and so on.

When this information is plotted on a graph, which is the conventional method of dealing with correlational data, the figure below is generated. Known as a scatterplot, each plot indicates both a measure on the independent variable, and its associated dependent value. It is the practice in this type of plot to denote the independent, or causal factor, on the horizontal (x) axis, with the corresponding dependent variable on the vertical (y) axis – even in cases where we are merely assuming some element of causality between the variables.

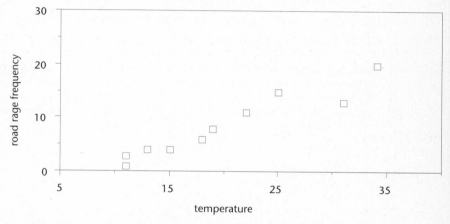

The relationship between incidents of road rage and temperature (°C).

The table containing the data has already indicated that a relationship exists between the two variables, a relationship depicted visually in the graph. Clearly, as temperature increases, so does the incidence of road rage.

Frequently we come across relationships which clearly demonstrate strong correlations between variables, but in which the direction of the relationship is different from that previously considered. In other words, as one variable changes in one direction, the corresponding variable changes in the other – a **negative correlation**. Box 2.13 offers the example of relating exam performance to the number of hours spent in social behaviour: going to

Box 2.13 Amazing facts about exams

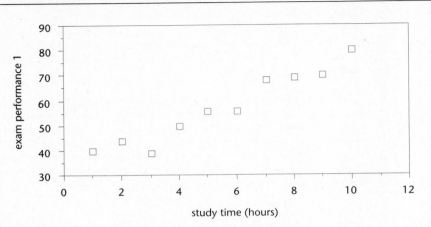

The relationship between study time and exam performance.

This first scatterplot demonstrates a strong positive correlation between the two variables: as one variable (study time) increases, so the other (exam performance) also increases. Moreover, as one variable changes, the other changes by an almost proportional amount. (Note: if the change were perfectly proportional, the plots would form into a straight line.)

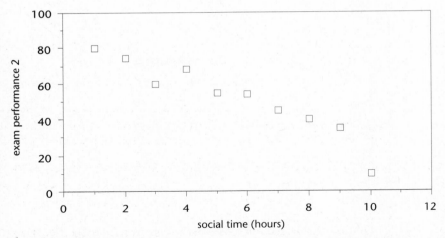

The relationship between the amount of socialising behaviour and exam performance.

In this second example, there is still a strong relationship between the variables, since as one changes, the other changes by a similar amount. In this instance, however, as socialisation time increases, exam performance decreases, indicating that the correlation is a negative one.

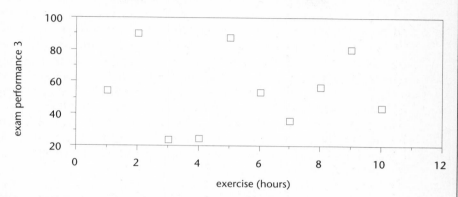

The relationship between exercise and exam performance.

In the final correlation example, the scatterplot shows a weak, if not non-existent, relationship between the two variables. In fact, with such a clearly unrelated pair of variables, without resorting to statistics (which would be pretty pointless in any case) it is impossible even to suggest whether or not such a relationship is positive or negative.

the pub, clubbing, watching movies, spending time with friends, etc. Almost as surprising as the previous finding, it would seem that the more time our hypothetical students spend socialising, the poorer is their exam performance, with those whose entire spare time is spent down the pub doing worst.

Both of these examples demonstrate strong relationships, but there are many instances in which two variables are only weakly related, or not related at all. The final illustration in Box 2.13 demonstrates the point, showing that varying amounts of physical exercise seem to have no bearing whatsoever on examination performance, which is precisely what we would expect.

The correlation approach is a popular and powerful research tool, especially in observational research, but, as with all attempts to study human behaviour, it is not without its own set of problems.

One of the difficulties encountered when looking at things which are related, is the fact that such relationships are not necessarily consistent. Consider the case of exam preparation and the common undergraduate problem of motivation. Most students would agree that without a certain level of motivation, studying is an extremely difficult, if not unlikely, activity. Not until examinations or assignments begin to loom and pressure begins to mount do many students find within themselves the ability to sit down with notes and textbook. We might then hypothesise that there will be a relationship of sorts between motivation level and examination performance, since the more motivated students will study more and therefore be better prepared. However, as most students will vouch for from bitter experience, this relationship between motivation and performance is not necessarily linear – it is by no means the case that continually increasing motivation levels will produce a consistent improvement in assessment performance. In the case of the poor students who have left their studying to within one week of a final examination (hard to believe, we know) while they may be highly motivated to study, the associated high level of psychological arousal (not to mention panic) might in fact interfere with their ability to concentrate. Motivated or not, the last minute studier might ultimately do worse than the moderately motivated student. Box 2.14 gives the idea.

There are many instances in which the curvilinear relationship can catch out the unwary researcher, especially when a study involves some developmental or age-related process. However, this would really only be a problem if purely statistical evidence of a relationship were sought. Relying on a

Box 2.14　Wanting it is not enough

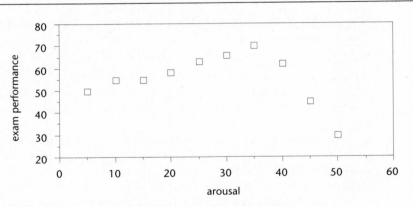

The relationship between arousal level and exam performance.

Motivation, as measured by a psychological arousal questionnaire, demonstrates a strong relationship with examination performance. However, this relationship is not linear, but curvilinear. Up to a certain point, increasing levels of psychological arousal relate positively to exam performance. Beyond this point, the direction of the relationship changes and increasing arousal produces a decline in performance.

numerical value as a measure of correlation (known as a **correlation coefficient**) would lead us to assume there was an extremely weak relationship between the two variables – the strong positive effect would be effectively cancelled out by the negative. A glance at the pictorial presentation of the relationship though would immediately show that these two variables are in fact closely linked; a salutary lesson indeed to the unwary researcher.

The most significant issue concerning this type of design involves the notion of causality. Normally, when a dependent variable is linked with some independent factor, the implication is that change in the outcome measure is in some way caused, or at least influenced, by the independent variable. This, by and large, is the point of all research and a great deal of this section has already been devoted to the many factors which can undermine attempts to demonstrate such a relationship. With correlational research, the cause and effect relationship is further complicated by the fact that two events occurring in juxtaposition need not be linked by causality. Box 2.15 provides a simple but effective example of this phenomenon.

By way of explanation, let us take a closer look at our temperature and road rage example. (The authors recognise the bizarre nature of the

Box 2.15 Is it real or is it not?

There are many things in our universe which are related – our mistake is often to assume that such relationships are meaningful in some way, when in fact they might be related merely because they happen to be in the same universe.

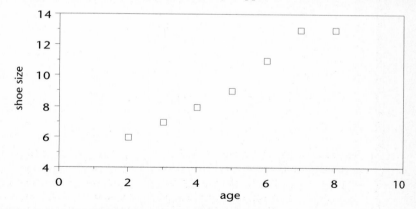

Showing the relationship between age and shoe size.

In this example we observe that as young children age, their shoe size increases. Not surprising since, in our early years, the maturation process includes physical growth.

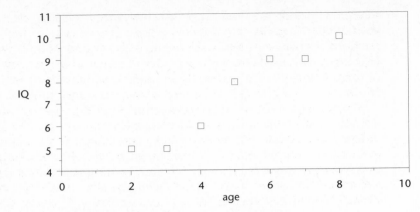

The relationship between age and a measure of IQ.

As with the previous example, there is a relationship between certain aspects of intellectual functioning and age (5-year-olds perform better on some intellectual tasks than 4-year-olds. Four-year-olds do better than 3-year-olds, and so on). Once again, intellectual development is a part of the age-related maturational process.

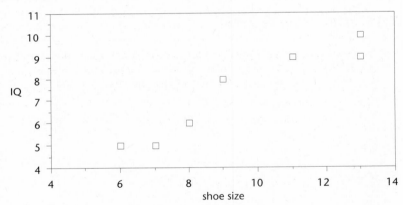

The relationship between shoe size and a measure of IQ.

This final example demonstrates the ground-breaking discovery that the bigger your feet, the brighter you are likely to be. The authors firmly believe, however, that this apparent relationship is purely accidental, or spurious. The two events are related only because they occupy the same universe – they appear to be related because they are both surface expressions of a deeper, more fundamental process – the profound and all-encompassing developmental process which occurs with age.

illustration, but at least there are no frogs!) The example so far has demonstrated that as temperatures rise, so the number of incidences of road rage also increases. By implication, changes in temperatures cause variations in rage, but to assume this would be to make a serious mistake, and one which even experienced researchers have made in their time. The essential fact about correlations is that they merely comprise observations of events which coincide – this relationship though could just as readily be spurious, coincidental or serendipitous as causal (see Box 2.15). On the face of it, temperature and rage rates do seem to be related, but supposing this is an accidental relationship? We could hypothesise that what is actually happening is somewhat more complex, and that the major player here is sun-spot activity, an astronomical event which when on the increase is known to have a number of effects on our climate. Certainly increased global temperatures are associated with solar activity, but what if an additional consequence were an intensification of the warm winds which sweep Europe, Asia and North America in the summer months. Such winds (sometimes called the faune, mistral and other local names, depending on where you happen to be at the time) have been associated in the popular press with increased depression, irritability and emotional changes in some individuals. If this is indeed the case, then the increase in road rage incidents could well be due to the raised irritability levels which attend these winds. Temperature changes, while related to rage, are merely an associated – but not causal – event.

This is a common problem with correlational research, and due to our old adversary, multicausality. As we have pointed out previously, for any piece of behaviour there will be many influencing factors – some important, some minor and some which simply interfere. And correlational research is no less a victim of this phenomenon than any other methodology.

2.5.2 | Developments in correlational research

The procedures for controlling for or incorporating the effects of other variables in correlational studies is much the same as in the group-comparison approach. We can attempt to keep other potential influences constant, we can decide that the influence of other factors is important and therefore incorporate them into our design, or we can control for extraneous variables statistically.

The first option is not always available in correlation research, since we are often dealing with naturally occurring events over which we can exert no or little control (this is why correlation studies are often regarded as quasi-experimental procedures). However, there are some things we can do: in our temperature example for instance, if we had taken temperature readings from different countries across the world, along with corresponding, local road rage reports, it might be possible that the variation in these traffic incidents was largely based on cultural factors, or other variables of a national or geographic origin. The logical solution here would be to restrict our observations to one particular location – then, if we still generated the same relationship between temperature and rage, we could be more certain that the key factor was indeed temperature changes, and not the geographic region in which the observations were made. Of course if, having removed the effects of geographic region, we no longer observe our relationship, then we have made a major error in judgement.

In situations where, rather than trying to eliminate the effects of one or more additional independent variables, we wish to include them in our design, then the second of our options can be applied. In this instance, instead of the usual bi-variate (two-variable) approach, we adopt what is known as a multicorrelational design. In its implementation this is a straightforward procedure, involving merely the simultaneous gathering of data on all the variables which are believed to be interrelated. Determining the combined effects of several variables on some outcome though is more complex, requiring sophisticated statistical analysis and familiarity with the procedures of multiple correlation and regression analysis. Complex as these techniques are, a number of statistical computer packages exist which deal with the process in a manner accessible even to undergraduates. However, at this stage it is enough to mention that the procedure exists – later sections of the book will look more closely at analytical techniques.

Unfortunately, the opportunities for the experimental control of confounding variables is often unavailable in correlational research – usually because the variables under investigation may be naturally occurring phenomena which don't lend themselves to manipulation. Continuing our road rage example, we may well recognise that sun spot activity is an important variable in determining these rates, but if we wish to somehow minimise its effects so that we can concentrate on the temperature effect, we might find it impossible to do so: solar activity may vary continually, or may be so interrelated with temperature that restricting observations to one particular level of activity results in only one temperature. In a situation like this, the only recourse is statistical control. If two variables are so inextricably linked that there is no way experimentally to eliminate the effects of one so as to assess the effects of the other, the technique of **partial correlation** can be applied. As with regression though (to which partial correlations are linked) this is a complex procedure and will be dealt with later. For the moment it is useful to realise that, when all else fails, some variables can be manipulated statistically in correlational research, with the effects of one extraneous factor – or even many factors – being controlled for as part of an analysis.

2.5.3 | Complex designs

Early on in this Chapter, the relationship between cause and effect was considered (Sections 2.3.6 and 2.3.7). The key point made was that human behaviour is complex and therefore subject to many influences or, to use the language of experimental design, any dependent variable is likely to be influenced by a number of independent variables. So far, however, most of our discussion has revolved around the one independent variable case, with other possible causal factors being regarded as nuisance variables to be controlled for and their effects minimised. Sometimes though we are prepared to enter the murky waters of multicausality and accept that more than one factor, or independent variable, might determine variation in some outcome measure. And once we have taken this step, we have travelled far beyond the relatively straightforward – but nonetheless respectable – world of two-group comparisons into a much more complex environment. And to understand a complex environment, we need complex designs.

As far as correlation research is concerned, the issues involved in moving from bi- to multivariate research are discussed in Section 2.5.2. With studies involving group comparisons however, although the concepts are similar, the procedures differ.

2.5.4 | Factorial designs

When we take a multifactor approach to the study of behaviour we design studies which have two or more independent variables present, each of which can have two or more conditions. Moreover, not only are we looking for differences between every possible combination of conditions, but we are also looking for interactions among them. This type of study is termed a factorial design, and is carried out as follows.

Let us return for a moment to our hypothetical study of frogophobic cyclists. In this example it has been argued (not unreasonably) that performance on the task would be largely a function of level of skill – with performance measured in the number of errors made, or poor frogs run over. Previously, while it was accepted that other factors might also have an impact on performance, these additional elements were treated largely as nuisance variables to be eliminated or controlled. However, should we decide that these other factors are important in their own right, and that, far from having their effects minimised, they should themselves be regarded as causal factors, then we have moved to a many-independent variable study. In a variant of our frog example, assume that we have identified two main factors likely to cause variability in performance: skill level (novice or expert) and terrain (easy or difficult). A study set up on this basis would be termed a 2 × 2 (two by two) factorial design: there are two factors, or independent variables in the study, the first of which comprises two conditions, or levels, and the second of which also has two conditions. Had we identified three levels of skill and two levels of terrain, this would give us a 3 × 2 factorial design. Moreover, if we proposed the existence of a third independent variable, such as personality Type A or Type B, then we would have a 3 × 2 × 2 design.

If all of this sounds unnecessarily complicated, it is because factorial designs don't consider just the isolated, or main effects of variables. If this were all we were interested in there would be nothing to prevent us carrying out a series of isolated experiments in which each variable was considered on its own: we would perform one study in which performance is measured for skilled and novice cyclists, and a second study in which performance is measured for easy and difficult terrains. What we would miss with this approach is the possibility of an interaction: for example, that skill level on its own might not dictate performance, but that its impact depends on the type of terrain. Box 2.16 illustrates how the two factors might interact.

The great advantage of this type of study is that not only can we observe the main effect of each independent variable on its own, but also, because every possible combination of conditions is considered, any **interaction**

Box 2.16 A factorial design with interactions

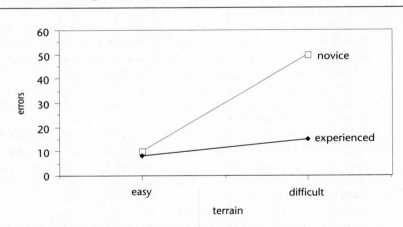

Effects of skill level and terrain on performance.

The results of our study on cycling show that while skill level is a key determinant of performance, its effects depend on the second factor, terrain. When the ground is easy, experienced and novice riders produce similar numbers of errors. It is only with difficult terrain that the effects of skill level can be observed.

effects can be seen as well. This opportunity to explore interactions is of immense importance since, as we have now ascertained, behaviour is the outcome of a large number of interacting factors – and to appreciate behaviour fully we must have access to these interactions.

2.5.5 | Mixed designs

There are occasions when our research question is not concerned merely with differences between groups of subjects, or changes which might occur over a number of trials, or treatments. Sometimes we are interested in finding out what happens to group differences over time, or from one situation to another – in particular, we wish to know if there is an interaction between the two events. In other words, we are considering a design which comprises both between- and within-subject elements.

By way of example, we may wish to explore the debate on the value of exercise on reducing hypertension levels. The general feeling among many general practitioners is that blood pressure can be controlled by exercise alone and without the need for medication. Less clear is the type of exercise which is most beneficial and we may wish to compare the effects of general fitness or cardiovascular training (running, cycling, etc.) against strength training (weight lifting). On the face of it this is simply a single factor (type of exercise) two-group comparison study (fitness versus strength). However, as most medical and sports practitioners would argue, the effects of training vary over time, and we might want to introduce a temporal element into our study. Specifically, we want to test for a cumulative effect of exercise at four different times – a within-subjects element.

What we now have is a mixed design in which the effects of the different type of exercise can be evaluated in terms of the different times at which measurements are taken. In statistical terminology this would be termed a two-way mixed ANOVA in which one factor is between-subjects and the other within-subjects. The final box in this section, Box 2.17, demonstrates this.

2.6 Review

In this chapter we have explored the basic elements of research design, beginning with a consideration of the types of variables encountered in a study and outlining the various ways in which variables can be related. The classical designs have been discussed in terms of comparing different groups of subjects, or using the same subjects repeatedly, along with the relative merits and disadvantages of each approach, and an introduction has been made to more sophisticated layouts. By the end of this section you should be able to plan an effective study, identify independent and dependent elements

Box 2.17   Mixing it up

In a mixed design, two groups of hypertensive subjects participating in either a fitness or strength training programme are measured over four time periods, each separated by one month. As this particular design is exploring the cumulative effects of exercise over time, no counterbalancing is required.

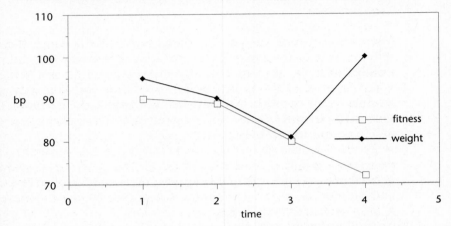

Diastolic blood pressure at T1 to T4 as a function of training condition (fitness or weight).

The figure indicates that during the first three time periods, blood pressure declines for both training groups (a within-group effect, but no between-group effect). In the fourth time period, although the fitness group experiences a continued decline in blood pressure, the weight group exhibit a dramatic reversal (a between-group effect).

and devise ways of dealing with extraneous factors. It should also be clear how a particular study fits in to the traditional between-subjects, within-subjects or correlational designs. As a final check on how well the various design matters have been explained in this section, the flow chart at the very beginning of Chapter 2 should be reviewed, hopefully with a far greater understanding of design issues than before reading this section.

2.7   Explanation of terms

Between-subjects design   An experimental design in which comparisons on some outcome variables are made between different groups of subjects.

Condition   A subject profile characteristic or element of an experimental manipulation which distinguishes one group of subjects from another (in between-subjects designs), or one observation period from another (in within-subjects designs).

Control   Any mechanism, device or manipulation whose function is to minimise the effects of some extraneous or confounding influence in a study.

Control group   A group which receives no treatment in an experiment, usually to provide a basis for comparison with an experimental group on some outcome measure.

Correlation   A relationship between two variables, assumed to be connected in some meaningful way. Specifically, if one variable changes, the other, correlated, variable will also change in some systematic manner.

Correlation coefficient   A numerical value which indicates the magnitude and nature of a correlation. It is expressed as a value between 0 and 1, and is either positive or negative.

Counterbalancing   A method of manipulating the order in which subjects experience experimental treatments in a within-subjects design. The technique eliminates, or reduces, the effects of repetition, such as practice, boredom, fatigue or experience.

Cross-sectional designs   Refers to research in which simultaneous observations are made on different subjects.

Design   The formal plan of a research study in which all the elements necessary to test a hypothesis are identified and detailed – such elements include independent and dependent variables, extraneous elements and controls, relevant experimental manipulations and significance levels to be applied.

Double-blind control   A method of eliminating the effects of 'knowledge of the experiment' on the outcome of an experiment, in which neither the subjects nor the experimenter know the nature of a manipulation. The term 'double' is appropriate since both elements of the experimental situation (subjects and experimenter) are blind to the manipulation. See also 'single-blind control'.

Experimental group   The group which is subjected to some form of treatment in an experiment.

Extraneous variable   A variable present in an experiment which might interfere with or obscure the relationship between an independent and a dependent variable

Independent groups design   A between-subjects design.

Interaction effect   The varying influence exerted by an independent variable on some outcome measure, as a result of some other factor.

Interval scales   A system of measurement in which observations are made on a scale comprising equal intervals. (The distance between two adjacent units on this scale is the same as the distance between any other two adjacent units.) Temperature, for example, is usually measured on an interval scale. See also Nominal, Ordinal, Ratio scales.

Level   The commonly used term for a condition in factorial designs.

Longitudinal   Research in which repetitive observations are made on a sample of the same subjects over a lengthy period of time.

Main effect   The influence exerted by an independent variable on some outcome measure, without the effect of any other linked or related factor.

Matching   A process whereby subjects in each group in a between-subjects design are matched on a number of key characteristics (between-subjects, matched groups design).

Mean   A statistic which provides a measure of central tendency and is simply the arithmetic average of a number of observations. The statistic forms the basis of comparison in between-subject studies.

Mixed designs   An experimental design which incorporates both between- and within-subjects elements.

Negative correlation   A relationship in which, as measures on one variable increase, measures on the other decrease.

Nominal scales   A system of measurement in which observations are placed into categories which differ from one another qualitatively. The variable sex is nominally scaled. See also Ordinal, Interval, Ratio scales.

Ordinal scales   A system of measurement in which observations are placed into categories which differ from one another quantitatively; the differences between categories are in terms of relative magnitude (greater than; less than). See also Nominal, Interval, Ratio scales.

Outcome variable   An alternative term for dependent variable.

Partial correlation   A statistical technique in which the influence of a third variable is removed from the relationship between two correlated variables.

Positive correlation   A relationship in which, as measures on one variable increase, measures on the other variable increase also.

Randomisation   A process whereby subjects are randomly assigned to groups in a study, the purpose being to compare them on some outcome measure. See also between-subjects design.

Ratio scales   A system of measurement in which observations are made on a scale comprising equal intervals and on which there is a true zero point. Measurement of *response time* on an experimental task would be on a ratio scale. See also Nominal, Ordinal, Interval scales.

Repeated-measures design   A type of experimental design in which a series of observations is repeated on the same subjects within a single experiment or study. See also Within-subjects design.

Repetition effects   The possible influence on an observation of previous trials or treatments in a Within-subjects design. Such effects can be of a generalised, practice effect in nature, or can be more specific and unpredictable.

Scatterplot   A special type of graphical presentation in which the relationship between two variables is plotted.

Single-blind design   An experimental design in which subjects are unaware of the particular experimental condition they are participating in whether control or experimental. The term 'single' is appropriate since only one element of the experimental relationship (the subject's) is blind to the precise nature of the manipulation. See also Double-blind control.

Treatment   The experimental manipulation to which subjects are exposed in an experiment.

Within-subjects design   An experimental design in which the same subjects are tested on some outcome measure at different times, or under different conditions.

2.8   Recommended reading

Dyer, C. (1995). *Beginning Research in Psychology: A Practical Guide to Research Methods and Statistics*. Oxford: Blackwell.

Shaughnessy, J.J. and Zechmeister, E.B. (1994). *Research Methods in Psychology, 3rd edition*. New York: McGraw-Hill.

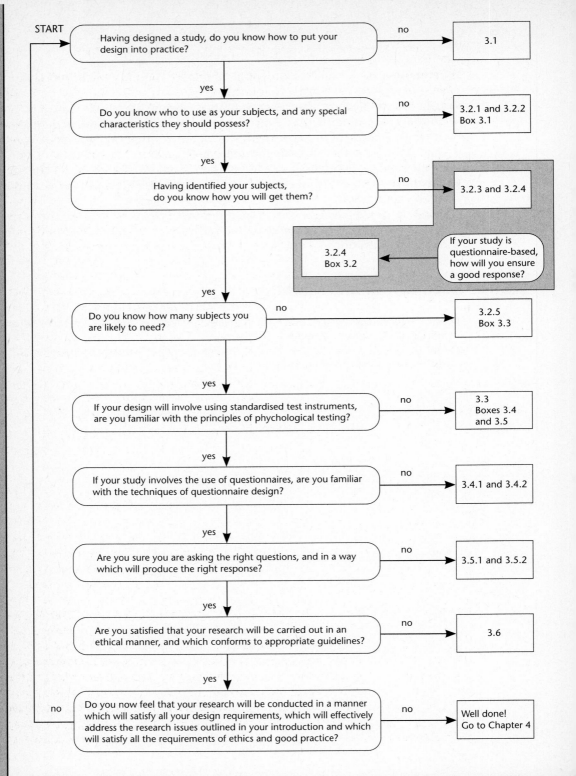

START

Having designed a study, do you know how to put your design into practice? — no → 3.1

yes ↓

Do you know who to use as your subjects, and any special characteristics they should possess? — no → 3.2.1 and 3.2.2 Box 3.1

yes ↓

Having identified your subjects, do you know how you will get them? — no → 3.2.3 and 3.2.4

If your study is questionnaire-based, how will you ensure a good response? → 3.2.4 Box 3.2

yes ↓

Do you know how many subjects you are likely to need? — no → 3.2.5 Box 3.3

yes ↓

If your design will involve using standardised test instruments, are you familiar with the principles of phycological testing? — no → 3.3 Boxes 3.4 and 3.5

yes ↓

If your study involves the use of questionnaires, are you familiar with the techniques of questionnaire design? — no → 3.4.1 and 3.4.2

yes ↓

Are you sure you are asking the right questions, and in a way which will produce the right response? — no → 3.5.1 and 3.5.2

yes ↓

Are you satisfied that your research will be carried out in an ethical manner, and which conforms to appropriate guidelines? — no → 3.6

yes ↓

Do you now feel that your research will be conducted in a manner which will satisfy all your design requirements, which will effectively address the research issues outlined in your introduction and which will satisfy all the requirements of ethics and good practice? — no → Well done! Go to Chapter 4

no

CHAPTER 3

Carrying out a study – the procedure

'How many subjects do I need?'

'Where can I get subjects?'

'What do I do if no-one returns my questionnaire?'

'From where do I get numbers?'

Let us assume you have now designed the perfect study, you've identified the key variables, considered everything that could go wrong and built failsafes into your plan. The next step is to put your plan into practice: this chapter deals with all the procedural details of implementing a design – how to carry out an experiment, conduct an observation study and design a questionnaire. The different kinds of measuring instruments are discussed, along with the related issues of reliability and validity, and consideration is given to contemporary psychometric tests. Practical problems, such as obtaining subjects, preventing various sources of bias and data collection, are also dealt with. And because your design is so detailed and absolutely foolproof, what can possibly go wrong? Read on . . .

3.1   The role of procedure

In Chapters 1 and 2 we looked at what might be regarded as the intellectual, or thinking components of a study: carrying out a literature review, identifying research issues, designing the study, and so on. Now, though, it is time to get out there and put your design into practice – known technically as the methodological, or procedural part of a study. For some, this can represent a daunting moment, being the point at which all their ideas must now be put into action with all the attendant possibilities for disaster. Others though find the actual implementing of a study the most satisfying part of the whole exercise – an opportunity to see their plans come together, and the point at which real data begin to emerge, perhaps providing the first evidence in support of a theory. Either way, the process is not without its own set of pitfalls, and what follows is an attempt to identify the common procedural problems and offer ways of dealing with them.

3.2   The stuff of research – whom will you use?

One of the most commonly expressed concerns of undergraduates every-where relates to subjects: what kind of subjects should they get? How do they get them? How many do they need?

The first question ought to be a straightforward one to answer since, in many respects, the whole research issue in general, and the research question in particular (see Chapter 1), will probably have identified a number of important subject characteristics, especially if the study is along quasi-experimental lines in which the independent variables are themselves subject, or profile variables. If, for example, a study is exploring gender effects on some index of social behaviour, it is clear that our subjects would have to comprise a mix of males and females. If we are concerned with attitudinal differences among university students taking different degrees, then our subjects would of course be students, differentiated by course of study, and so on.

The design section of a research project (see Chapter 2) will have further refined our subject characteristics, since the purpose of a design is to develop a plan which will answer the research question while at the same time preventing extraneous or confounding factors from interfering with the study. Since many such interfering factors are themselves subject variables, dealing with them is often enough to narrow down our subject requirements even further. By way of illustration, our gender and social behaviour example had logically required that subjects be of both sexes. However, in the design of an appropriate study, we may have concluded that, if genetic factors contribute to social behaviour in females but not in males, such differences will become diluted over time, as boys acquire the skills which girls are potentially born with. Therefore our subjects are not just males and females, but males and females young enough for the effects of hereditary factors to be still visible. In short, we may decide that our subjects should be of pre-school age.

In our student example above, if our review of the relevant attitudinal literature intimates that the predicted differences might evolve over time, then not only are we looking for students following different career paths, but students in their later, or final years.

The key to grasping the significance of the 'whom do I study?' problem lies in an understanding of the relationship between **samples** and **populations**, and an appreciation of how what we are studying varies within the population. By population, we mean the entire set, or subset, of entities

Box 3.1   Choosing subjects

Research topic	Possible subjects
A study investigating gender differences in social behaviour.	Males/females of varying ages.
A study investigating sex differences in social behaviour, controlling for the effects of acquired factors.	Male and female children of pre-school age.
A study investigating sex differences in social behaviour during the performance of a psychomotor task.	Male and female cyclists of varying ages.
A study investigating revenge behaviour of tailless, web-footed amphibians of the genus Rana, on perambulating socially aware hominids.	Frogs, of varying ages.

In most instances the nature of the subjects required for a particular study can be readily identified by the nature of the research topic itself.

which comprise the group we are interested in: this could be the population at large, representing humanity in general, or it could be pre-school children or particular personality types, or it could even be other species. Whenever we carry out a piece of research the ultimate aim is to demonstrate that what we discover in our experiment, questionnaire or survey is relevant to the wider population. Of course, the ideal way to ensure this relevance would be to test everyone in that population; this way we could say with a certain surety that 'this is what people do,' or 'pre-school children behave in this way in this situation'. Unfortunately, testing an entire population (currently standing at some 7,000 million people) is just a bit impractical, with even subsets of this group being so large as to be out of reach, so research, even the most impressively funded, tends to concentrate on a smaller version of a population – a sample. The trick of course is to ensure that the subjects who comprise our sample are really representative of the population we wish to explore, an issue briefly considered in Chapter 1 (1.4.4). However, irrespective of the size and scope of the population, the aim in studying a sample will always be representativeness: if our population contains both males and females, our sample must have the same distribution of sexes; if there are varying ages in the population, our sample must reflect such age differences also. And if the proportion of males to females in the general population is uneven, then our sample too should reflect this imbalance.

It is worth noting, however, that the cause of representativeness can be overstated: slavish adherence to its principles can generate unnecessary complications in a study when the object of investigation is not susceptible to particular sources of variation. In certain areas such as reaction time and signal detection or in studies involving the physiology of the visual and auditory systems it might be safe to assume that measures will not vary as a result of, say, sex and social class, or regional location and culture. In instances like this, while it might not be true to say that any old subjects would do, it is likely that the much-put-upon undergraduate would be an acceptable subject here. What we learn about taste and olfaction from a student sample is likely to be true of the population at large, up to a point – for even these relatively universal functions will vary with age and so generalisations from an undergraduate sample would have to be made with caution. When studying more complex, interacting variables however (attitudes, motivation, stress, coping behaviours, voting intentions) – when measures are likely to vary among individuals and groups of individuals – the issue of representativeness becomes central.

When research involves dependent variables which are known (or assumed) to covary with other factors (age, sex, class, etc.) the need for subjects in a sample to truly reflect the important characteristics of the population becomes an important requirement – otherwise we would find ourselves in the position of claiming that a finding is true of the particular group studied, but not necessarily of anyone else, a problem known variously as **sampling bias**, **situational bias** and **situation specificity**, all reflecting the possibility that particular groups might be over-represented or particular context factors emphasised in a study. While all researchers should be aware of this issue, the problem of sampling is particularly keen when research is based on survey procedures. How often have opinion samples, market research surveys and political polls been discounted or proved wrong because the sample studied failed to accurately reflect the population at large? The voting polls taken prior to the 1992 general election in the UK were way off the mark in predicting a Labour landslide largely as a result of sampling problems, in addition to a gross underestimation of the 'last minute' factor in voting behaviour. In survey research, the choice of sample is often *the* issue. So how do we ensure that a survey adequately taps the true range of population characteristics? The next section may provide some answers.

3.2.1   *Sampling techniques*

There are two major methods for ensuring that subjects for our study are a fair representation of the general population. The first of these is termed **random sampling**, whereby, as the name suggests, a number of individuals are picked from the population totally at random and in the absence of any selection criteria whatsoever. The advantage of this approach is seen in its fairness and objectivity, since every single person in the population has an equal chance of being selected (the approach is sometimes known as probability sampling). The only problem is in ensuring that the process of drawing subjects is truly random, that a crofter on the Isle of Skye has as much chance of becoming a subject as a stockbroker in London. In reality – and this is a mistake often made by undergraduates – many so-called random samples have more in common with what is sometimes known as area sampling, a process of restricting the available population to particular areas, clusterings or locations. The undergraduate who randomly samples from his own neighbourhood, rather than travelling the country in his search for subjects, is guilty of this, running the risk that the particular section, or subset of the population from which he is drawing his sample is in some way unusual; a pre-election opinion poll taken in the West of Scotland for instance would generate very different findings from a similar poll in the English home counties. Having said this, however, most undergraduate studies rely on a highly restricted population for subjects, using for example schools in the area, or business premises in the neighbourhood. Provided the dangers of using a local population are understood – people in one location being more similar than if the entire population were considered, or even certain rare characteristics being overrepresented – the approach is acceptable, not to mention pragmatic. The random approach is of course the preferred method for drawing subjects from a population, especially useful in that it allows us to gather data from a population even when we know little about the characteristics of that population. However, to prevent us from oversampling from a particularly rare group, or underestimating common features in a population, sampling has to be extensive with large numbers of subjects drawn. The magnitude of this task makes the approach really only viable for major research, marketing or government organisations, with the unfortunate undergraduate restricted to more local populations, and all the attendant problems.

One of the advantages of random sampling mentioned above was that we didn't need to know all that much about a population in order to draw a fair, representative sample from it. However, in many cases we actually know a great deal about populations: how they are structured, the different subgroupings or strata which comprise them and the relative proportions of people who fall into the various categories. We know for example that people can be classified by social status, by earning bracket, by educational qualification and so on. Researchers have been able to use this knowledge to modify their sampling procedures such that much smaller samples can be drawn, in which the sample represents a smaller version of the population as a whole. The procedure, particularly useful to those involved in survey procedures, is termed, not surprisingly, **stratified sampling**, in which a population is divided into a number of predetermined subgroups on the basis of existing groupings or strata, or according to some predetermined design characteristic. The market researcher standing at a street corner watching passing shoppers, is probably trying to identify a quota of particular types of people: for example the study might require that individuals from different ethnic groups are interviewed, or the study might be on different socio-economic classes, or age ranges and so on. The great advantage of this approach is that, knowing how the population is structured, we can ensure that all relevant groupings are represented in our sample. This increases our confidence in the **generalisation** of findings to the population of interest since the typicality of our sample should be ensured. The trick is to know how the population is structured, not easy once we go beyond the clearly identifiable traits such as sex, age, weight and class; identifying the proportion of high to low income individuals can be gleaned readily through census and household survey material, but what is the proportion of introverts to extraverts?

Much easier than either of the above is the situation in which the independent variables in a study are the subjects' characteristics themselves, making it relatively easy to identify whom should participate. Going back to our earlier examples, if we are investigating social behaviour within pre-school children, then we are interested in a highly specific group. There is no need to randomly sample from the population at large – we need merely identify members of that single group and draw from them. Of course, sampling from highly specific groups should itself be random, to eliminate concentrations of particular characteristics but again, in most undergraduate research, even sampling from specific groups tends to be localised – inevitably raising the problem of situation specificity. Pragmatism though will still govern most student projects and as long as the problems are understood these limitations are likely to be tolerated. After all, few pieces of undergraduate work will be of the ground-breaking variety, the aim being primarily to provide an important learning experience.

In the case of a true experiment, where the independent variables are a matter of some form of manipulation, or experimental treatment, the problems are slightly different. On the one hand, if the key factors in our study are what we do to subjects, and not the subjects themselves, then it does not matter who we use. This is even more true when extraneous effects are subject to experimental controls. In a study comparing two different problem-solving approaches for instance (in which the independent variable is a strategy taught to subjects by the experimenter), we might have identified problem complexity as an interfering or interacting factor. To reduce the influence of this element we can ensure that problem complexity remains constant across both conditions of strategy or, if we are actually interested in interactions, we can incorporate this factor into our experiment as an additional independent variable. Either way, any old subjects would do for this kind of study, providing there was nothing present in the sample which in itself might affect the experiment.

In the event that we suspect subject characteristics might produce their own effects we might attempt to reduce individual differences through the process of randomisation (a procedure discussed in Chapter 2), in which subjects are randomly assigned to one or another of the experimental conditions. Alternatively, if a particular subject characteristic is deemed to be important enough, it can be dealt with by matching subjects in each group on this, or other, factors.

3.2.2 | *Subjects – how to get them*

It is all very well knowing whom you want to take part in your study; getting them is another matter altogether. In the case of an observation study in some kind of natural setting there is really no problem, since everyone in the situation is potentially a subject. Studying behaviour unobtrusively in a bank would automatically incorporate all customers, tellers and bank staff into your subject pool, although there are certain restrictions on this kind of study which must be understood before it can be implemented. Section 3.6 on ethics is of particular relevance here.

The real problem in obtaining subjects is that, with the notable exception of naturalistic observation research, all subjects in a study must be participating willingly. Commendable as this notion is, it does give rise to problems of its own: given the previous discussion on representativeness, how typical can our sample be of the general population if introverts, or neurotics, or heavily stressed individuals refuse to participate in our study – especially if these characteristics are known to be sources of variation within our dependent variable? Having said this however, all the various codes of practice governing the behaviour of social and behavioural researchers are in agreement on this point: no one should be a participant in any research without their consent, against their will or without their knowledge. So how are you going to get people flocking to take part in what you might well regard as cutting-edge research but which, from the subject's perspective, is as stimulating as watching paint dry?

For the majority of undergraduate research projects, subjects are usually drawn from other undergraduates, with the keen, first year student taking the brunt of the offensive. Indeed, some colleges and universities make it clear that there is an expectation for students – psychology undergraduates in particular – to participate in departmental research, whether carried out by fellow students or academic staff. The argument is that a student of a behavioural science is likely to learn as much about the processes of research by participating as by conducting, providing a detailed debriefing forms part of the experimental experience. However, true as this argument might be, it is nevertheless at odds with the general principle that experimental subjects should be willing volunteers. Moreover, making such expectations explicit detracts from the fact that most students are genuinely interested in what other people are up to, and will quite happily volunteer, if only in the knowledge that some day they too will be looking for subjects.

As a population, undergraduates are often suitable as a basis for research: when projects are designed for demonstration purposes or when dependent variables are pretty universal within the population at large (not affected by age, social class, region, etc.) rigorous sampling procedures are unnecessary.

Occasionally, though, undergraduates will prove inappropriate as experimental subjects – in situations where an understanding of certain psychological principles or phenomena would interfere with the course of a study, you clearly don't want psychology students. After all, how valid would an experiment be on visual illusions if your subjects have detailed knowledge of how these illusions operate and the mechanisms whereby they produce their misleading effects? There is also the more widespread problem that, as a group, the student population is not typical of the population at large. Students tend to be well-educated, bright and highly motivated; if they are also volunteers, then you have an unusual group indeed. Consequently, any findings which emerge from a student-based group might not generalise well to the population at large, simply because of their atypicality – in some respects this can be regarded as an extreme case of a **local sampling effect**. Having raised this point though, sometimes the student population represents the only practical group: an experiment, possibly one requiring repeated measures with the same subjects over a period of time, is unlikely to be popular, let alone possible, with members of the general public; fellow students may represent the only practical group for this type of study. As ever, though, the decision on which subjects to use rests with the experimenter and must be made based on a judgement balancing the relative importance of design needs and practicality, and weighing up the extent to which our dependent variables are likely to covary with other factors not present within the student sample.

3.2.3 *Special groups*

When a research project is of the quasi-experimental variety – that is when the design revolves not just around any particular manipulation on the part of the experimenter, but on the selection of particular types of subject – access to special groups must be sought. In the past it has not been unusual for undergraduate researchers to explore developmental processes among nursery children, to compare vocational aspirations among third form school pupils in deprived as opposed to wealthy communities, or to study work motivation among managerial staff in various organisations. Some enterprising individuals might even have obtained access to local maternity units in order to evaluate differing coping strategies among mums-to-be. However, while such creative work has been possible in the past, it is becoming increasingly difficult for researchers of any stature – let alone undergraduates working on final projects – to work with certain, special groups. Part of the problem relates to a growing sensitivity, particularly within educational and health institutions; recent developments concerning changes in status and accountability have made many individuals at managerial level in these organisations extremely cautious about, if not suspicious of, any research which might reflect badly on policy, practices and procedures. Indeed, it is now a common requirement that any proposal for research in a health or educational sphere, no matter what the source, be considered by an appropriate committee and assessed on the grounds of ethics, potential disruptiveness and public relations. Moreover, since such evaluation committees tend to meet at irregular intervals, the time constraints on most student projects make the use of such groups impractical.

Occasionally an individual might, by dint of personal background, experience or contacts, have access to groups which might otherwise be inaccessible. Some students work part time in offices, some act as helpers in nurseries or school libraries, and some even offer their spare time for voluntary work among the deprived, the homeless or the addicted. In such cases it is often possible to carry out a practical study within a special subject group, not as a result of some back-door enterprise, but simply because approval is more likely to be granted as a result of a personal request from someone known, than if a proposal arrived cold, through the post from some anonymous source. It wouldn't be the first time that a tutor, trying to guide a supervisee towards a practical research topic, asks if the student has access to some particular group. More than a few studies have evolved not from some burning research issue, but simply because of the availability of a particular section of the population.

3.2.4 | *Ensuring questionnaire responses*

In some ways experimentation at undergraduate level is the easiest to organise: the population is relatively captive and most of your peers will co-operate with whatever strange experimental scenario you have devised. When your study involves a questionnaire though, or attempts to survey members of the wider population, problems can arise. Approaching people in the street can be a soul-destroying experience – just recall the deftness with which all of us manage to avoid the desperate looking market researcher in the high street and you will recognise the difficulties. Most of us don't like being diverted from our goals and everyone striding down a busy street is going somewhere – to the shops, to meet friends, to the office after an overextended lunch; it is much better to catch people whose goals have been attained, or even thwarted. Waiting rooms, queues, libraries will likely provoke more co-operation than trying to stand in the way of some poor woman, laden down with shopping and children who just knows she's going to miss the last bus home. At least though, in a face-to-face situation, once you have caught someone's attention, the chances are they will be reasonably happy to answer your questions or fill in your questionnaire. This is by no means true in the much more anonymous case of postal questionnaires.

Many surveys use the device of postal questionnaires for the obvious reasons that they are cheap – no more than the price of a stamp – and huge sections of the population can be reached quickly. Unfortunately, the approach is also prone to generating the poorest response rate of all data gathering techniques – with one or two notable exceptions. The problem is that few people see any reason to respond to a 'cold' questionnaire; in the face-to-face scenario, there are all kinds of subtle pressures and rewards present which make it likely that someone will take the time to answer your questions, no matter how banal – you provide a distraction to a boring wait at the bus stop, they like your face or they are touched by your expressions of relief and deep joy to find someone who isn't running away from them. Either way, despite its own set of problems, the direct approach will usually produce a co-operative response due to factors which are simply not present in the more distant postal approach.

Receiving a questionnaire through the post lacks the warmth and human reinforcements of the direct, one-to-one approach. Add this to the requirement of not just filling in the questionnaire, but also posting it back – a chore, even if a stamped addressed envelope is provided – and we should be surprised that anyone takes the bother to respond at all. Most people would probably prefer to expend the energy in steaming the stamp off the envelope than to answer questions on a form. The exceptions are when there is a legal obligation, as in the case of the national census – there is a threat of fine or imprisonment for non-compliance; when there is a positive reward on offer – as when we fill in forms to obtain credit; or it is implied that answering questions and returning on time will make us eligible to win ten million pounds; or when it is clearly in the interests of respondents to comply. If none of these conditions can be met then it would seem that another method must be sought to collect data.

| 3.2.5 | *How many subjects?*

Along with 'Whom should I choose?', 'How many should I get?' ranks as one of the most common questions asked of tutors. Unfortunately it also seems to trigger the most common of responses, as in 'How long is a piece of string?', or the equally unhelpful 'How many can you get?'

Box 3.2 Getting a response!

There are three tried and tested methods of increasing response rate to postal questionnaires.

1. Legal sanctions
'Failure to comply could result in a fine or even imprisonment' (Few undergraduates will be in a position to enforce threats of this nature. This is usually left to national governments or the power companies.)

2. Offer of financial reward
'Reply within seven days and you could be entered in our million pound prize draw, or be eligible to win one of our other wonderful prizes' (Student loans are unlikely to extend to offering real financial incentives to potential respondents.)

3. Implication that a response might provide something of benefit, either to the respondent or to others.
'Your responses, and the responses of others in your situation might help in some day finding a cure for. . .' (A cynical sounding statement, obscuring the fact that most people like to be helpful and are willing to share their experiences, especially when those experiences are in some way unusual or abnormal. The abuse of this approach is both unethical and unforgivable.)

There are some techniques for estimating appropriate sample sizes from particular populations, but in the case of most student research, where the entire population is simply not available, rule-of-thumb guides are probably more useful. The most important thing about choosing a sample to study is to bear in mind just exactly what it is you are doing and why. Remember, the whole point of any research is to find out something about people in general, or the population at large. The impracticalities of studying such a large group though make it necessary to work with a small sample, and then generalise up to the larger population, but to be able to do this without falling into the trap of situation specificity (see 3.2.1) we must ensure that our sample is typical, or representative of the whole population. Now if the population at large were a relatively stable, homogenous group, containing little in the way of variability, then our sample could be relatively small. In a study of cloned frogs, for instance, where each member of the population was almost identical to every other member, a sample containing a mere handful of specimens would suffice; any findings stemming from studying this sample would probably be true of the whole population. Studying people is another matter altogether.

Throughout the course of this book the authors have been continually reminding its readership of the complexity of human behaviour. No two people are ever truly alike – even genetically identical twins cannot occupy the same space so will be subject to different environmental influences – and humanity in general comprises a vast range of traits, needs, wants, attitudes, perceptions, experiences, predispositions and aspirations. Indeed it is the sheer variety of the elements which make up human nature which makes people such a rich and fulfilling research area. Unfortunately, for the same reason, the study of human behaviour can be the most taxing and frustrating.

Part of the problem revolves around the sampling issue – if there is so much variation within the population, no sample, unless it is huge, is going to contain enough of the same variability to reflect honestly the larger world. Small samples will always run the risk of missing out important elements of a population, or even overrepresenting particular groups.

'I have bad news – the human race is shrinking!'
'I have worse news – there are only seven people in your sample, and none of them are over four feet.'
'Ah...!'

By and large, the rule has to be: as many subjects as you can get. A sample containing 50 subjects will say more about the population from which it has been drawn than a sample of only 10. In terms of analysis moreover, proving hypotheses statistically will be more successful when a large number of observations are available than when only a few are present. Consider a situation in which a spatial test suggests a tiny superiority of male subjects over females. If our sample were small, say, 20 subjects (10 of each sex) then it would be highly likely that any observed differences, unless they were huge, would be due merely to chance, or individual differences. Statistical analysis would probably agree, producing inconclusive findings when the two groups are compared. However, if such a marginal difference were maintained, and was still present when our sample size grew to 200, then we may well have discovered a real effect.

Sample size then is really a question of balance, and judgement. If the effect we are exploring is likely to be large, then a relatively small sample size will probably demonstrate it. If the anticipated effect is small, however, we would want a much larger number of observations.

Design factors must also be a consideration: repeated measures designs require fewer subjects than between subjects designs (see Chapter 2); and between-subjects designs with many conditions will need a larger pool of subjects (see Box 3.3).

So far, much emphasis has been placed on ensuring sufficient numbers of subjects in our sample. Only then can we conduct appropriate statistical tests and generalise to the wider population, and by and large this is true. However, there is a danger in emphasising a quantitative approach if it causes us to ignore potentially rich supplies of information, marred only by the fact that it comes from a limited source. While there is still a small band of researchers who continue to believe that if you can't work out means and standard deviations, or subject your data to parametric analyses, then there's no point

Box 3.3 Conditional on conditions

A questionnaire-based study investigating attitudes towards dental hygiene identified a number of factors, each with varying numbers of levels.

Gender   male   female

Age   <10   11–20   21–30   31–40   41–50   51–60   >60

To maintain even a minimum of five subjects in each possible condition (male 11–20; female 31–40, etc.) would require a sample of 70.

If a third factor of social class were to be considered (comprising five different class levels) a stratified sampling procedure would require some 350 subjects. Using a random sampling procedure, a draw of the same sample size might result in one or more of the conditions not being filled (i.e., even out of 350 randomly selected individuals it is possible that not one will be male, skilled and in the 21–30 age group).

in doing the research at all, most contemporary workers in the field recognise the value of working with small samples or conducting qualitative research.

One aspect of working with small samples involves what has become known as small-n research. This describes a particular technique of studying behaviour commonly found in the clinical setting. Extensive measurements are taken on particular behaviours before and after some form of intervention – be it therapy, drug treatment or whatever – and comparisons made, very often on the basis of only one subject. Alternatively, rather than concentrating on precise measurements, qualitative information can be sought, relying on a subject's introspections, expressions of feeling or other sources of descriptive information to describe behaviour. While work in a clinical setting is likely to be a rare experience for the undergraduate, the general procedures for working with small (or even single subject) samples can still be applied. There is a great deal which can be learned from small but unusual subject groups using non-quantitative procedures, and the later section on qualitative techniques (Chapter 6) provides considerable discussion on this very issue.

3.3 Data collection – using standard instruments

Most studies at some point are likely to make use of a standard instrument, such as a psychological test, either as a device for assigning subjects to different experimental conditions, or as a key source of data, as in an outcome measure. This could be an existing personality test used to classify subjects as Type A or Type B personality types, extraverts or introverts, tender-minded or tough-minded, or whatever – categories which will comprise the various elements of an independent variable. Alternatively, standard instruments could provide us with our dependent measure, as in a stress or wellbeing questionnaire measuring the impact of unemployment, or a job satisfaction instrument assessing responses to different supervisory styles in industry. By and large, using existing tests as part of a study can make life a little easier for the researcher; normally, before a test can be released on to the market, it must demonstrate that it is fit for its purpose – a great deal of preparatory work then has invariably gone into the design and construction of a psychological test. This provides the researcher with a useful measurement or classification tool without the need for the lengthy process required in developing a new instrument from scratch. However, using a psychological test correctly requires familiarity with the general principles underlying psychometric measurement, in addition to the essential characteristics of any particular test. Such a level of competence can only be attained through many years of experience with testing instruments; furthermore, the major publishers and distributors of psychological tests have for some years provided training courses in various aspects of assessment while, more recently, the British Psychological Society (BPS) has introduced an accreditation scheme whereby potential test users are obliged to undertake specific training before they are regarded as qualified to use particular tests. This is an important consideration, since failure to understand how a test has developed, or what specific responses mean, or a failure to prevent bias in administering or scoring can lead to misinterpretation of scores and misleading – or even damaging – information being fed back to the testee. Equally dangerous is the potential for exploitation when tests are used by unqualified or unscrupulous people and it is largely for these reasons that the BPS has introduced its accreditation scheme.

The observant reader might have realised by now that most undergraduates are unlikely to have either the experience or training to include existing psychological tests as part of their research. The assumption though is that it is the competence of the supervisor and the department to which they belong which allows the use of such instruments, not the student, although in all cases the user will be expected to familiarise themselves thoroughly with whichever test they will be using.

3.3.1   *What you need to know about psychological tests*

While it would be nice to test every aspect of a behaviour under investigation, such that we could explore someone's entire personality, or measure every single aspect of their life as it relates to the issue we are interested in, this is clearly impractical. Any such test would be not only unwieldy, but would probably take a lifetime to administer. What tests actually do is study a small but carefully chosen sample of an individual's behaviour, in the hope that we can generalise from the specific to the global, in much the same way that a survey, while its main interest is the entire population, can only ever explore a small section of that population. Hence, a vocabulary test cannot address every single word in a person's repertoire; rather it deals with a sample of what the individual knows.

To be of any use in predicting or describing behaviour in general, this sample must be **representative** of the overall area, both in terms of *type* and *number* of items. An arithmetic test using only five items for instance, or only items on multiplication, would be a poor test of arithmetic skill. A good test on the other hand would have to include items on addition, subtraction, multiplication and division. Furthermore, we might be unhappy if such a test omitted items involving fraction or decimal calculations and we might also expect some measure of computational abilities such as dealing with square roots, power or factorial calculations. The underlying point here is that it would be impossible to develop a good, representative test of any aspect of behaviour, unless the composition of that behaviour had been fully considered in advance.

While we expect test designers to demonstrate a sound knowledge of their particular area, it is equally important that we, as ultimate users of tests, also understand a good deal about the behaviour we are testing. How else could we judge whether or not a test was a good one for our purposes, or, given a number of similar tests, how would we know which was the best?

3.3.2 Standardisation

Even the best test in the world will be wasted unless we can ensure that scores reflect the behaviour that we are interested in, as opposed to some other factor. Notorious 'other factors' which can affect apparent performance on a test are instructions given to subjects, anxiety of the test-takers, motivational factors, methods of collecting data and scoring procedures. Unless every individual who completes a test does so under identical, standardised conditions, any observed differences might simply reflect **procedural variations** rather than actual differences in behaviour. Box 3.4 illustrates the point.

Box 3.4   Testing IQ or motivation?

Instructions given to a group of college students prior to the administration of a standard intelligence test.

Instruction A
'The test you are about to complete is one of the most advanced tests of intellectual functioning yet devised. Your scores on this test will be considered by a team of experts and their decision will partially determine whether or not you are allowed to enter the honours stream next session. It is therefore important that you do well in the test.'

Instruction B
'I'm afraid today's video presentation is cancelled due to technical difficulties so, for want of anything better to do, I've got this intelligence test here. It's not an especially good test but it might be a bit of fun and it will give you something to do.'

Each of the above sets of instructions is in its own way inappropriate (and also unethical) in that they actively cue respondents to approach the test in particular ways. We would not be surprised to obtain two completely differing sets of scores but in this case measuring not intelligence, but more probably, motivation or – especially among those receiving Instruction A – test anxiety.

Fortunately, many test constructors are well aware of this issue and are able to employ several procedures to reduce the effects of administration variability. The Eysenck Personality Questionnaire (EPQ) (Eysenck and Eysenck, 1975) is a good example: a preprinted test with restricted response categories and instructions clearly printed on every copy. Even scoring has been taken out of the hands (or judgement) of the administrator, being achieved via standard scoring stencils. Finally, interpretation of individual profiles can be guided by reference to printed norms, a procedure with which all test users must become familiar.

3.3.3 | *Norms*

Contrary to popular belief, there is no predetermined pass or fail level in psychological tests – it would be nonsense to talk of passing a personality test for instance, although the notion might seem less bizarre if we are dealing with something like intelligence. In fact, in the majority of tests, individual scores are compared against other scores which have previously been collated by the test designer. This comparison function is obtained by first administering the test to a large, representative sample of those for whom the test will subsequently be used (**the standardisation sample**). This provides us with a **norm**, which is simply a measure, or series of measures, indicating how people typically (or normally) perform on this test.

Norms can take various forms, although usually they comprise a measure of average performance (being the arithmetic average, or mean of the scores of all the participants in the standardisation sample), and a measure of the extent to which scores tend to vary above and below this average (given as a standard deviation, see Chapter 4, Section 4.4). The point of these measures is that, provided the people who tried out the test during these initial stages are representative of the broader population, what is true for the sample should be true for everyone. And this is a crucial point – for statistical purposes a standardisation sample of 600 or so subjects would be fine, providing that what we are measuring is pretty stable in the population. If, however, a test is being designed to measure some trait which is known (or suspected) to be influenced by many factors (it can vary with age, sex, social class, occupation, etc.), then the sample would need to be much larger to allow the different sources of variability to be reasonably well represented. (This issue has been discussed more fully in 3.2.1.) In the development of the EPQ, one of the better known instruments of its type, the authors used a standardisation sample of more than 5,000 subjects. With a sample this large, they were able to explore the major traits of psychoticism, extroversion and neuroticism by age, sex and some 47 different occupational groups, a diversification which would not have been possible with smaller numbers of subjects. The point of this protracted discussion on norms and samples is that, if a test is to be used as part of a student project (or indeed for any research purpose), it is important to be aware of how relevant norms are to the group being studied: a standardisation sample which is small, or which does not allow for sources of variation, might be of limited value in describing the larger population.

Returning to the EPQ, the large standardisation sample allows us not only to state that the average extraversion score for all males in the sample was 13.19 and for females 12.6, but also that the average for male students was 13.8 with female students 13.49. Similar information is available for many other occupational categories.

Providing an average measure of performance on a test is a common method of presenting norms, but there are others. Most typical, and more informative in some ways, are norms which are expressed as **percentiles**: a measure of the percentage of the standardisation sample which scored at or below a particular level. Hence, if a test manual informs us that a score of 35 on an abstract reasoning test is at the 50th percentile, then we know that approximately 50 per cent of the standardisation sample scored 35 or less; if we are told that a score of 59 lies at the 95th percentile, then we know that 95 per cent of the standardisation sample scored 59 or less, and so on. For a fuller discussion on proportioning test scores, and for alternative methods of presenting norms, Kline (1993) should be consulted (see Section 3.9).

3.3.4 | Test reliability

Every measuring instrument, if it is to be of any use, must possess a number of important qualities. The first of these is that it must be sensitive to whichever aspect of the environment it is measuring – be it some physical property or a psychological phenomenon – and accurately detect any changes which might occur. Equally important, it must not indicate change where no change has taken place. This may sound strange, but consider an everyday measuring instrument, such as a ruler. If we measure the height of a table on a Monday and obtain a measure of 1 metre, but on the Tuesday obtain a height of 1.3 metres, there are two things which can have occurred. The first is that the table (for some bizarre reason) has changed its dimensions in the course of a day and is now 0.3 metres taller than it was on Monday, a change which has been accurately detected by our ruler. Alternatively, the table has not changed, rather it is the ruler which has changed – possibly some temperature-sensitive metal was used in its manufacture and the thing actually shrank overnight. The point of this example is that, with a psychological test, we always try to ensure that the first case is the typical one – when a change is signalled it must be the aspect of the environment which is changing and not the instrument itself. In other words, a test must demonstrate consistency, or *reliability*. There are a number of ways in which this might be done:

Test-retest reliability. The simplest and most direct method for demonstrating that a test is behaving consistently is to measure the same thing twice: the same test is administered to the same subjects and the two scores compared, using a form of correlation (a statistical technique for exploring the relationship between two variables or, in this case, two tests – see Chapter 4, 4.10.1 to 4.10.3). Obvious problems here are **practice effects**, which could actually produce a poor comparison between two presentations of the same test and lead us wrongly to assume the instrument is not reliable when in fact the opposite is the case – the test has been sensitive to the change in behaviour. Alternatively, if subjects recall their original responses and attempt to reproduce them, an artificially high correspondence between the two measures might occur, demonstrating more the reliability of subjects' memories than the stability of the test. Only tests not affected by repetition can be assessed in this way.

Alternate-form reliability. When there is a danger of straightforward repetition producing a misleading reliability measure – as in the memory issue – two different forms of the test can be given to the same subjects and the scores correlated. Care should be taken to ensure that the two forms of the test are truly equivalent and of course practice can still influence performance.

There is a method for assessing reliability without the need for two repetitions of the same, or parallel, forms of the same test – **split-half reliability**. In this variant, a test is administered once only, the items split in half and the two halves correlated. Sometimes a straight split is made, with the first half of a test compared with the second half, while at others, the split is in terms of odd-numbered items versus even-numbered ones. However, this method is not so much a measure of temporal reliability (consistency over time) as of internal consistency, and should not be regarded as an alternative to either of the previous approaches. If a good comparison is achieved, the individual items are deemed to be consistent and the test largely reliable. There are of course a number of problems in attempting to demonstrate reliability, with practice and memory effects having already been discussed. Equally important though are procedural and administration factors – any variations between successive repetitions of a test will adversely affect reliability measures. Nor is the split-half approach without its problems, with the strength of comparisons often varying depending on how the split is made. There are statistical ways of dealing with reliability problems, and the actual correlation between two testings is not the conventional calculation most undergraduates are familiar with, but rather a development which attempts to counterbalance the deficiencies of the reliability procedure in general. The manuals which accompany all tests ought to provide details of the procedures used to establish reliability, together with the associated **reliability coefficients**. For illustrations on the calculation of these statistics, any of the references dealing with psychometrics at the end of this chapter are suitable.

3.3.5   *Test validity*

The next crucial quality that a test should possess is validity. This is simply an expression of the extent to which a test is actually measuring what it is supposed to be measuring, although the methods available to demonstrate this quality are often far from simple. In terms of test characteristics validity is possibly even more important than reliability. After all, reliability only tells us that whatever the test is measuring, it is doing so consistently. It doesn't necessarily inform us about what the test is actually measuring. If a test is demonstrably valid, though, we know it is doing what it claims to do. Unfortunately, in the historical development of psychological testing some of the early forms of intelligence test were proved invalid when it was observed that they could not be completed successfully without a conventional educational background – they had more to do with scholastic aptitude than that which people regard as pure intelligence (whatever that might be). This is validity, and this example also offers an idea of the scope of the problem. Given that many tests attempt to measure aspects of behaviour which are largely implicit and assumed to exist through indirect observation and inference (creativity, personality, intelligence, etc.), and whose presence remains a subject of fierce debate among theorists, the problem of validity becomes a huge and, some might argue, insoluble one. Having said this though, a number of methods are available which go some way towards demonstrating the fitness of particular tests, and the different types of validity are discussed in the following sections.

Content validity. If a test is to demonstrate content validity then the content of the test must accurately and adequately reflect the content of the behaviour under investigation. In the case of an attitude measure for example, the content of the test should be based on a thorough under-standing of the attitude, its correlates, associated measures and likely values expressed; knowledge tests should be a fair representation of the topics which comprise the information base – your psychology exam for instance should be a good expression of the course of study, reflecting topic diversity, issues raised and references given. If it does not, students have every right to complain about the lack of content validity present in their exam (the content of the test failed to reflect the content of the course). However, many such tests can become overloaded with items which lend themselves to objective testing. While it is easy enough to explore an individual's familiarity with information aspects of an issue, how do you measure something like critical appraisal? And, as previously mentioned, early intelligence tests comprised primarily items on academic skill rather than abstract reasoning, creativity and the like. Achievement tests in particular will invariably be examined in terms of their content validity.

Face validity. This is often confused with the previous test feature, since, as with content validity the concern is with the appearance of a test. However, face validity is not a true indication of validity, being concerned only with what a test appears to measure, and having little to do with what is actually being measured (on the face of it, what does this test seem to be measuring?). Nevertheless, this represents a useful feature of any test because there will be a relationship between how people view a test and their willingness to participate; if we see an instrument as childish, irrelevant or even insulting, we will certainly not give it our full attention. Box 3.5 illustrates this issue.

Note, in some cases, especially in the area of attitudinal research, it is not always possible to ensure face validity – in a situation where a subject may not respond honestly if the true purpose of the test is known, we may be tempted to disguise part of the test content. This of course must be done with extreme caution and only with considerable justification. It should be understood that this approach actively deceives subjects and adherence to ethical guidelines (as published by the BPS) must be ensured. See Box 3.6 for an illustration of the problem, and also the section on questionnaire design in which this issue is further explored.

Criterion-related validity. When a test is developed to diagnose something about an individual's present circumstances, or to predict something about a person's future, validation can sometimes be effected by comparing test scores to some other indicator (or criterion) of what the test is trying to measure. An occupational selection test for example can be checked against later job performance (which is actually how such tests are validated);

Box 3.5 On the face of it. . .

Orange ice lollies cost 50p each, raspberry lollies 35p and lemon ones 40p. If a schoolboy has £1.60p to spend in his tuck shop, and he wants to buy at least one of each for his friends, of which flavour of ice lolly can he buy two?

The above problem would be a good (valid) item in a test of general arithmetic reasoning. However, if the item appeared in a test designed for trainee electrical engineers, the response would more likely be derisory laughter than the correct answer (which is raspberry lollies for the computationally challenged). For this particular group the item would not have face validity. Some rephrasing however would achieve the desired result:

1 millimetre cable costs £35 per 100 metre drum, 1.5 cable £40 per drum and 2.5 millimetre cable £50 per drum. If a project buyer needs electrical cable of each size and has £160 to spend, of which diameter cable can he buy 200 metres and stay within his budget?

This is the same item as the previous one, except, for this particular group, it now has face validity. (By the way, the correct answer is 1 millimetre cable, in case you haven't got the idea yet.)

Box 3.6   How needy?

Armed with a limited budget and charged with identifying the most needy 20 per cent of pensioners most in need of additional subsistence payments, you devise a questionnaire to determine differing levels of deprivation.

Please indicate on the scale below, how adequate your pension is in meeting your individual needs.

1	2	3	4	5
totally inadequate	inadequate	acceptable	pretty good	wonderful

If other items on the questionnaire are like this, approximately 99 per cent of our sample will fall into our most needy category – simply because it is obvious what the questionnaire is about, and what the consequences of particular responses will be. Modifying the appearance of items however might provide a more subtle route to the information you are looking for, e.g., if items appear to be measuring more general behaviour than obvious levels of deprivation:

Please indicate how often you enjoy a hot meal in the course of a week?

Approximately how much do you spend on fuel in the course of a week?

On average, how many times do you go shopping during the week?

Items like this allow us to infer certain things about respondents, indirectly, and it could be argued that for some types of information this form of deception is the only way of ensuring an honest or accurate response. However, an approach of this type is deceptive and runs counter to the spirit of openness which forms the basis of current ethical principles. Such approaches also tend to encourage the sense of mistrust in which psychology is often regarded by others. The question is, is the need for such information so great that the means by which we obtain it are justified?

a neuroticism test can be checked against counsellor's records, or friends' ratings of behaviour. A scholastic achievement test can be checked against assignment ratings, and so on. Within this general procedure of relating test scores to some other criterion though, there is a particular condition concerning the temporal relationship between the test and its criterion measure (i.e., when we actually obtain this validating information). This relationship is determined by the nature of the test itself – whether or not it is measuring something about an individual's current circumstances, or whether it is predicting something about the future.

Concurrent. The criterion against which scores are to be checked is obtained at the same time. This is the type of proof which is necessary when a test is assessing some aspect of a current condition (as in a diagnostic test).

Predictive. In a test which predicts something (as with aptitude tests), a follow-up study is carried out to test the strength of the prediction. Most selection tests are obliged to demonstrate criterion related predictive validity, since everything from an interview to a job sample test is predicting something about job candidates. If a selection test is described as having predictive validity, then during its design phase it might have been administered to job candidates as part of a general selection and recruitment process. Subsequent assessment of individuals actually hired by the company would be compared with the predictions made on the original test, and if a good match is obtained, the test is declared valid. Only then would it be developed for future use in the selection process.

A problem here is criterion contamination, in which the independent measure can become contaminated by knowledge of the test results and therefore ceases to be truly independent.

'He looks sick, what do you think?'
'Yeah, now that you mention it . . . '

Construct validity. This indicates the extent to which a test measures some theoretical construct or concept, such as intelligence, creativity or personality. Not surprisingly this represents the most difficult form of validity to demonstrate, since the concepts being measured – as the name suggests – are really theoretical entities whose existence is inferred by observation of related activities. Consequently, validation of such concepts is also indirect – measurements of activities which are believed to be related to, expressions of, or caused by, some underlying factor.

Age differentiation is one such indirect method of validation: if a trait is expected to change with age, performance on the test should reflect this change. For instance, if the understanding of certain linguistic concepts is part of a developmental process, we should be able to observe this by comparing older children with younger ones.

Correlation with other tests is another commonly used validation method whereby a new test should compare well with existing tests of the same trait.

Administration to extreme groups offers another method of validation, such that if two groups are known to differ on a trait, again the test should reflect this difference (a personality test for instance might clearly distinguish between extreme extraverts and extreme introverts). This is a particularly crude measure however, since it will only demonstrate that a test is capable of identifying broad differences and not how well it measures fine distinctions.

In fact, in the case of construct validity, a number of independent measures would be used to provide a comparison function, and most manuals for specific tests will offer extensive detail on how precisely the test was validated.

All of the foregoing discussion from Section 3.3 onwards represents essential reading for anyone contemplating using a standard testing instrument as part of a study. It is important to understand how a test was devised, how reliable it is and what steps were taken to prove its validity. Familiarity with test norms are also vital, since this information tells us for whom the test is suitable, and what particular scores are likely to mean. Apart from being a major factor in determining your competence to use a given test, you will also be required in a final report to justify fully the use of a particular instrument. And none of this is possible unless you *read the manual.*

While standardised tests form a common element in undergraduate research, there will be occasions when no existing test is suitable for a particular design, or when an issue is being explored using questionnaire or survey methods. This is usually the case when a contemporary attitudinal issue is being investigated or when some kind of behavioural measure is being devised. In such cases researchers must develop their own instrument, a task sufficiently demanding that sometimes the design of a measure – with all the attendant requirements of reliability and validity – becomes the study itself.

Whether the development of an instrument is part of a broader study, or whether it is seen as an end in itself, there are a number of guidelines which can make the task easier. The next section covers these issues.

3.4   Using questionnaires in research

3.4.1   Questionnaire design – how to get information

So far, we have decided on the research issue we are going to explore, we know whom we are going to use as subjects and we have decided on the key components of our hypothesis (i.e., we are exploring sex differences, relationships or whatever); we also know what kind of information we want from our subjects, the precise data needed to test our hypotheses and to explore the research issue in question. So how are we going to get this information?

Some research designs will use standardised tests to generate information (stress measures, neuroticism scores, etc.), others will rely on an outcome measure of a laboratory experiment (reaction times, frequency of correct responses to stimuli or changes in decision times). Many designs though will require custom-made procedures to gather information, as researchers devise questionnaires to assess attitudes to numerous issues, to obtain information on what people do in various situations or to explore the distribution of different categories in the population. Gathering information in these ways is not without its problems, but the following sections attempt to make the process a little easier, explaining the pitfalls and offering solutions.

Probably the simplest rule of information gathering is: 'if you want to know something, ask', and, by and large, this is the most useful rule to follow when designing a questionnaire or interview schedule. Just ask your subjects to tell you what you want to know. Most people are honest, disingenuous and, once they have agreed to participate in a study, usually willing and co-operative. Unfortunately, a common perception of psychology is one of a somewhat sneaky profession, relying on methods of deception and misdirection for its research. Even among students of the discipline, there is a view that subjects have to be tricked in some way into giving honest, objective responses and, unfortunately, such a view will only continue to encourage the sense of suspicion and mistrust directed at the profession by outsiders. While such a lamentable state of affairs may have its justifications in the type of research allowed before the guidelines set up by the BPS and its American counterpart, the *American Psychological Association* (APA) contem-porary views frown on the needless use of deceptive techniques. In most instances – with certain qualifiers – the direct approach is best: if you want to know something, ask. The qualifiers though are important.

The general rule of ask and ye shall be answered holds true most of the time. Sometimes though, the nature of response can be influenced by who does the asking and how the asking is done. Consider the following question: 'Have you ever, at any time in your life, committed a crime?'

A simple enough question, if asked by a social science researcher guaranteeing absolute confidentiality. Consider though the nature of response if the same question was asked by a serving police officer conducting research into criminal behaviour among undergraduates. So the 'Who' of a question is important and what all researchers must ask themselves is: 'Will the fact that *I* am asking a particular question affect the response?'

The other major qualifier is the 'How' of a question. The example above: 'Have you ever, at any time in your life, committed a crime?' can only generate either a Yes or No response. Modifying the question to: 'What crimes, no matter how small or insignificant, have you ever committed in your life?' is likely to produce a very different class of response. Aside from the fact that this could be described as a leading question (it assumes people do commit crime) the asker has no control over the type and quantity of response. Anything from a 'How dare you . . .', to a two-page list of guilt-ridden confession is possible. And so, the 'How' of a question is an important quality consideration. The following section describes the most common ways of asking questions and the kinds of response each produces.

3.4.2 | Types of scale

There are two broad types of question available to the researcher: one in which the compiler controls the nature of the response and one in which the subject is free to respond in any way. Both have their uses and their disadvantages, and the decision as to which method to apply is one the researcher must make in terms of the context of the research and the quality of the information required.

1 Closed-ended questions

This is where the possible range of responses is predetermined by the tester: the opportunity for free response is closed to the person answering, e.g. **Dichotomous** – A question offering only two answer choices.

Are you enjoying this book so far?

              Yes   No

The type of data questions like this produce are in the grand tradition of survey techniques, as outlined in Chapter 1 of this book (1.4.8 and 1.4.9). Subjects respond by selecting one or another of the nominally-scaled categories and sample data can be presented simply, by referring to the numbers, proportions or percentages of subjects who selected each category. Table 3.1 and Figure 3.1 demonstrate the economy and elegance of this approach.

Both Table 3.1 and Figure 3.1 offer an 'at a glance' summary of the data, and the Yes/No distinction represents one of the simplest; and most common item formats available to researchers. However, care must be taken not to confuse simplicity with impoverishment; true, the Yes/No response options provide only limited information but, when other variables are introduced, the basic dichotomous distinction suddenly becomes quite sophisticated.

Consider the above example when we wish to analyse further the Yes/No choice in terms of the student's sex, or age group, or study options; suddenly we have more than straightforward descriptive data – we can begin to make comparisons and to make inferences. We have now moved, and quite

Table 3.1   Responses of 200 psychology students to an attitude measure

Item: Are you enjoying this book so far?		
Response	N	per cent
Yes	120	60
No	80	40

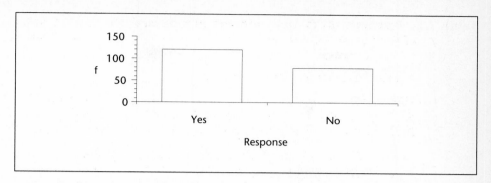

Figure 3.1   The frequency (f) of response of 200 psychology students to the item 'Are you enjoying this book so far?'

painlessly at that, to a point where the obsessive, number devouring statistician begins to take an interest.

However, the dichotomous example is only one of a variety of closed-response formats. There is no reason why we should stick to just two possible responses when, with most questions we might want to ask, there are invariably several types of response possible:

Multiple – A question offering three or more choices for the respondent:

e.g. This year, are you going to:

a. Work harder than before?   ☐

b. Find a more interesting course?   ☐

c. Try and marry money?   ☐

d. Stay in the pub?   ☐

Just as with the previous example, the response categories are independent of one another: i.e., there is no relationship of magnitude between any one category and another, only of difference – the essence indeed of all nominal scales. Similarly, the display of data is equally straightforward, as Table 3.2 and Figure 3.2 demonstrate.

Rating scales – A scale which rates some attribute from positive to negative, low to high, strong to weak.

Moving along the continuum of sophistication, but still retaining control of how subjects can respond, are scaled items. Instead of requiring subjects to choose from a number of response categories which differ in type from one

Table 3.2   Responses of 200 students to an attitude measure

Item:
This year are you going to:

Response	N	per cent
a. Work harder than before?	20	10
b. Find a more interesting course?	50	25
c. Try and marry money?	100	50
d. Stay in the pub?	30	15

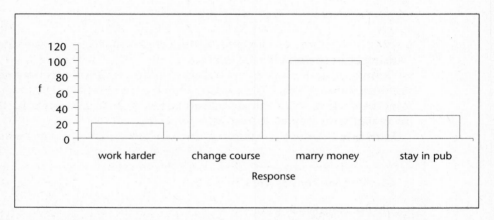

Figure 3.2   The frequency (f) of response of 200 students to the question 'This year are you going to. . .?'

another (as in the dichotomous and multiple examples above), we focus on just one single category and require subjects to indicate their strength of feeling on the issue. In the 'are you enjoying the course so far' example, subjects could only state that Yes, they were or No, they weren't. Interesting as such responses are, they nonetheless obscure possible variability within either category. i.e., one Yes respondent might be transcendentally ecstatic about the course, whereas another might merely be adopting a 'yeah, it's OK' attitude. This kind of internal distinction is lost in fixed category items, but is accessible in rating scales in which, at its most basic level, nominally-scaled responses are transformed into ordinally-scaled ones. Consider the restructuring of the previous Yes/No item.

e.g. I am enjoying the course:

A great deal   Not at all
      1   2   3   4   5

      ☐   ☐   ☐   ☐   ☐

Not only does this provide a more detailed picture of how subjects vary within an issue, it also moves the information generated away from the descriptive towards the more traditionally quantitative. What this means is that, while in the previous examples subjects differed in the **type** of response they could make, now subjects differ in terms of, at the least, order, and even **magnitude**, or quantity of response. It also moves the analysis of data into a format with which many people feel more comfortable – we now have measures of central tendency (average) and variability to play with!

However, the presentation of such data is no less straightforward than for the earlier examples, provided we are familiar with the concepts of sample statistics. Table 3.3 and Figures 3.3 and 3.4 demonstrate this.

Translating back to our original attitude item, we can now readily interpret these numerical values in terms of the scale itself (see Figure 3.3).

As with our qualitative examples we can of course make our analysis more sophisticated with the inclusion of additional independent profiles, or subject variables. For instance, we can compare the different sexes on the same scale, or different seminar groups, or whatever. Figure 3.4 demonstrates this.

A special variant of scaled items comes to us from Likert (1932). In this approach, subjects are asked to provide their level of agreement with a statement. Usually (though not always) corresponding numerical values are absent and appended only later when the researcher converts response categories to quantitative equivalents. For example, in the following

Table 3.3 Mean response rates to an attitude item

Item	μ (mean)	σ (SD)
I am enjoying the course	3.75	0.64

The mean provides a measure of central tendency (average) on the issue and SD (standard deviation) a measure of how much on average, scores varied around this value. Sections 4.3.1 and 4.3.2 in Chapter 4 explain these concepts in greater detail.

In this illustration the median, or middle value, indicated by *, is approximately 3.7, the interquartile range (the range of scores from the lower quarter to the upper quarter of the distribution of scores), as indicated by the upper and lower limits of the enclosed rectangle, is approximately 3.2 to 4.2, and the overall range of responses shown by the upper and lower 'whiskers', is approximately 3.0 to 4.4. This particular method of illustration, the boxplot, is further explained in Chapter 4, Section 4.3.3 and Box 4.9.

Figure 3.3 Boxplot showing median, IQR (interquartile range) and range of the responses to an attitude item

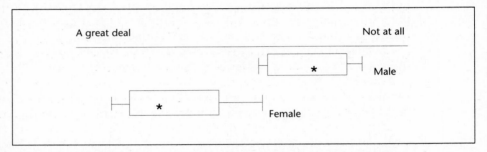

Figure 3.4 The response positions of males and females to an attitude item

illustration, subjects choose one of the agree/disagree categories. The choice made will ultimately place their attitude on some kind of linear scale and means, standard deviations and all kinds of comparisons can be produced in the time-honoured manner of parametric statistics. (Note: if these statistical terms are foreign to you, the next section introduces basic statistical concepts.)

Likert scale – A statement with which the respondent indicates the amount of agreement/disagreement with an issue.

This method whereby actual scale values are obscured can have its advantages. A problem with asking subjects to choose a numerical value indicating a particular view or attitude, is that sometimes people are unclear as to how their feelings can convert to a number; or they may be reluctant to select extreme values, or they may be unsure of how one scale value differs from the next. Replacing numbers with choice categories (as in the Likert scale) will sometimes alleviate this problem, in addition to making items e.g., Projects are a good idea

Strongly agree	Agree	Don't care	Disagree	Strongly disagree
(+2)	(+1)	(0)	(−1)	(−2)
5	4	3	2	1

Normally, with this type of item, respondents are presented with only the written response options (Strongly agree, Agree, etc.). The numerical scales are shown to indicate how the researcher might transform actual responses to numerical scale values.

more 'user-friendly'. A development of this approach in which subjects are indirectly placed on some scaled position is the semantic differential, shown below.

Semantic differential – The respondent rates an issue on a number of bipolar categories. The choice of pole can indicate intensity of feeling on the issue. In its simplest form, items at one pole can be given a positive value, with items at the other, negatively valued. A simple arithmetic count of both positive and negative choices can produce an overall score which will be indicative of the general attitude towards an issue.

e.g. Psychology projects are (choose one of each pair of response options):

Good	Bad
Easy	Difficult
Useful	Worthless
Challenging	Problematic
Interesting	Boring

2 Open-ended questions

This is where *S* is free to offer any response.

With this type of question the researcher is relinquishing control of how the subject can behave. In fact, open questions are not really questions at all. Rather they are scenarios or situations created artificially in which respondents are encouraged to respond. In this respect they have much in common with the projective techniques used in a clinical setting, or for the measurement of personality variables. Given free choice, we all tend to project some part of ourselves onto a situation, and this is the principle behind the open-ended question. What we say or write in response to an unrestricted item is an expression of our feelings, values and opinions, for instance.

Unstructured items – The subject can answer in an unlimited fashion.

---

e.g., **What do you think of this book?** . . . .

Note, in an item of this type the researcher has some control over at least the magnitude of response, if not the content itself. Leaving the item as it stands invites a very brief response, possibly only a single word. Allowing several blank lines though, or even a page, invites a much fuller response.

Word association – The subject is asked to respond with the first thing that comes to mind on presentation of the cue word.

---

e.g., **What is the first thing you think of when you hear the word:**

PROJECT   EXAM   LECTURE   SEMINAR

Sentence completion – The subject is offered an incomplete sentence and asked to continue in their own words.

---

e.g., **I chose to study psychology because** . . . .

Note, the comment about controlling the length of a response as encountered in the 'What do you think of this book?' example earlier, is relevant here.

The great advantage in not restricting responses is that the full variety of human thoughts and feelings is available to the researcher. The disadvantage is that it is available in a totally unstructured and uncontrolled form. Responses to any of the above can range from a few words to hours of introspective rambling. This makes analysis problematic: given the wide range of possible responses, considerable judgement is required and each subject's response must be inspected for common themes or threads of thought which offer an insight into the unique nature of the individual

As a general principle, unless the components of an issue and the range of possible responses to a question are well understood, a study would normally be piloted using some form of open-ended enquiry. This would identify the type and range of responses likely, any sources of ambiguity, overlap among items, and so on. Only then would the more direct, closed-type items be used. The rule in closed-type items is simple: you will only get the information you ask for, so you had better have a good idea of what you are likely to get!

3.5 Special techniques

3.5.1 *Focus groups*

The previous section on questionnaire design ended with the sage advice that if you don't ask the questions, you won't get the answers. But how do you know which questions to ask? Or how much of an issue is important? Or relevant to your subject group?

It would seem then that, even before we consider our very first questionnaire item, we should know in advance what we are looking for. In many cases, this will have been established following an appropriate literature review: issues would have been identified at this stage and hypotheses developed. However, there are certain situations in which a research issue, or its key components – and hence a workable hypothesis – cannot readily be identified in this way; many elements of attitudinal and behavioural research are simply not accessible via the standard route and have to be explored in a more direct manner. One particular method of doing this, which evolved within the marketing sphere, is the focus group.

One of the key functions of the marketing process is to find out how people are likely to respond to new products, publicity campaigns and marketing information. If this is done well, when a product is released on the market we, the consumers, respond positively and (so the manufacturers hope) go out and buy it. Poorly done, the result is a marketing disaster and possible bankruptcy. The attempt by Ford to launch America's first small, economical automobile in a culture of gas-guzzling monsters was an abysmal failure, and even today comedians make jokes about their parents being the first in the street to buy an Edsel. Similarly, the attempt by British Leyland in the 1970s to persuade us that an Allegro with a square steering wheel was a must, ended in fiasco (oddly enough, the square-wheeled Allegro is now something of a collectors item).

These examples represent classic marketing disasters – public opinion was seriously misjudged and important informational cues missed. By and large, however, marketing strategists tend to get it right (or right enough) relying on a variety of techniques to gauge opinion, evaluate campaigns and judge consumer response. One of the mainstays of the approach is the focus group.

Much as the term suggests, focus groups are essentially discussion groups comprising in some cases randomly composed, or in others, carefully selected, panels of individuals brought together to discuss, or focus on, specific issues. Discussion can be free-flowing or controlled, but usually under the guidance of a moderator, or facilitator, whose role is to maintain the focus of the group's attention on the issue, and to probe further or develop important themes. As exploratory instruments, focus groups are superb sources of information, allowing a skilled researcher excellent insight into the values, beliefs, fears and aspirations which comprise most attitudes. Not surprisingly then, the approach has become an important tool in recent years in psychological and social science research. Opinion though is divided as to both the value and the procedures involved in focus groups.

In some quarters, the focused approach is seen as a preparatory procedure only, a way of refining ideas, getting to grips with the scope of a particular issue or developing a theory sufficiently to generate hypotheses. For others, the focus group is an end in itself, with the information generated providing the essential and necessary data for a study. And certainly, given the vast amount of potential information generated in this format (hours of audio tape, pages of transcriptions, etc.) its appeal as a qualitative research tool is obvious. However, it is in the first context that focus groups are probably of most use to undergraduate researchers, providing as they can a way of coming closer to an issue, of developing a greater understanding of the components of attitudes and of identifying key or relevant issues which will ultimately form the basis of a questionnaire.

With its increasing application within the social sciences, several guidelines have evolved covering the use of focus groups and related procedural issues – how to sample, optimal group sizes, the composition of groups (whether or not members should be strangers or people known to each other), and so on. There are views on the roles of moderators, on how to collect information and whether or not to analyse data in qualitative or quantitative terms. For the majority of undergraduate studies though, a focus group *approach* is probably of more value than adopting a full procedure – in most cases a student is merely interested in identifying or refining important issues so that questionnaire instruments can be designed which will ask the right questions and provide sufficient coverage of an issue to deal appropriately with a given research topic. Such a scaled-down version though will still require planning: subjects have to be recruited to participate; subject characteristics have to be identified if these are going to be important variables in a study; topics for discussion have to be prepared, along with procedures for guiding or focusing discussion, dealing with awkward individuals and recording data. And, of course, some thought must be given as to how the information gained here can be developed into a standard instrument.

By and large, many undergraduates tend to underestimate this procedure, calling brief, informal discussion meetings with relatively few individuals, failing adequately to control discussion and not recording data in any systematic way. Often this process is seen merely as a precursor to the more important business of questionnaire design, forgetting that they will ultimately have to justify every issue covered, and every item contained in any instrument. This can only be done if the issues have been properly explored and understood in advance.

For a more detailed review of focus groups, their history and their application, several excellent references are provided at the end of this section, particularly Asbury (1995).

3.5.2 | *Pilot research*

Most of us feel that by the time we reach the stage of implementing our research design, we have worked everything out to the last detail: we have completed our literature review and therefore know how other practitioners have fared in their research, we have identified all potential sources of bias and we have used an appropriate procedure to focus on the key issues and develop a foolproof questionnaire. However, complacency at this stage is to admit to a poor regard for the vagaries of human nature: misunderstanding instructions, misperceiving the researcher's intent, refusal to co-operate, and so on are all events which can ruin the best conceived study. The solution of course is to pilot your work – try it out on a small sample of the population you will eventually be working with. This is the only way to refine the elements of a design, to identify questionnaire items which are misleading, confusing or offensive. Such pilot work need not be extensive – indeed in designs where subject pools are limited, pilot studies must be constrained – but it can be thorough; an experiment, survey or questionnaire in addition to some kind of focused interview can be useful in identifying limitations and areas of improvement. Mistakes at this stage can be easily remedied; identifying flaws only after a major study has been implemented is hugely wasteful, not to mention demoralising. And if our research is more qualitative in nature, some kind of pilot or practice study is essential to identify appropriate classification and coding procedures.

3.6 Conducting ethical research

It is important to be aware that, before you can inflict a study on an unsuspecting public, you are bound by certain constraints on your behaviour – especially concerning your subjects. Aside from the implicit moral obligation of any researcher to prevent distress among subjects (whether human or animal) there exist a number of guidelines which should always be considered in the design and implementation of any study. Developed over many years of research, and based on universally accepted moral and ethical values, an explicit set of guidelines has been produced by the BPS and is available in full in their various publications, relating both to human and animal subjects.

A summary of the main points in the BPS guidelines is offered below and students should note that most supervisors would decline to supervise an undergraduate project if the guidelines are not adhered to. Moreover, as we appear to be evolving into an increasingly sensitive, not to say litigious, society, academic institutions are themselves becoming more cautious about the nature of research carried out under their names. In any event, ignoring these points should only be considered in exceptional circumstances, and with the strongest possible justification since, by and large, they reflect powerful human values and not simply professional ones.

1 Sampling

Where subjects are to be drawn from specific populations (workers in an organisation, patients in a hospital, pupils in primary schools), you should be aware of any possible disruption to normal institutional functioning which your study may cause. It is therefore important that approval or authorisation be sought from appropriate individuals or bodies before your work can commence. Indeed, some institutions (e.g. hospital boards) require research proposals to pass their own form of ethics committee before approval can be given. Furthermore, any reporting on the findings of a study must include details of all procedures used to obtain subjects, to ensure their consent and to seek the approval of relevant bodies.

2 Apparatus

Apparatus refers to any instrument, device or questionnaire which is used to aid the collection of data. In the case of standard equipment, such as a tachistoscope (a device for back-projecting images onto an enclosed screen for predetermined durations) it is important that all operations are fully understood and the regulations governing use are fully adhered to. In the case of standard questionnaires and psychometric tests, the instructions for administration and scoring must be followed. Further, no such instrument should be used without a thorough awareness of norms, limitations, applications, reliability and validity studies, such that in no way can subjects be disadvantaged by a lack of familiarity with the manual. (This issue is covered in detail in the section 3.3, What you need to know about psychological tests.)

In the case of non-standard equipment, full details of, for instance, circuit diagrams, if applicable, safety precautions and usage should be included in a report. In the case of non-standard questionnaires, a full copy, with a rationale for each item, must also be included as part of the report (See Chapter 7, 7.3.8). The reason for so much detail is not simply replicability, although this is always an aim of any good research, but also to ensure that ethical standards are seen to be maintained. If a researcher is unable to provide such depth of information or, worse, is unwilling to do so, then the research is clearly suspect.

3 Procedure

Participation in any psychological study is normally voluntary and you must ensure that subjects are aware of this, and that they are able to withdraw *at any time* during a study, without prejudice (i.e., without any fear of sanction and with an assurance of no negative consequences of withdrawal), a right which extends even beyond the data-collection stage. At no time must you coerce or use deceit to obtain co-operation, which is not in itself a part of the study. In the event that some form of deception forms part of the experimental manipulation, you must ensure that subjects are fully debriefed.

If a situation is encountered in which subjects are not able to provide some form of informed consent, steps must be taken to protect the individual – if people with brain damage, young children or individuals exhibiting other forms of cognitive disorder are to be approached as subjects, consent must be obtained from those who have the interests of your potential subjects at heart. This could be relatives, parents, carers or medical staff. And even then, unless there is sound reason for pursuing a particular research interest, such individuals should not be used in a study. Increasingly, academic departments are now requiring subjects to sign a consent form, stating that they fully understand the purpose of the study in which they are participating and that they are aware of their rights, both legally and morally.

If the data collected in a study are to be confidential, you must take steps to ensure that not only is this so, but that it is seen to be so, particularly by your subjects. This is especially true if the data might be considered private and personal to participants. Again, reported research is now expected to include details of how the confidentiality of responses has been ensured.

As a general rule, subjects should never be placed under undue stress, unless there are sound methodological reasons to do so. However, should induced stress form a part of a study, advance preparations must be made in terms of controlling such stress, and for preventing possibly catastrophic consequences (both physiological and psychological). Generally speaking, no undergraduate would be permitted to conduct a study along these lines nor, unless in exceptional circumstances, would an experienced researcher. The days of Milgram, in which subjects were placed under great personal stress in the false belief that they were inflicting pain on others, have gone!

4 General

All of the above are merely guidelines to enable you to conduct yourself and your research in an ethical, humane and fair manner. They should not be regarded as constraints, rather as a series of reminders that when you carry out a piece of research you are dealing, not with abstract sources of data, but with real people (or animals) with rights of privacy, sympathy, and expectations of fairness of treatment to which all of us are entitled.

5 Current issues

The importance of adhering to a common set of moral and ethical standards in the treatment of other people is unassailable, and professional bodies like the British Psychological Society and the American Psychological Association have an important role in reminding members of their obligations. Recently, the BPS (1997) has taken the position that even the use of the term 'subject' is in itself unethical. The view is that it is impersonal and that 'psychologists owe a debt to those who participate in their studies and . . . people who are willing to give up their time, even for remuneration, should be treated with the highest standards of consideration and respect.' (p. 295). Consequently, the recommendation in the BPS code of conduct is that more suitable terms are 'participants', 'respondents', 'individuals', or some other non-controversial term.

Debate on the issue continues, with some people arguing that this most current of recommendations is merely a logical extension of an ongoing process of ethical development, while others see it more as a form of misguided extremism. The authors for their part await the outcome of this debate, choosing in the meantime to retain the use of the term 'subject', as intimated in the Introduction to this book.

3.7 Review

In this chapter we have considered the practical aspects of carrying out a study. By this stage you should now have a good idea of how many subjects you require, how you will recruit them and who they will be. You should also know precisely how you are going to collect your data – whether you will be using an existing measure or devising a measurement instrument of your own. If you are developing your own instrument, you should now appreciate the various options available in terms of item design, the advantages of the different approaches and the associated pitfalls. You will also have sufficient familiarity to ensure that your study will be carried out in an ethical manner.

3.8 Explanation of terms

Alternate form reliability A measure of reliability obtained by administering equivalent or parallel forms of a test to the same subjects on separate occasions. Using different forms of a test in this way is seen as a control for memory effects.

Closed-ended questions A type of questionnaire or interview item in which the range of responses possible to a respondent is determined by the experimenter.

Concurrent validity A version of criterion-related validity in which the comparison measures are taken at the same time as the test findings become available.

Construct validity The type of validation necessary for any test attempting to measure some psychological concept or construct. This is not really a measure in itself and does not describe one single procedure – rather construct validity is demonstrated using a variety of techniques.

Content validity Demonstrated when the content of a test – in terms of the type and scope of items – comprises a fair and representative sample of the trait, behaviour or knowledge base being measured.

Criterion-related validity A method of demonstrating test validity by comparing test findings to some other measure, or criterion.

Dichotomous scales Measuring scales on which there are only two kinds of response (as in yes/no).

Face validity A characteristic of measurement instruments whereby a test seems to be measuring what it claims to be measuring. This is an aspect of a test's appearance and its apparent relevance to subjects. The term is potentially misleading since it provides no indication of true, objective validity, but it does influence the attitudes of participants and their level of co-operation.

Focus groups A type of discussion group established to explore particular issues. They can be used as a primary source of data in their own right, or as a preliminary to a more structured data-gathering methodology.

Generalisation The ability to apply findings gleaned from a sample to the population at large. This is only possible when samples truly reflect population characteristics, otherwise findings are situation-specific.

Informed consent The agreement of a subject to participate in research, based on a full understanding of the aims of a study, and of their own rights in respect of confidentiality and ethical treatment.

Likert scale A type of rating scale in which the numbers are replaced by response categories, usually in terms of how much a subject agrees with a particular statement. Possible responses are typically: strongly agree; agree; don't know; disagree; strongly disagree.

Local sampling effect A possible consequence of a practical constraint on some research, describing an effect of restricting sampling to a local community. Inadvertently such samples can become overloaded with unusual or extreme localised characteristics. See also sample bias and situation specificity.

Norms Measures of typical or normal performance on psychological tests, usually measured in terms of mean scores and measures of spread for specific subsections of the population, though sometimes presented as a proportion or percentage of a sample producing particular scores. See also percentiles.

Open-ended questions A type of questionnaire or interview item in which there are no restrictions on the range of responses possible to a respondent.

Percentiles In psychometrics a cumulative measure of the proportion of individuals who score at, or below, particular points on a measuring scale.

Pilot research A small-scale study usually carried out in advance of the main research, the aim being to identify problems before the study proper begins.

Population   The entire set of entities which comprise the group, or subgroup of subjects which are the object of study, and in which the entire range of an outcome measure is represented.

Practice effects   A tendency for performance on certain types of test to improve over time simply as a result of practice. The effect can often lead to artificially reduced measures of reliability.

Predictive validity   A version of criterion-related validity in which the comparison measures are taken some time in the future, after test findings have become available.

Procedural variations   An occasional tendency for apparent differences among subjects on particular tests to reflect variations in testing procedures as opposed to actual variations on some trait.

Random sampling   A procedure of drawing subjects from a population in a totally random fashion; every single individual has an equal probability of being selected.

Rating scales   Measuring scales on which there is a range of numerical responses available to the respondent.

Reliability coefficient   The statistic which offers a numerical indication of test reliability. The statistic is based on a modified version of correlation, in which such factors as the number of items in a test are controlled for.

Representative   A term used in different contexts but meaning the same thing. In psychometrics, it refers to a highly desirable characteristic of tests, in which the item coverage is a fair reflection, or representation, of the area under investigation. In sampling procedures, it refers to the importance of ensuring that subjects comprising a sample for study are a fair reflection, or representation, of the population from which they have been drawn.

Sample   A subset of a population which forms the subject basis for a study. It is assumed that the sample will be representative of the population from which it has been drawn such that observations on the sample will allow inferences to be made about the population.

Sample bias   The result of a particular sample being over (or under) represented on some characteristic which makes the sample atypical of the population from which it was drawn. This has the effect of limiting the extent to which inferences about the population can be made.

Semantic differential   The responses available lie at two extremes of a single continuum, e.g., good/bad.

Situation specificity   Describes the tendency for many research findings to be relevant only to the sample or situation in which the study was carried out. A function of rigorous sampling and controls which remove a particular study too far from real life.

Split-half reliability   A measure of reliability which measures the relationship among the items of a particular test. By splitting a test into two halves, and comparing the scores of subjects on each half, it is possible to measure the internal consistency of a test.

Standardisation In the context of psychological testing, standardisation refers to the process of ensuring identical procedures for administration, data collection and scoring.

Standardisation sample The particular subset of a population who first experience a particular test, the aim being to identify typical or normal scores (norms).

Stratified sampling A procedure of drawing subjects from a population according to some predetermined strategy. Normally, if a population is seen to comprise certain strata (socio-economic divisions, ethnic groupings, etc.) a sample should reflect the same structure and in the same proportions.

Test reliability A measure, or indication of the extent to which a test produces consistent results across time and situations.

Test-retest reliability A measure of reliability obtained by administering the same test to the same subjects on two separate occasions.

Test validity An indication of the extent to which a test is actually measuring what it is supposed to be measuring. Unlike reliability, validity is not necessarily demonstrated statistically, although there are instances in which it can be.

3.9 References

Eysenck, H.J. and Eysenck, S.B.G. (1975). *Manual for the Eysenck Personality Questionnaire*. London: Hodder & Stoughton.

Likert, R.A. (1932). A technique for the measurement of attitudes. *Archives of Psychology*, 140, 256.

3.10 Recommended reading

Asbury, J.E. (1995). Overview of focus group research. *Qualitative Health Research*, 5, 414–420.

Beech, J.R. and Harding, L. (1990). *Testing People: A Practical Guide to Psychometrics*. Windsor: NFER-Nelson.

British Psychological Society (1991). *Code of Conduct: Ethical; Principles and Guidelines*. Leicester: British Psychological Society.

Cooper, P. and Tower, R. (1992). Inside the consumer mind: Consumer attitudes to the arts. *Journal of the Market Research Society*, 34, 299–311.

Kline, P. (1993). *The Handbook of Psychological Testing*. London: Routledge.

Lindsay, G. (1995). Values, ethics and psychology. *The Psychologist*, **8**, 493–498.

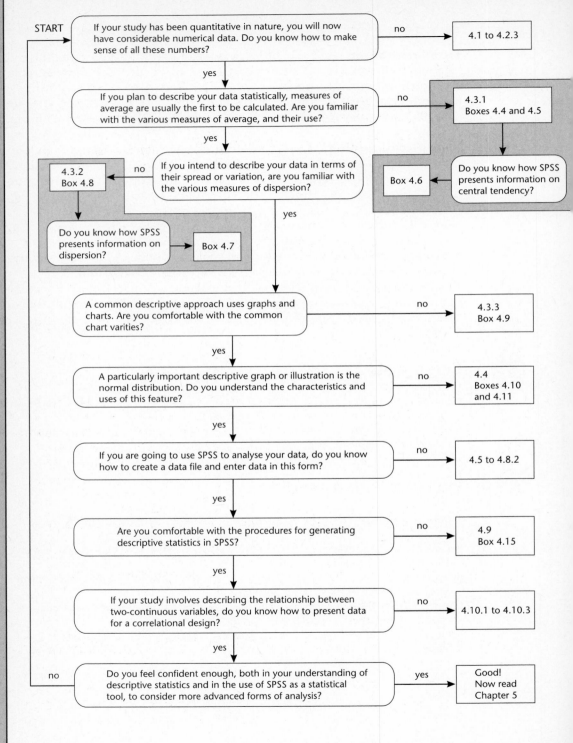

Flow Chart 4

START

If your study has been quantitative in nature, you will now have considerable numerical data. Do you know how to make sense of all these numbers? — no → 4.1 to 4.2.3

yes

If you plan to describe your data statistically, measures of average are usually the first to be calculated. Are you familiar with the various measures of average, and their use? — no → 4.3.1 Boxes 4.4 and 4.5

yes

4.3.2 Box 4.8 ← no — If you intend to describe your data in terms of their spread or variation, are you familiar with the various measures of dispersion?

4.3.1 Boxes 4.4 and 4.5 → Do you know how SPSS presents information on central tendency? → Box 4.6

Do you know how SPSS presents information on dispersion? → Box 4.7

yes

A common descriptive approach uses graphs and charts. Are you comfortable with the common chart varities? — no → 4.3.3 Box 4.9

yes

A particularly important descriptive graph or illustration is the normal distribution. Do you understand the characteristics and uses of this feature? — no → 4.4 Boxes 4.10 and 4.11

yes

If you are going to use SPSS to analyse your data, do you know how to create a data file and enter data in this form? — no → 4.5 to 4.8.2

yes

Are you comfortable with the procedures for generating descriptive statistics in SPSS? — no → 4.9 Box 4.15

yes

If your study involves describing the relationship between two-continuous variables, do you know how to present data for a correlational design? — no → 4.10.1 to 4.10.3

yes

no ← Do you feel confident enough, both in your understanding of descriptive statistics and in the use of SPSS as a statistical tool, to consider more advanced forms of analysis? — yes → Good! Now read Chapter 5

4

Descriptive techniques – setting up data in SPSS

'What do I do with all these numbers?'

'Should I be using bargraphs, histograms or boxplots?'

'Help!'

Chapter 4 deals with the data generated in research: what do we do with the numbers produced by a survey or experiment, how do we present them and what is the most appropriate form of descriptive analysis. Initial sections deal with the basic concepts in describing data, using tables, graphs and introducing descriptive statistics, while later sections are concerned with the practical issues of setting up data files and working with modern statistical software, in particular the SPSS statistical package which is becoming one of the most frequently encountered descriptive and analytical tools in academic and government departments. (SPSS is an abbreviation of *Statistical Package for the Social Sciences*, although the acronym is sometimes expressed as *Superior Performance Statistical Software*.) By the end of this chapter you should be able to create a file for your data in SPSS, generate a variety of basic, descriptive statistics and produce appropriate graphs. As with all sections of this book, however, the aim is merely to introduce essential concepts; those interested in more advanced ideas and techniques should pursue some of the articles cited in Section 4.13.

4.1   Understanding numbers

So, the study is complete and you will now have amassed a great deal of information. For some, those of you who opted for a qualitative approach, this will be in the form of notes, video and transcriptions, but for most, your data will be quantitative in nature – i.e., numbers. Scores on a personality test; the number of correct responses in a series of memory trials; measures of attitude on rating scales – these are all typical. In addition, you will also probably have information on your subjects: profile information such as gender, age category, social class and similar. These too will probably be in the form of numbers, and here is an important point – the central philosophy of a quantitative approach is that everything in the universe can be represented numerically. This allows widely diverse elements to be compared using a common system. Hence, the strength of an attitude on any issue might be expressed as a value between 1 and 7; extraversion can be represented as a single score on the EPQ. Even membership of a particular experimental group can be expressed numerically: for example, control subjects might be identified by the value 1, and experimental subjects by the value 2. Once the notion of numbers as mere symbols which represent other things is understood, the next stage in the quantitative process is to make use of the significant characteristics of numbers – they can be added, subtracted, multiplied and divided. In other words, they can be manipulated.

4.2   Making sense of numbers

Choosing to represent the world numerically is only the beginning of the quantitative process. After all, taking a series of measurements on a sample of subjects – be it height, age or scores on some personality variable – will only provide you with a list of numbers. And if this is a long list the numbers quickly become meaningless. Yet the quantitative approach is intended to make sense of the world, so techniques have evolved to do this.

At the most basic level of analysis quantitative methods aim to reduce large amounts of data into something meaningful; **descriptive techniques**, as they are known, are designed to summarise, simplify and explain. Their tools are tables, graphs and statistics.

4.2.1 Tables

At their most basic, tables allow us to organise numerical information in a way that imposes some order on our data, and in this way they serve the functions described in Section 4.2, of summarising and simplifying.

Imagine a research scenario in which we are interested in the performance of skilled versus unskilled individuals on some co-ordination task. (Readers are alerted to the imminent return of amphibian-based analogies.) As part of our study we may feel it relevant to report on, or describe, the key characteristics of our sample, and what better way to do this than in a table.

Tables 4.1, 4.2 and 4.3 below are good examples of simple tables which reduce, summarise and describe information in a way which is both easy to follow and meaningful; they are particularly effective for the presentation of nominally-scaled information, as is the case here, in which a sample is described in terms of its relevant descriptive characteristics.

The first two tables are known as **frequency tables** (the frequencies with which subjects fell into each category – m/f; skilled/unskilled – are reported) while the third is slightly more sophisticated, being a **crosstabulation** (frequencies are reported across two different variables – in this case we are

Table 4.1   The distribution of males and females

Gender (sex of subject)

	Value	Frequency	Per cent	Cum. Per cent
male	1	14	46.7	46.7
female	2	16	53.3	100.0
Total		30	100.0	100.0

Table 4.2 The distribution of skilled and unskilled subjects

Skill (skill level of subject)				
	Value	Frequency	Per cent	Cum. Per cent
skilled	1	15	50.0	50.0
unskilled	2	15	50.0	100.0
Total		30	100.0	100.0

Table 4.3 The distribution of male and female cyclists by level of skill

Gender (sex of subject) by skill (level of skill in cycling)				
Count		SKILL		
		skilled 1	unskilled 2	Row Total
GENDER				
male	1	8	6	14 46.7%
female	2	7	9	16 53.3%
Column Total		15 50.0%	15 50.0%	30 100.0%

presented with information on individuals who were both male and skilled, etc.).

While most studies require that their researchers report on the characteristics of their subjects, this is especially true of survey-based research, in which the disposition of a sample is often the whole point of the study: how many subjects claimed they would support Conservative at the next election, as opposed to Labour; how many respondents voted yes on the issue of a single European currency, and so on. However, tables are not the only way to represent this type of information which can sometimes have a more immediate impact when presented graphically.

4.2.2 Graphs

While no one would deny the importance of tabular illustrations, it must be said that not everyone is comfortable with this approach. Aside from the fact that many of us seem to have an inherent fear of numbers, causing us to shy away from even the most informative of table, presenting information pictorially often has more immediate impact. Graphs can be colourful, striking even; moreover, apart from appealing to an apparent liking for visualisation, they can often emphasise effects which could easily be overlooked in the dry world of tabulation. Figures 4.1a, b, c reproduce the information displayed in the preceding tables.

Each of these figures has been produced using the full range of display options usually available to the user of modern computer software. This has

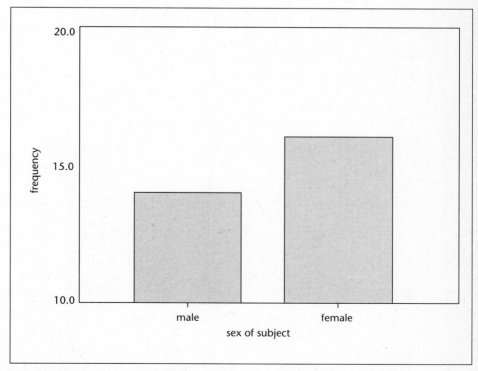

Figure 4.1a   The distribution of males and females

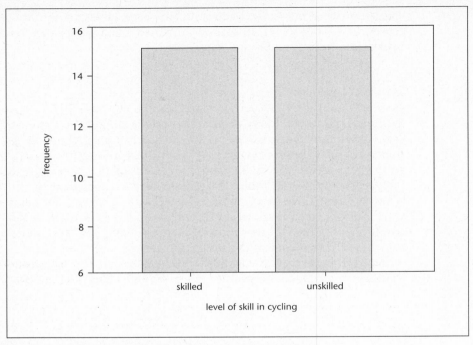

Figure 4.1b   The distribution of skilled and unskilled subjects

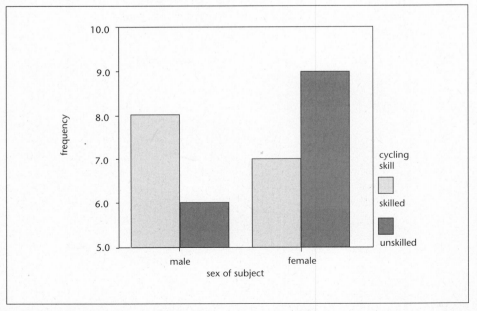

Figure 4.1c   Skill distribution by gender

been done deliberately to illustrate the potential impact of figurative illustrations; without doubt figures like these are impressive. They are also, it must be admitted, pretty ghastly.

Generally speaking most researchers tend to shun overembellishment, partly as a matter of taste, and partly because overcomplexity in an illustration might obscure those very characteristics of the data which the figure is attempting to demonstrate. On a practical note, complex, multi-coloured illustrations are expensive to reproduce and many publishers of papers, journal articles and book chapters will often prefer a simpler way to make a point. Consequently, in this particular textbook, aside from the above examples, you will find the majority of graphs and charts presented in a relatively straightforward manner.

4.2.3 Statistics

The third method for making sense of our universe is quite different from the previous two: tables and graphs both tend to provide a broad view of the data, with illustration and description being their primary function. Statistics on the other hand can express and summarise substantial amounts of data with a single value. This is what a statistic is – a symbol, and an associated numerical value, which represents a body of data. Moreover, a statistic is often merely the first step in a more complex analysis – in the way that a measure of average can often be used as the basis for comparison with other measures of average. The next section illustrates the point.

4.3 Using statistics to illustrate and describe

4.3.1 Statistical measures – central tendency

When trying to describe or illustrate the typical characteristics of a variable, we often opt for some measure of central tendency which best represents our information. Consequently we describe the heights of a group of under-graduates in terms of an average and, because we are used to using this kind of statistic in our everyday lives, we readily understand that the average is only a part of the story; while most people will cluster around some central measure, we nonetheless accept that some people will score higher than this, and some people lower. Observing that the average height of a group of undergraduates is 5' 9" recognises the fact that there will be some students who measure 5' 10", or even 6'. Similarly, there will be some people who measure 5' 9" or 5' 7", but by and large, most of the people will measure round about the 5' 9" mark. This is what average is all about, the almost universal tendency for anything we care to observe to cluster around some central or typical measure.

The term 'average' is usually taken to represent the arithmetic average, in which all the scores or values in a set of observations are summed, then divided by the number in the set. Statistically, this is known as the arithmetic **mean** (symbolised by $\bar{x}$) and it is the most precise of all the different measures of centrality, based as it is on actual scores. However, there are situations in which the mean, irrespective of its accuracy, may not fulfil the function of indicating typicality. This can occur when a distribution contains one or more extreme scores, or outliers, as in the following examples.

In example (a) Box 4.1, the arithmetic mean works out as 8.3, which is fairly typical of the way scores are clustered in this group. In example (b), however, the mean is 18 which clearly is typical of none of the members of this particular group. (If you are wondering, by the way, how such an extreme score as 120 could find its way into a group whose real average is closer to 8, admittedly this is unusual. Perhaps a passing alien of outstanding intelligence joined the class to see what we humans were up to, or perhaps we made a mistake in measuring our subjects. Either way, the calculated mean is going to be misleading.)

To deal with such problems, which are really quite common (not the part about the alien), an alternative measure of central tendency is available to us which is not so sensitive to extreme outliers. This is the **median**, which is simply the middle value in a range of scores (arranged in order from lowest to highest that is, rather than simply jumbled up). In example (a), the median would be 8. In case (b) the median is also 8, a much more representative value than the arithmetic average, and a statistic not in the least influenced by the extreme score of 120.

This tendency for the middle value in any range of scores to provide a good measure of average is a universal phenomenon, such that the measurement of every human characteristic will always produce a clustering of observations which will typify the majority. Height, shoe size, intelligence, whatever –

Box 4.1   Central tendency

(a) mental age scores of male undergraduates

5, 6, 7, 7, 8, 8, 8, 9, 9, 10, 11, 12

(b) mental age scores of female undergraduates

5, 6, 7, 7, 8, 8, 8, 9, 10, 11, 120

there is invariably a measure, or range of measures, which is most typical of that particular trait. Hence, the middle value will invariably fall within this common, or most typical cluster, which is why the median is usually a good measure of average.

There exists a third measure of central tendency, which is really a 'rule of thumb' indicator, termed the **mode**. The mode, or modal value, is the most frequently occurring score in a series of observations. Providing the trait or characteristic being measured is of the kind where most people are scoring around some typical level, the mode will give a similar value to the other two measures. In both the above examples, the mode is 8. Box 4.2 illustrates all three measures of central tendency.

Box 4.2   Different views of central tendency

If people are drawn at random from the general population and their shoe size measured, the following arrays of scores might be produced.

1.   2,2,2,3,3,4,5,5,5,5,5,6,6,7,7,8,9

Each of the three measures of average is suitable here, with the mean, median and mode giving a typical score of 5 – a nice, dainty shoe size.

2.   5,5,6,7,7,7,7,8,8,9,9,10,10,10,10,11,11,12,13,14.

Here, the mean is 8.95, the median, 9 and the mode – in fact, there are two modes, making this measure of average inappropriate here. Both the mean and median are the most useful measures of central tendency in this case. And if you are wondering why there appear to be two groupings of 'typical' sizes, this could be attributable to the fact that this particular sample comprises a mixture of males and females, and that their shoe sizes are sufficiently different to give two distinct clusters.

3.   5,5,6,7,7,7,8,8,9,9,10,11,25,37.

In this final example, the occurrence of two extreme scores at the top end of the range will artificially pull the calculated arithmetic average towards this extreme. Hence, the mean here would be 11. The median however, immune as it is to the effects of such extreme scores, would be the much more reasonable 8, with the mode not far away, with 7. (Note: in the event that a median fails to land on an actual middle value, as will be the case with all even-numbered arrays, the procedure is to take the average of the two adjacent scores. Thus, a median falling between the values of 5 and 6, would become 5.5.)

Finally, most contemporary statistical software, if it is good enough, will make allowances for the fact that extreme scores are possible in any study. The SPSS output shown in Box 4.3 is a typical example, in which the true arithmetic mean is printed alongside an adjusted mean, which has removed the top and bottom 5 per cent of values from its calculations (5 per cent Trim). This serves the purpose of eliminating much of the influence of extreme scores. It also, however, reduces the size of the data set, which must be taken into consideration, especially where sample sizes are already small.

Box 4.3   Big foot

1. SHOESIZE – shoe size (inches)					
Mean	**4.9412** Std Err	.5107 Min	2.0000 Skewness	.1785
Median	**5.0000** Variance	4.4338 Max	9.0000 S E Skew	.5497
5% Trim	**4.8791** Std Dev	2.1057 Range	7.0000 Kurtosis	−.6410

2. MORESHOE SIZE – shoe size (inches)					
Mean	**8.9500** Std Err	.5642 Min	5.0000 Skewness	.2372
Median	**9.0000** Variance	6.3658 Max	14.0000 S E Skew	.5121
5% Trim	**8.8889** Std Dev	2.5231 Range	9.0000 Kurtosis	−.5653

3. EVENMORE SHOE SIZE – shoe size (inches)					
Mean	**11.0000** Std Err	2.3950 Min	5.0000 Skewness	2.4317
Median	**8.0000** Variance	80.3077 Max	37.0000 S E Skew	.5974
5% Trim	**9.8889** Std Dev	8.9615 Range	32.0000 Kurtosis	5.6386

The three examples above are extracts from SPSS outputs based on the data shown in Box 4.2, relating to measurements of different shoe size. While a great deal of information is generated by this programme, for the moment our concern is with the measures of average. In each example, SPSS has offered us three measures of centrality – a mean, a median and a trimmed mean, in which scores at either end of the range have been eliminated. In most instances, this will have little impact except reducing the range of values on which the calculation of average is based – as in examples 1 and 2. In example 3 however, where there are two extreme scores (see Box 4.2) the mean becomes inappropriate as a measure of average. The 5 per cent Trim gives a more representative value, which is reinforced by the very similar median score. (Note: a useful hint for embryonic statisticians is to compare the mean and median values in a distribution. If the distribution is normal, as in some middle clustering of values, with a few tailing off at either side, then the median and the mean will be similar. However, if there are extreme scores present, this will adversely affect the calculation of the mean and a noticeable difference will be observed in comparison to the median.)

4.3.2 │ *Dispersion*

In describing the characteristics of a variable it should now be clear that relying solely on measures of central tendency provides only part of the picture. Much of the discussion in the previous section involved problems associated with how widely or unevenly scores varied around some central measure, and this aspect of any variable or distribution is of considerable interest to researchers.

Much in the same way that even the layman has an intuitive grasp of the concept of average, so too do most of us have a working understanding of dispersion, even if we lack the statistical skills to generate appropriate measures.

Think back to school days and class exams: if you scored 46 in an arithmetic test and stated that the class average was only 45, you would be more likely to impress parents and friends by pointing out that the top mark was 47. Alternatively, if we scored 50 to the same mean of 45, we might just keep quiet about the fact that the total range of marks was from 0 to 100!

What we have been applying here is the simplest measure of dispersion, the **range**, which is a statement of the lowest score to the highest. Box 4.4 illustrates this, with SPSS providing both the range and a minimum and maximum value.

As we have already discovered with central tendency, trying to reduce a large amount of information to a typical, representative value is not without its problems – in particular the misleading effects caused by extreme scores. In much the same way, a simple range, or a statement of minimum and maximum values, can be equally inappropriate when extreme scores are present. Box 4.4 illustrates the point: the minimum and maximum values are given as 5 and 37 respectively, with a corresponding range of 32. This implies

Box 4.4   The spread of feet

EVENMORE – shoe size (inches)

Valid cases: 14.0

Mean	11.0000	Std Err	2.3950	**Min**	**5.0000**
Median	8.0000	Variance	80.3077	**Max**	**37.0000**
5% Trim	9.8889	**Std Dev.**	**8.9615**	**Range**	**32.0000**
				IQR	**3.5000**

A closer look at the shoe size data demonstrates that, just as there are a number of ways to express central tendency, there are alternative measures of dispersion.

a broad spread of scores, yet we know that the majority of subjects in this group had shoe sizes in the 5–11 range (see Box 4.2). Fortunately, just as with measures of average there exist alternative ways to represent spread which are not susceptible to extremes.

One such measure is related to the median and is known as the **interquartile range**, or IQR. Just as any array of scores can be divided in two by the median, or middle value, so can it be further subdivided: if we take the lower half of a distribution and divide this in turn by half, we obtain two quarters. Similarly, if we take the upper half and further divide this, we also obtain two quarters. These two further subdivisions are known as the lower quartile and the upper quartile (or Q1 and Q3):

```
5  5  6  7  7  |  7  7  8  8  9  |  9  10  10  10  10  |  11  11  12  13  14
        Q1              median                  Q3
        7                 9                     10.5
```

All we need do is subtract the value at the first quartile from the value at the third (Q3 – Q1), and we have the interquartile range, which is a measure of spread in which the top and bottom quarters have been removed, thus eliminating any extreme values. In the above example the IQR would be 3.5, the same value interestingly enough as that shown for the example in Box 4.4.

There exists a third measure of spread which, like the mean, is based on the actual scores or values found in a distribution. Termed the **standard deviation**, this provides an indication of how much, on average, scores deviate from the mean. Because it is based on actual values it is a very accurate and powerful statistic. For the same reason however, it is also susceptible to extreme values and if a distribution becomes too skewed in one direction, the standard deviation ceases to be of value in representing a distribution.

4.3.3 | *Graphs*

We have noted previously how useful graphs can be for illustrating large amounts of data. The bargraphs at Figures 4.1a, 4.1b and 4.1c (see Section 4.2.2) are extremely effective and high-impact illustrations of their respective nominal categories – not only clearly describing the characteristics of each group, but allowing an immediate, visual comparison of different groups. Similarly, the type of data on which means and standard deviations can be calculated (i.e., interval data) is also susceptible to graphing techniques, again allowing alternative methods for presenting the same information.

Box 4.5   Standard deviation

Consider the example of the shoe sizes of a group of undergraduates, shown below:

$$2,2,2,3,3,4,5,5,5,5,5,6,6,7,7,8,9$$

The calculated mean (obtained by adding up the individual sizes and dividing by the number of observations) is 4.9. To find out how much each score varies or deviates from this value, we perform a simple subtraction:

mean	score	mean-score
4.9	2	2.9
4.9	2	2.9
4.9	2	2.9
4.9	3	1.9
.	.	.
.	.	.
.	.	.

In approximately half the cases, taking each score from the mean will produce a positive value, as above. Because, however, about half of the scores in a distribution will be greater than the mean, the results of some of these calculations will be negative values, as below:

mean	score	mean-score
.	.	.
.	.	.
.	.	.
4.9	5	−0.1
4.9	6	−1.1
4.9	7	−2.1

In many statistical calculations, negative values are irritations. In the calculation of the standard deviation, they are eliminated by squaring the result of each subtraction:

mean	score	mean-score	(mean-score) squared
.	.	.	.
.	.	.	.
4.9	5	−0.1	0.01
4.9	6	−1.1	1.21
4.9	7	−2.1	4.41
.	.	.	.
.	.	.	.

The total deviations can now be obtained by adding up all these squared values but what we really want is an average of these, obtained simply by dividing by the number of observations. However, just when you thought you had the answer, we mustn't forget that we are currently dealing with squared scores and not the original values, and this must be rectified. Taking the square root will finally provide the statistic known as the standard deviation.

In summary, the standard deviation is obtained by:

subtracting each score from the mean; squaring this value; summing these values and taking an average; taking the square root.

Alternatively, for those comfortable with statistical expressions, this can be shown in formula terms,

$$SD = \sqrt{\frac{\sum(x - \bar{x})^2}{N}}$$

Referring to Box 4.3, the standard deviations for each of the shoe size examples are shown, and the exaggerated measure caused by the extreme scores for example 3 is apparent.

The following examples shown in Box 4.6 are further illustrations of how SPSS produces a range of charts in support of underlying numerical data.

Box 4.6   Picture this

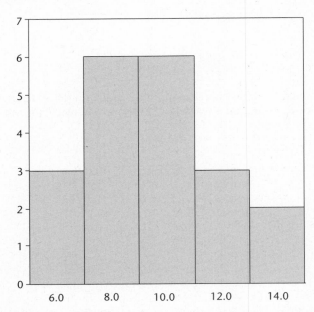

The **histogram** above provides an 'at a glance' representation of the moreshoe data shown in Boxes 4.2 and 4.3. Immediately apparent is that the most frequent shoe sizes are occurring around some central value between 8 and 10, and that the range of shoe size is from 5 to 15. (The actual values were mean = 8.9 and range 5–14, making our visual judgement on the basis of the histogram pretty impressive.)

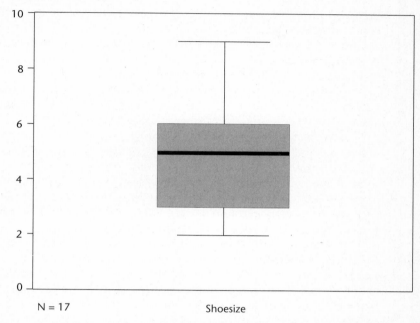

N = 17   Shoesize

The figure above, based on the shoesize data shown in Boxes 4.2 and 4.3, is known as a boxplot and is another frequent illustrative chart, utilising the measures of median, IQR and overall range. Many people, new to this mode of presentation, find boxplots unintelligible, yet once their principle is understood, they quickly become an indispensable tool for the researcher.

The median value is indicated by the black bar running through the coloured box (in previous versions of SPSS this was shown by a simple asterisk). The upper and lower quartiles are shown by the upper and lower limits of the rectangle itself, while the overall range of values is shown by the horizontal lines resembling the plunger on a syringe (actually termed the 'whiskers' of the plot).

Inspection of this chart would suggest that the average shoe size is just over 5, the interquartile range about 3 and the overall range of sizes going from 2 up to 9. (The actual values were, median = 5; IQR = 3.5; range = 7 – again, an impressive judgement from a chart.)

4.4   The normal distribution

A major characteristic of human behaviour is the tendency for certain patterns to repeat themselves. One such pattern observed whenever we measure a human trait is the tendency for most people to congregate around some middle value, with fewer and fewer people falling into more extreme categories. This always happens if the group we are observing reflects the normal population – normal in that there is the expected variation among individuals in the group we are measuring.

We have already witnessed this effect with our previous examples on shoe size (see Boxes 4.2 and 4.3) but the notion holds true for most other traits, such as IQ or certain aspects of personality.

Studies of general intelligence, for instance, show that most of us will cluster around some average measure, usually given the arbitrary value of 100 (based on the Terman and Merrill (1960) development of the original Binet Mental age and Chronological age relationship). As with height, there will be some people who will score in higher ranges (105–10), but there will be fewer of these. At more extreme ranges (110–20) there will be fewer still. This typical pattern is illustrated in Figure 4.2.

This pattern, of course, will only occur providing the group being measured is normal: if, by some chance, the observations on intelligence were made on an unusually bright group (e.g., a group of MENSA members) there would be more than the usual (or normal) proportion of intellectually superior people in our sample. Therefore the distribution of scores would reflect this 'skew', as illustrated in Box 4.7.

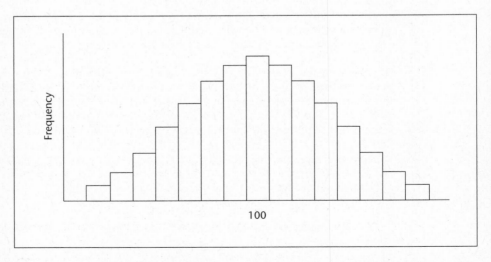

Figure 4.2   Histogram showing the distribution of IQ scores around the mean of 100

Box 4.7   Skew

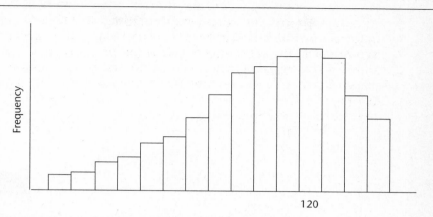

Histogram showing a skewed distribution of IQ scores

When a distribution contains more than the usual proportion of observations near one of the two ends of the measurement scale, it is said to be skewed. In this example, there is a disproportionate number of observations close to the top end of the distribution. This is known as a left, or negative skew. (Note: the expression 'left' refers to the elongated tail of the distribution, and not the direction of the most intense concentration of scores.) This tendency for some distributions to deviate from the expected shape can be represented statistically, as shown below:

Mean	112.5000	Std Err	.6270	Min	70.0000	Skewness	−.9191
Median	115.0000	Variance	176.9321	Max	135.0000	S E Skew	.1151
5% Trim	113.2778	Std Dev.	13.3016	Range	65.0000	Kurtosis	.8212

The skewness statistic of −.9191 is calculated using a formula which considers how much each score deviates from the mean, and interprets these differences in terms of the standard deviation. Fortunately, SPSS does all this for us and all we need do is inspect the coefficient of skewness for magnitude. If necessary, a simple rule of thumb method for estimating skewness is to compare the mean with the median, reminding yourself of the tendency for the mean to be affected by extreme scores in a way in which the median is not.

In most instances the kind of skew illustrated in Box 4.7 will not occur if the group we are observing is typical, or normal, or the sample an honest reflection of the population at large. You might recall the discussion in Chapter 3 in which sampling issues were considered: in particular, the problem of inadvertently overrepresenting particular groups was noted, a problem which could easily give rise to a skewed distribution. If sampling is carried out properly though, and if what we are measuring conforms to the typical human pattern, the type of distribution we obtain (as in Figure 4.2) is called a **normal distribution.** Statisticians usually prefer to display such trends, not in the form of histograms, but in the form of a 'bell-shaped' or 'inverted U' curve, as in Figure 4.3. All normal distributions share this typical shape, and they also share similar characteristics:

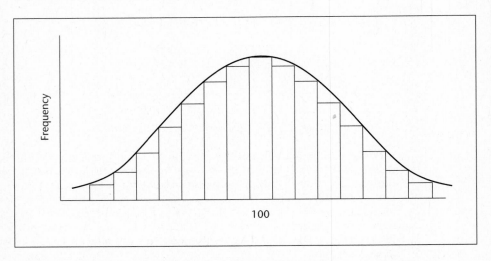

Figure 4.3   Bell-shaped curve superimposed on the histogram shown in Figure 4.2

1.   The shape of the distribution is always symmetrical.
2.   The highest point of the distribution represents the mean, and because this distribution is so symmetrical, this point will also represent the median and the mode.
3.   Furthermore, due to this symmetry, each half of the distribution will account for 50 per cent of the scores (see Figure 4.4).
4.   Dividing the normal distribution into equal halves is only the beginning of the descriptive potential for this particular shape: e.g., we can identify the particular score below which only 25 per cent of the sample falls (Figure 4.5). Likewise, we can identify a similar score at the other end of the distribution, above which 25 per cent of the sample falls. This is a procedure we have already considered in the section on dispersion, when the concept of quartiles was introduced (see Section 4.3.2).

In case no one has noticed, it's worth pointing out that we have actually progressed from looking at specific examples involving a sample, some kind of measure and a range of scores, to what is in effect a theoretical model of

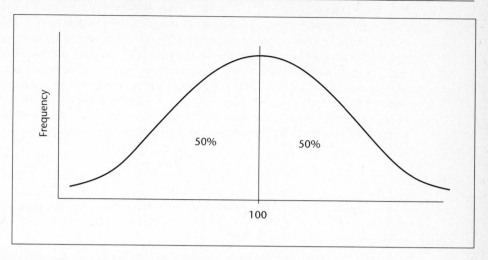

Figure 4.4 The proportion of the distribution on either side of the mean

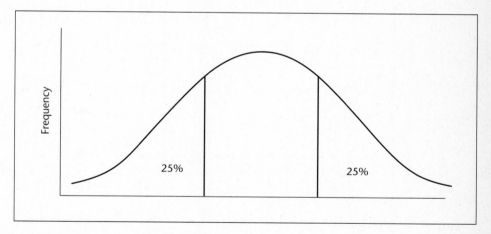

Figure 4.5 Subdividing the distribution

just about any human characteristic one might think of. Just as the mean is simply a useful statistic which typifies or symbolises a range of scores, so too the **standard normal distribution** (as it is termed when it serves as a model, rather than a representation of some concrete measure) merely offers a general picture of the way most human behaviours and characteristics look – a lot of people clustering around some middle value, with the number of cases declining the further removed they are from this point.

The point of this evolution from the real to the theoretical is that if most actual human characteristics conform to an approximation of this normal shape, then whatever can be deduced from the standard normal distribution (i.e., the theoretical model) will hold true for real life. Consequently, because all normal distributions share the same symmetry, it is possible to identify standard distances from the mean, and to know what proportion of scores falls on either side of these points. For this, we use the formula for the standard deviation (SD), already encountered at Box 4.5:

$$SD = \sqrt{\frac{\sum(x - \bar{x})^2}{N}}$$

This formula allows us to divide our distribution into three equal proportions on either side of the mean: 1, 2 and 3 SDs above the mean, and -1, -2 and -3 below the mean, as in Figure 4.6.

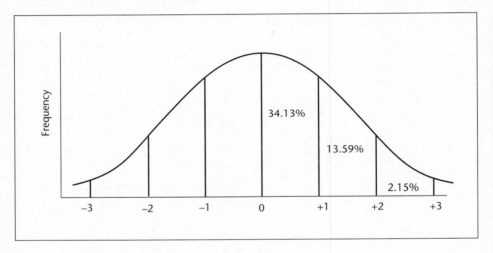

Figure 4.6　Standard deviations from the mean

In case we are in danger of losing anyone at this point, it is worth recalling that in this perfectly balanced distribution, a line down the centre will divide the distribution into two equal halves. Similarly, a distribution based on some real human characteristic, be it intelligence, extraversion or reaction time, as long as it conforms pretty well to the now typical shape, will also be divided in two by some measure of centrality – in other words, the mean. By way of illustration, if intelligence is normally distributed, with a mean of 100, we know (because of our increasing understanding of the characteristics of this kind of shape) that 50 per cent of the people measured have scored close to or below this value, while the other 50 per cent scored close to or above.

Developing from here we can now return to the notion of the standard deviation, recognising that what this particular statistic does is to divide a distribution (providing it approximates the characteristic shape of the normal curve) into six segments, or intervals, based on the absolute range of scores. And because all normal distributions are symmetrical, we can expect to find that about 34 per cent of the scores are between the mean and one SD above. Another 34 per cent are between the mean and one SD below. Since the number of cases decline the further away we travel from the mean, the interval between the first and second SDs will comprise 13.59 per cent of all observations, with the third and last interval containing the remaining 2.15 per cent.

For example, if we discovered that the IQ distribution had a mean of 100 and an SD of 5, we would know that the dividing points above the mean are 105; 110; 115. Similarly, the dividing points below the mean are 95; 90; 85.

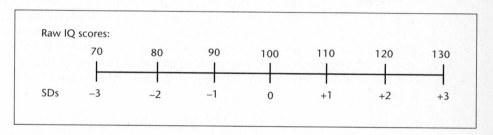

In this sample, therefore, about 68 per cent of the IQ scores fall between 95 and 105 (see Figure 4.7).

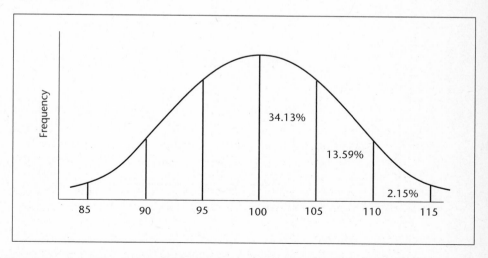

Figure 4.7   The proportion of scores falling between standard deviation units

Thus for any normal distribution, if we divide the distribution into three equal parts above and below the mean, we know that the proportion of scores falling between the particular values will always be: 34.13; 13.59 and 2.15 per cent. While these proportions remain constant, the actual values which represent the different standard deviation positions will obviously change.

For example, Figure 4.7 is based on an IQ distribution which ranged between scores of 85–115. If we conducted another study, we might find that, although our mean was again 100, the range of scores was from 70–130. With individuals spread out across this range, then our standard deviation value would be different: i.e., 10. Figure 4.8 illustrates this point.

Therefore, while the shape of our new distribution would be the same as in the original example, and while the proportion of scores falling between any given standard deviation points would be the same, the actual raw scores reflecting these standard units would be different.

To calculate where any individual score falls in a distribution, we need to transform it into the same kind of score as standard deviation scores – reminding ourselves that the standard deviation allows us to divide up a distribution in terms of percentages. Known as a **z-score** this tells us how many SDs a score of, say, 103 is above the mean, or how many SDs a score of, say, 94 is below the mean. The significance of this information is demonstrated in Box 4.8.

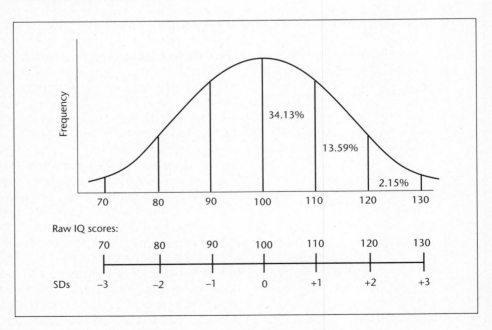

Figure 4.8   Normal distribution of IQ scores ranging from 70 to 130

Box 4.8   z-scores

To understand the relationship between a single score and a distribution of scores of which it is a part, the score must be transformed into a form which can be interpreted in terms of our standard normal distribution. Once this transformation has taken place, we can now view our score in terms of percentage differences above or below the mean.

Transforming a score into a z, or standardised score can be achieved via the formula shown below:

$$z = \frac{x - \bar{x}}{SD}$$

With a mean of 100 and an SD of 10, a raw score of 103 converts to a z-score of +0.3, and a raw score of 94 has a z-score of −0.6. With a mean of 100 and an SD of 5 (as in Figure 4.7), a raw score of 103 has a z-score of +0.6, and a raw score of 94 has a z-score of −1.2, and so on. However, aside from offering a visualisation of how far a particular score deviates from its mean, more precise information can be offered – recalling that normal distributions can be subdivided into standard deviation units, each with its own known percentage of observations, it ought to be possible to interpret any individual score also in terms of percentages. This is precisely what can be done with z-scores.

Consulting the statistical tables which invariably form an appendix to any modern statistics textbook will identify the tables of proportions of area under the normal curve. Such tables state the proportion, or percentage of cases which, for a given mean and standard deviation will fall between a z-score and its mean, or which will fall beyond z.

By way of example, if our score of 103 above generated a z-score of +0.6, the appropriate statistical tables indicate that 22.57% of all the scores which made up that particular distribution fall between this score and the mean. Alternatively, the same tables will indicate that 27.43% of all scores fell above this score.

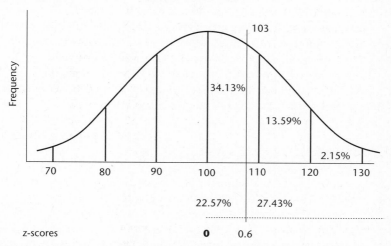

The position of an individual score on the standard normal distribution

To summarise this section we restate that all human characteristics possess the same approximate characteristics – most observations will congregate around some central value, with decreasing numbers falling above and below. Presenting these common characteristics graphically invariably produces an approximation to the normal distribution, a theoretical distribution which nonetheless allows us to predict the proportion or percentage of observations which will fall between any two points, irrespective of the actual scores which comprise the real distribution.

4.5 Computer analysis and SPSS

In the last decade the advances in statistical computing have been extremely rapid, with numerous systems proliferating in an attempt to capture a section of a huge market. Initially available only as mainframe facilities in large academic departments, such systems became progressively accessible to owners of small portable machines until today, when anyone with a half-decent computer now has at their disposal the type of analytical power once only available to major universities.

Software too has undergone a revolution with the once cumbersome command-driven packages giving way to the more user-friendly menu driven approach. This method of manipulating files and carrying out complex operations has proved extremely successful and now, with the advent of Windows [Windows is either a registered trademark or trademark of Microsoft corporation in the United States and/or other countries] software for PC owners, advanced statistical software is now in reach of us all.

There are many different varieties of statistical software, and departments, and individuals within those departments, all have their own preferences. However, increasingly, one particular system has been developing – at least in Europe – as the academic industry standard, the system known as SPSS (Statistical Package for the Social Sciences). It is this particular system which will form the basis for the following illustrations.

4.6 Creating files in SPSS

Let us assume that the superb piece of research which you so painstakingly designed has been completed and now you find yourself staring at a small mountain of data: numbers, ratings, responses or reams of dialogue. The chances are that for many, the thoughts which accompany such piles of information go along the lines of 'what am I going to do with all these numbers?' The answer couldn't be simpler: these numbers are going to be sorted, simplified and summarised; they will be reduced to statistics which will impose meaning on the trait or behaviour they represent and they will be

Box 4.9   Common statistical symbols and their meaning

X	a score, or the column heading for a variable in univariate analysis. Where more than one variable is present, the notations become X_1, X_2 . . . .X_n.
Y	a score, or the column heading for the second variable in bivariate analysis. Also the variable heading for the dependent variable in 3-group comparisons.
$\sum$	the sum of . . . (whatever follows)
$\sum X$	the sum of the scores
X^2	the square of the score, or scores
$\sum X^2$	the sum of the squared scores
$(\sum X)^2$	the sum of the scores, which is then squared
$\sqrt{}$	the square root
!	factorial
$\bar{X}$	a sample mean. Obtained by $\sum X/n$
s	a sample standard deviation, used as an estimate of the population standard deviation
μ	a population mean
σ	a population standard deviation
n	the number of observations in a sample
N	the number of observations in a population
s^2	sample variance

used to draw inferences and test hypotheses. They will also form the basis for a variety of graphs and charts which will illustrate, highlight and describe. But before any of this is possible, we must create a space to store our information: we must create an SPSS data file.

Those new to computer statistical software might be daunted by the scale of a package like SPSS, but in its use, nothing could be simpler, as the following sections will demonstrate.

4.7 The basics of working with SPSS

4.7.1 Setting up variables and data entry

The first contact with SPSS takes the form of a blank spreadsheet, a kind of template which opens automatically when the programme is activated (by clicking or double-clicking on the SPSS icon similar to that above). At this stage the spreadsheet comprises merely a grid of empty cells, devoid of data and not even titled, but forming the basis of a file in which all the information from any study can be stored. However, the SPSS spreadsheet is more than simply a bin for information, offering the capacity to manipulate data and perform complex analyses via the symbols and menu options which form a part of it. The figure below illustrates the major elements of a typical blank spreadsheet: there are a number of empty cells (many thousands of these in fact, although only a screen's worth will be visible at any one time).

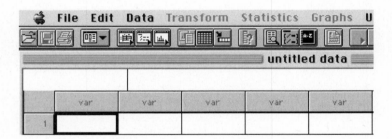

The title of the particular spreadsheet or data set is also shown, although initially this appears as **untitled data**. Not until you actually enter some data into the spreadsheet and save your work are you given the opportunity to give your data set, and your file, an appropriate name.

Above the title area is a ribbon of buttons, a series of small symbols which, when selected (by a single mouse click), perform various functions – some switch the view from the data spreadsheet to charts, some change the way the data appear and one initiates printing:

Not all of these buttons will be available until the spreadsheet contains data, and in fact when the first untitled file is opened several of the symbols will be 'greyed out', indicating that they are currently deactivated. In the sample empty spreadsheet above for instance, the printing symbol is unavailable, and will not become active (as above) until there is something to print.

The final part of this window (a window is whatever is currently on the screen) is the menu bar running along the top. Opening any of these menu items (by clicking and holding the mouse button depressed, or simply clicking in the PC versions) will display the various functions available under each heading. Generally speaking the main categories of operation are file handling (opening new files, saving, etc.), editing (copying, pasting and moving information about), and statistical functions. Box 4.10 offers an example of the menu items at work.

4.7.2 | Coding data

Once a study is complete you will have available large amounts of data. Some of these will be what are termed **profile** or **subject data,** which comprise descriptive information on the individuals who participated in the study. For example, you will probably have numbered your subjects to enable you to

Box 4.10 Using menus in SPSS

All operations and functions within SPSS are accessed in the same way: using the mouse and selecting any of the menu items a single button click will explore all the operations available under each heading.

File	Edit	Data	Transform
New...			⌘N
Open...			⌘O
Connect to ODBC Database...			
Read ASCII Data...			
Close			⌘W
Save Data			⌘S
Save As...			

Opening the file menu at the top of the data spreadsheet will allow access to the type of functions shown above. Selecting a particular function is achieved by dragging the arrowhead over each activity until the desired one is achieved. Releasing the mouse button at this point automatically selects the highlighted option and SPSS will happily carry out the specified sequence of operations. This is the case whether the system used is a Macintosh version, as above, or the PC version, below:

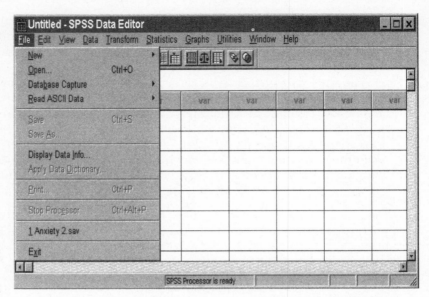

All the other menu items work in the same way although, as with the assortment of toolbar symbols beneath the menu, not all operations will be available at any particular time. It is also worth noting that many operations can be carried out using a combination of keystrokes (e.g., Ctrl+O to open a file). These are always shown on the menu if they are an option and many experienced users sometimes prefer to work this way because of its speed.

identify cases while at the same time ensuring the anonymity of the actual participants. You are likely to know if they were male or female, how old they were, whether married or single, working or unemployed, Type A or Type B personalities, and whether they cycled or not (or whatever was relevant to the particular study). If the study took the form of a true experiment, you will also have information on the experimental condition to which subjects were assigned (e.g., control or experimental), and finally, you are likely to have a number of outcome measures – responses to questions on a survey, scores on a number of questionnaire items or performance measures on some experimental task.

Not all of this information though will necessarily be numerical – the subject profile details are likely to be categories into which individuals can be placed (male or female; control or experimental). Likewise response or outcome data will often be in a non-numerical format – many survey data are in the form of nominal categories chosen by respondents (yes/no/don't know). Likewise, scaled responses on questionnaires are often in the format 'strongly agree/agree/uncertain/disagree/strongly disagree'. However, if the intention is to carry out some form of quantitative analysis on your data, all of the relevant information must be transformed into a numerical format.

This process of changing category information into numbers is known as **coding**, and nothing could be simpler. A subject who happens to be male is represented in the 'gender' variable by the value '1'; females are represented by the value '2', and so on. Moreover, statistical software is at its most contented when dealing with numbers so the procedure has many merits; in fact, the only problem is when the researcher loses track of what all the numbers mean, although this is rare. Box 4.11 illustrates the point about coding.

Box 4.11 Coding

When collecting data during the course of a study it is sometimes not possible, and occasionally undesirable, to record information numerically. Subject profile information is invariably presented in terms of specific categories (male/female; married/single), while some response variables are often more comfortably expressed qualitatively. Many subjects for instance are happier when allowed to respond to descriptive categories rather than numerical scales. Compare the examples below.

$ How satisfied are you with your course of study so far?

completely unsatisfied	unsatisfied	neutral	satisfied	completely satisfied
☐	☐	☐	☐	☐

$$ Please rate on the scale below your level of satisfaction with the course so far. Selecting 1 indicates complete dissatisfaction; selecting 5 indicates complete satisfaction.

1	2	3	4	5
☐	☐	☐	☐	☐

While qualitative categories might be preferable for some subjects, if the ultimate aim of a study is quantitative analysis, such descriptive categories must be recoded – which simply means replacing category information with an appropriate numerical value.

Item			Code
Subject No			7
gender	M ☐	F ☑	2
marital status	single ☑	married ☐	1

condition   control   experimental

☐   ☑   2

How do you feel about the book so far?

brilliant   good   limited   awful

☑   ☐   ☐   ☐   4

In the above example, all of the items offer descriptive, qualitative responses to subjects. However, in order to analyse the data in terms of, for example, the percentage of males and females responding to a particular attitudinal category, or even to determine the number of single versus married subjects who participated in the control and experimental conditions, it is necessary to convert this information into a format which is more accessible to conventional statistical software. Hence, male subjects are coded with the value '1', and females, '2' (One of the contributors to this text wishes to point out that the convention of using 1 = male and 2 = female should not convey any sense of order or magnitude; the numbers merely differentiate between the classes on a nominal scale.)

Likewise, other profile information can be coded numerically – *married* can be represented by the (arbitrary) value '2', with *single* coded as '1', or the other way around, it doesn't really matter. Responses on outcome measures are coded in the same kind of way, with the proviso that when response alternatives indicate degree, as in 'greater than' or 'less than', the numerical codes must reflect this. Consequently, coding of an item along the lines of: 'to what extent do you agree with...?' would generate an ordinal scale (1 2 3 4 5) in place of the categories 'strongly agree', 'agree' and so on. Many researchers take the additional step of regarding ordinally-scaled categories as representative of points on a continuous scale. This allows for a number of operations to be carried out, such as calculating a mean response across a number of related categories, as in the example below:

$1. What do you feel about the book so far?

brilliant   good   limited   awful

☑   ☐   ☐   ☐   4

$2. How good do you feel the statistical explanations have been?

brilliant   good   limited   awful

☐   ☐   ☐   ☑   1

$3. How effective do you feel the graphical illustrations are in this text?

brilliant   good   limited   awful

☑   ☐   ☐   ☐   4

If we represent the descriptive terms of *awful* to *good* by the numbers 1 to 4 (with the higher values reflecting a more positive attitude) then an average value of 3 would represent the above responses. Overall, the attitude towards the textbook is positive.

4.7.3 *Entering data and naming variables.*

Each variant of statistical software has its own set of preferences concerning data handling, but all share certain conventions, the most fundamental of which relates to how data are entered. The typical format – and that required by SPSS – is that all cases are identified by a subject or case number, in a single column. Traditionally this is the first set of data entered into any dataset, although with the current version of SPSS this is no longer strictly necessary, since all the rows in its spreadsheet are numbered, and actually identified by the system as case numbers. However, the authors have found it a useful discipline to begin all data entry by identifying, numerically, each subject who participated in a study. This sets the scene as it were and makes it easier to deal logically with subsequent data entry.

Many undergraduates experience difficulty with this initial stage, and understandably so since the common method of presenting data in journals and textbooks distinguishes among subjects in terms of group or category, as Table 4.4 illustrates:

Table 4.4 The number of correctly recalled words following a memorising trial under a control condition of no noise and an experimental condition of intrusive noise

Control (no noise)	Experimental (noise)
25	15
22	12
19	18
21	14
22	19
–	–
–	–
n	n

When dealing with data in this format the intuitive way to enter it into a statistical spreadsheet is to mimic the two-column table above. While this is fine for publication or illustration purposes, it is not the way most statistical software works, as the next section demonstrates.

4.7.4 *Data entry – between group designs*

The trick in error-free data entry is to begin, as mentioned in Section 4.7.3, with a single column listing of every subject or observation which comprised a particular study. Each successive column contains information relevant to its associated subject, whether it be subject or grouping characteristics, or outcome measures on some experimental task. Table 4.5 illustrates the point.

Table 4.5   Recall scores of subjects in both the experimental and control conditions

Subject	Condition	Recall score
1	control	25
2	control	22
3	experimental	15
4	experimental	12
5	control	19
6	experimental	18
7	experimental	14
8	control	21
–	–	–
n	–	n

All between-group data are organised in this way, with a separate column devoted to each variable as it relates to individual subjects. In Table 4.5, subject 1 participated in the control condition and returned a score of 25. Subject number 3 was in the experimental group and returned a score of 15, and so on. The approach can of course be extended to allow for any number of variables, as is the case with traditional social science research – much survey data and a great deal of government statistics are based on considerable quantities of information, such that for each individual participant there can be several dozen associated measures.

4.7.5   Data entry – within-group designs

When entering data for a within-subjects design, the general principle of one subject column followed by separate columns for each related variable still holds. For example, if in the memory experiment outlined in Tables 4.4 and 4.5 above, we decided that differences between the control and experimental groups were being confounded by the effects of individual differences, we might opt instead for a within-subjects design in which the same subjects participated in both conditions, as in Table 4.6.

Here again, there is a single column devoted to identifying the subject or case number, with successive columns providing information relevant to each subject. By way of example, Subject 1 correctly recalled 25 words in the 'no noise' condition, but only 15 in the 'noise' condition.

Table 4.6 The recall of subjects in a no noise and a noise condition

Subject	Recall under Condition 1 (no noise)	Recall under Condition 2 (noise)
1	25	15
2	22	18
3	19	12
4	20	17
"	"	
"	"	"
n	n	n

4.8 Setting up data in SPSS – practicalities

4.8.1 Working with SPSS

The first step in setting up a data file in SPSS is to recognise that all computer-based analytical systems appear initially dim, unhelpful and occasionally intransigent. Of course, software producers and distributors emphasise user-friendliness and sophisticated help functions yet the truth is that all such systems are designed not to be nice or awkward, but to obey. Few systems will make suggestions, none will make allowances and all of this makes life difficult for the novice. However, providing we appreciate that no statistical package will do any more than we tell it to do, then we are on the way to developing an effective working relationship.

Translated into actions this means that we must always explain what we are doing and what we expect in response. The majority of errors can usually be traced back to a failure adequately or fully to explain what is required. The next few illustrations demonstrate the main steps in setting up a data file in SPSS.

4.8.2 Naming and defining variables

For any analytical system to be able to work with a set of data – generate tables, draw graphs, make comparisons – it needs to be able to identify the variables which comprise the data set. This is the first task in data entry and it is initiated by clicking or double clicking (using the mouse button) on the column heading cell found at the top of the first empty column of data cells.

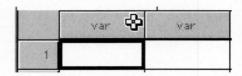

This procedure opens the first of many possible operational windows, some of which allow us to describe in detail the nature of each variable, and others of which let us select various descriptive and analytical options. This first window is the **Define Variable** window and serves the dual purpose of informing SPSS of the key characteristics of our data, and also incorporating descriptive information which can serve to remind us what the variable actually is. This might seem an odd thing to do, but in large data sets in which variables are identified by some cryptic abbreviation, it becomes all too easy to forget what the various wordings and codes originally meant.

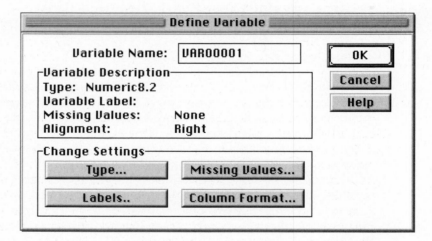

The define variables window (above) serves two purposes – it provides information describing important characteristics of a particular variable and, secondly, it offers the means to change that information.

The **variable name**, initially appearing as **VAR00001**, or just **var**, is readily changed to whatever is desired, with the proviso that any new variable name is restricted to a maximum of eight characters, without spaces or dashes. This limitation will often prove an irritation requiring the use of abbreviations which will inevitably vary in their usefulness.

The **variable description** part of the window indicates that the data to be entered under this particular variable are numeric, may be up to eight characters long, two of which are decimals. The **variable labels** section is blank at this stage, there are no **missing values** recorded yet (**none**) and any data will appear **right** aligned in the data spreadsheet.

These settings can be changed: selecting the **Type** button (by clicking) will open a new sub-window in which we can change the data type from numeric to, for example, comma (whereby 3000 becomes 3,000), and other variants such as string, which would allow us to enter actual words as values (referred to as alphanumeric data).

Selecting the **Labels** button opens yet another window, this time allowing us to provide a more detailed description of particular variables, and also to explain how nominal, category variables are subdivided. When dealing with small data sets, containing perhaps no more than two variables, this facility is often unnecessary, since we will probably remember what our study is about. Large data sets however, containing possibly many variables, each given some cryptic abbreviation, can lead to confusion if we forget which variable was which, or how we recoded the data. In cases like this the labels option comes into its own, allowing us at any time to review the characteristics of any variable. (Note: in the latest version of SPSS variable labels are shown merely by moving the pointer across the variable names in the data window. Older versions require that we return to the define variables option.) The procedure for this is potentially complicated and is illustrated in Box 4.12.

The **Missing values** button is an important one in SPSS; from time to time and for various reasons, some of our data for some of our subjects will be missing. Sometimes a survey respondent will refuse to answer a particular item on a questionnaire (they might object to the intrusive nature of an item, or question its relevance), some items will be omitted by accident and some will so obviously have been misunderstood that a response to a particular item might have to be ignored (as when a subject selects two options from a response scale). Similarly, the researcher can make mistakes in recording or transcribing responses – all expressions of a natural human fallibility which result in the occasional finding that some of our data are missing.

Most undergraduate researchers, not familiar with the peculiarities of computer software, or the significance of missing pieces of data, might take the line : 'so what?' 'So there are missing data, so Subject number 24 forgot to complete item 19, so I'm not sure if the response to this particular item is a "3" or a "5". Just type in a zero or leave the cell blank and go on to the next one.'

Neither of these options is recommended – a blank space, while it will be picked up by SPSS as a missing value in a list of values, might actually be caused by the person entering the data inadvertently miskeying, and SPSS will not discriminate between a genuine missing value and incompetence on the part of the operator – they all look the same, as it were. Using a zero is not a good idea either, since zero is often itself a value, or represents a category within a coded variable. However, it is important to let SPSS know if any values have been omitted – even a simple calculation like the arithmetic average will be undermined by miscounting the number of cases or values. Moreover, it is sometimes useful for the researcher to be able to identify cases or subjects who did not respond to particular items in the event that they represent an interesting subgroup of the population.

The convention for dealing with missing values is to enter an extreme, or bizarre value which could not form part of a conventional set of values within a specific variable, and which is clearly distinguishable from them. Hence, if a response to a given item is of the nominal Yes/No variety (typically coded 1 and 2 respectively) then no response at all could be represented by the value 9, or 99, or whatever. Providing SPSS is informed that whenever it encounters '99' it is to treat this as a missing value, then calculations won't be affected and any such cases can be readily spotted. Selecting the missing values button in the define variable window leads to an additional sub-window in which we can state which value (or values) will be used to identify missing data.

The **Column format** button controls the appearance of data in the columns – selecting this option allows you to specify whether data should be presented left, right or centre aligned.

Box 4.12 Dealing with category variables in SPSS

When a variable comprises a number of categories, as in subject or profile variables (male/female) some experimental treatments (control condition/ experimental condition) or nominal response variables (yes/no), a few additional steps are required at the initial stage of defining the variable. Aside from giving ourselves valuable practice in coding skills, this allows SPSS to deal with what is essentially qualitative data in terms of numerical symbols, with which it is much happier.

In the Define variable window, once we have named our variable, selecting the Labels... button will reveal the next-level window:

The purpose of this new element is to allow us to more clearly label or identify the characteristics of a variable. In particular we can do two things: (a) we can offer more information on the name or label which we have given the variable. This is useful since, restricted as we are to only eight characters for names, working out what a given variable actually represents can be something of a challenge; this is an opportunity to expand upon the cryptic label which appears at the top of a data column.

Consider an example in which one variable in a data set refers to the experimental condition to which subjects have been assigned. Due to the restrictions on number of characters, the variable name has been abbreviated to **condit**, a term which requires further explanation, as in the example below:

Define Variable	
Variable Name:	condit
	Define Labels:
Variable Label:	experimental condition

(b) we can identify the various components or categories which comprise a variable in terms of different numerical values, by defining the value labels. To do this we enter the first value in our range (e.g., 1) in the Value: box, then offer a description of what this value means in the Value label: box, as shown below:

Value Labels	
Value:	1
Value Label:	control condition

This information must be 'added' to the SPSS information store on what various value labels stand for, simply by selecting the Add button. On being returned to the Value: box, the next value label in the range can be entered, and so on. The finished product will look like this:

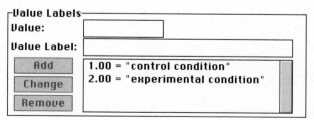

On the face of it this procedure might seem complex, but in its implementation the process is speedy. On completion, data entry couldn't be simpler – the values 1, 2 or 3 need now only to be entered and the associated labels will be recognised:

subject	condit
1.00	control c
2.00	control c
3.00	control c
4.00	experimen
5.00	control c
6.00	experimen

Moreover, in all subsequent tables and charts, the descriptive information entered to define the variable will be shown, or at least as much of it as SPSS is capable of:

CONDIT   experimental condition

Value Label	Value	Frequency	Per cent	Valid Per cent	Cum. Per cent
control condition	1.00	10	50.0	50.0	50.0
experimental condition	2.00	10	50.0	50.0	100.0
Total		20	100.00	100.00	

Valid cases   20   Missing cases   0

4.9   SPSS and descriptive statistics

So far in this chapter a large number of tables and graphs have been used to illustrate various points about measures of central tendency, dispersion and the general presentation of quantitative information. The remaining sections now deal with the procedures for generating this type of descriptive information, based around the sample data presented in Box 4.16. These data refer to the hypothetical example discussed earlier, on the word recall scores of two groups of subjects, one operating under a 'no noise' condition, and the other operating under a 'noise' condition. In fact, the source of the data is not especially relevant, since it merely serves as the basis for further explanation.

Descriptive statistics in SPSS are easily obtained through the Statistics menu which, when selected, displays the options available:

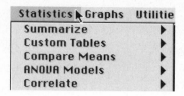

(Note: the contents of these menus vary depending on which version of SPSS is in use. For instance, in later PC versions the **ANOVA models** option has gone, replaced by the **General Linear Model** (GLM) option.) At this initial level, the aim is to summarise data, and selecting this further option from the menu takes us to the major descriptive functions possible.

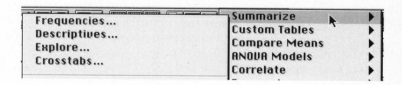

The basic summary operations available are shown above, and selecting any of them will lead to a further window which allows the identification of variables to be considered in analysis plus access to various options. Selecting **Frequencies**, for instance, will produce the following:

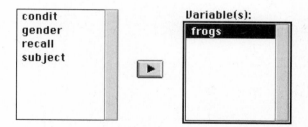

Selecting variables for any kind of analysis in SPSS follows the same general sequence – all the variables in a data set are displayed in a scrolling box on the left part of the window, where one or more can be selected using conventional mouse clicks. In the above example, a number of variables from our hypothetical noise and learning experiment are shown: the subject identification number, the condition to which they were assigned and their recall score. Also available are data on the sex of each subject, plus a measure of their liking for small amphibian creatures. An arrow button: ▶ transfers the selection to a variables window on the right from where, depending on the particular analysis being carried out, a number of additional options can be selected. A final OK will produce an appropriate output which will either be tabular, graphical or both. The table below illustrates this:

FROGS   liking for small, green amphibians

Value Label	Value	Frequency	Per cent	Valid Per cent	Cum Per cent
yes	1.00	18	60.0	60.0	60.0
no	2.00	12	40.0	40.0	100.0
Total		30	100.0	100.0	

The Frequencies command is suited to the analysis of a single variable which comprises category data: the number of males and females in a sample, the number of experimental subjects participating in a control or experimental condition, or the frequency with which respondents to a questionnaire item opted for a YES as opposed to a NO response. However, in the event that tables are not as informative as they might be – and this is a problem common to most statistical programmes – the option of seeing the same data presented graphically is usually offered:

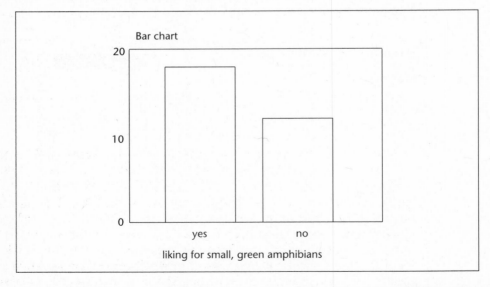

When the data are continuous, or interval-scaled the **Descriptives** command is appropriate, offering relevant parametric statistics on central tendency and dispersion. As with most SPSS operations numerous options are available, allowing the user to determine how much information will be displayed. In our learning and recall example, the Descriptives command produces the following table:

Number of valid observations (listwise) = 30.00

Variable	Mean	Std Dev	Minimum	Maximum	Valid N
RECALL Words correctly recalled	19.80	3.86	13	28	30

Considerably more information, however, is available via the **Explore** command which provides not only an extensive statistical breakdown of a given variable, but also a number of graphical views. Box 4.13 offers the entire output generated on the recall data.

Box 4.13 Explore and recall

The Explore command in SPSS provides the most comprehensive analysis of continuous data: detailed tables providing information on average, spread and skewness; Stem and Leaf tables and a variety of pictorial representations. In the example below, the recall data has been examined by the nominal variable of Experimental Condition.

RECALL:
Number of words correctly recalled, by Condition 1 . . . control (no noise)

Valid cases: 15.0   Missing cases: .0   Per cent missing: .0

Mean	21.1333	Std Err	.7676	Min	17.0000	Skewness .3214
Median	21.0000	Variance	8.8381	Max	26.0000	SE Skew .5801
5% Trim	21.0926	Std Dev	2.9729	Range	9.0000	Kurtosis −.8372
95% CI for Mean	(19.4870, 22.7797)	IQR			4.0000	SE Kurt 1.1209

Frequency	Stem & Leaf
5.00	1. 77899
7.00	2* 0012223
3.00	2. 566

Stem width:	10
Each leaf:	1 case(s)

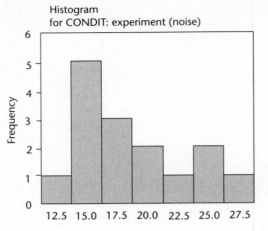

Histogram
for CONDIT: experiment (noise)

Std. Dev = 4.27
Mean = 18.5
N = 15.00

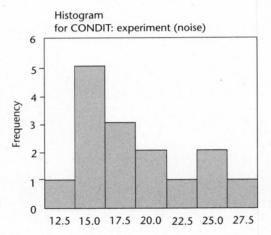

Histogram
for CONDIT: experiment (noise)

Std. Dev = 4.27
Mean = 18.5
N = 15.00

RECALL words correctly recalled
By CONDIT 2 experimental (noise)

Valid cases: 15.0   Missing cases: .0   Per cent missing: .0

Mean	18.4667	Std Err	1.1035	Min	13.0000	Skewness	.9263
Median	17.0000	Variance	18.2667	Max	28.0000	SE Skew	.5801
5% Trim	18.2407	Std Dev	4.2740	Range	15.0000	Kurtosis	.1677
95% CI for Mean	(16.0998, 20.8335)	IQR		7.0000	SE Kurt	1.1209

Frequency   Stem & Leaf

2.00	1* 34
9.00	1. 556677899
3.00	2* 244
1.00 Extremes (28)	

Stem width: 10
Each leaf: 1 case(s)

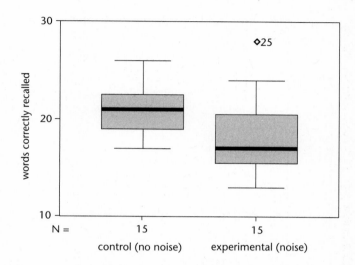

Authors' note: our discussions on the tabular output on the above variables have concentrated on the major aspects of the data being described. However, in the interests of completeness the **standard error** – short for the standard error of the mean – provides a measure of the extent to which the sample mean in question is likely to be close to the mean of the population from which it has been drawn. In general terms, the smaller this value is, the less error there is; moreover, the standard error is partly a function of the sample size, so the larger the sample the less error there will be. In terms of describing the characteristics of a variable this is not particularly important, but if we are interested in the extent to which a sample is a fair reflection of a population, the standard error becomes an essential piece of statistical information. CI in the table stands for **Confidence Interval** and, like the standard error, is concerned with estimating population characteristics. The values given here indicate the range within which we are 95 per cent confident that the population mean lies. The remaining statistic to be considered is **kurtosis**; as with skewness, this measure relates to the physical shape of a distribution, being, in this instance, an indicator of how steep or shallow is the curve comprising the normal distribution. Aside from that, the measure of kurtosis is of little real value in analysis, apart from being a pretty piece of statistical terminology.

The final option in the Summarise sub-menu is the Crosstabs command. Concerned with nominal – or ordinally-scaled data, Crosstabs provides frequency counts of pairs of related variables. The example below presents the typical tabular output – in this instance for the two category variables in the recall data set – experimental condition and gender.

CONDIT	treatment condition by GENDER		
	GENDER		Page 1
of 1			
Count			
Row Pct	male	female	
Row			
	1.00	2.00	
Total			
CONDIT			
1	8	7	15
control (no noise)	53.3	46.7	50.0
2	8	7	15
experimental (noise)	53.3	46.7	50.0
Column	16	14	30
Total	53.3	46.7	100.0

The type of table shown above is termed a 2×2 contingency table, there being two variables in the analysis, each comprising two categories. Occasionally the more informative notation of 2R×2C is used, making it clear how the data are laid out – with two categories in the *Row* variable, and two in the *Column*. In its basic format each cell displays only the number of observations or cases applicable to its particular categories, such that in this illustration we can see that, in the control group, there were eight males and seven females. More useful for descriptive purposes is the translation of cell counts or frequencies into percentages, thus reducing the sometimes misleading effects of uneven subject numbers represented in each category. In the setting up of this example, a subcommand allowed the specification of what actually appeared in the various cells: percentages were selected for the row variables and the cells now provide the additional information that, for the control condition, 53.3 per cent of the cases were male and 46.7 per cent female.

```
┌Counts──────────────┐
│ ☒ Observed         │
│ ☐ Expected         │
└────────────────────┘

┌Percentages─────────┐
│ ☒ Row              │
│ ☐ Column           │
│ ☐ Total            │
└────────────────────┘
```

The 2x2 case is the simplest of the crosstabulation relationships possible for, as we are aware, variables can be subdivided into many components. We could measure preference for beer or lager among different astrological signs for instance, and this would give us a 12x2 contingency table; we could obtain an impression of political bias in newspapers by equating the political affiliation of subjects with their most frequently read newspapers. If there are three major parties, and six possible national papers, we would generate a 3x6 contingency table, and so on. Box 4.14 offers a sophisticated application of crosstabulation in addition to providing a word of caution in the use of this procedure.

Box 4.14 Crosstabulation and cautions

In a hypothetical study exploring aspects of psychological health, a random sample of 150 subjects is drawn from the population. Occupational group is assessed by questionnaire and subjects are asked how many times in the past year they have consulted their GP for stress-related problems. Data are also available on the geographic region of each subject, allowing a breakdown of the basic two-variable relationship by a third, control variable, as is shown in the three tables below.

Presenting the data in this format, with the row percentages selected, allows us to view the proportion of skilled, managerial, and so on who have consulted their GP with varying frequency for stress-related problems in the past year. Moreover, because we have been able to use the geographic regions as a control variable, we can inspect each table and judge if the pattern of occupational group is consistent across all three regions.

There are some potential problems with this kind of table, the most important of which relates to the distribution of cases. While initially a sample size of 150 might have seemed adequate, when this is subdivided by six occupational

CLASS (Occupational class) by HEALTH (health) by GP visits
Controlling for . . .
REGION (uk regional category)   Value = 1.00   Scotland

HEALTH   Page 1 of 1

Count Row Pct	none	one – two	3 or more	Row Total
	1.00	2.00	3.00	
CLASS				
1.00 professional	4 33.3	5 41.7	3 25.0	12 24.0
2.00 managerial	6 40.0	5 33.3	4 26.7	15 30.0
3.00 skilled	2 25.0	5 62.5	1 12.5	8 16.0
4.00 semi-skilled	2 40.0	1 20.0	2 40.0	5 10.0
5.00 unskilled	1 20.0	1 20.0	3 60.0	5 10.0
6.00 other		4 80.0	1 20.0	5 10.0
Column Total	15 30.0	21 40.0	14 28.0	50 100.0

CLASS (Occupational class) by HEALTH (health) by GP visits
Controlling for . . .
REGION (uk regional category)   Value = 2.00   Wales

HEALTH   Page 1 of 1

Count Row Pct	none	one – two	3 or more	Row Total
	1.00	2.00	3.00	
CLASS				
1.00 professional	1 14.3	4 57.1	2 28.6	7 14.0
2.00 managerial	3 42.9	4 57.1		7 14.0
3.00 skilled	3 37.5	2 25.0	3 37.5	8 16.0
4.00 semi-skilled	4 40.0	6 60.0		10 20.0
5.00 unskilled	4 44.4	1 11.1	4 44.4	9 18.0
6.00 other	2 22.2	5 55.6	2 22.2	9 18.0
Column Total	17 34.0	22 44.0	11 22.0	50 100.0

CLASS (Occupational class) by HEALTH (health) by GP visits
Controlling for . .
REGION (uk regional category)   Value = 3.00   Midlands

		HEALTH			Page 1 of 1
Count Row Pct		none	one – two	3 or more	Row Total
		1.00	2.00	3.00	
CLASS					
professional	1.00		3 100.0		3 6.0
managerial	2.00	1 20.0	1 20.0	3 60.0	5 10.0
skilled	3.00	1 6.3	7 43.8	8 50.0	16 32.0
semi-skilled	4.00	3 27.3	2 18.2	6 54.5	11 22.0
unskilled	5.00	2 25.0	3 37.5	3 37.5	8 16.0
other	6.00	4 57.1	1 14.3	2 28.6	7 14.0
Column Total		11 22.0	17 34.0	22 44.0	50 100.0

classes, a random distribution would leave us with only about 25 cases per category. When subject numbers are diluted across three response classes the likely numbers falling into any cell are further reduced, and when these observations are spread over three geographic regions, our subjects are likely to be only sparsely distributed among all the possible cells. Inspection of the above tables illustrates the point: some cells contain only one or two cases, while there are even some in which there are none at all. The presence of percentage values in each cell is consequently quite misleading and should not be used to describe such impoverished data.

A related problem, which will be considered at greater length in Chapter 5, concerns the use of crosstabulations to analyse the distribution of observations. In a search for patterns among responses, or in an attempt to judge whether actual observations deviate substantially from our expectations, certain statistical techniques can be applied to crosstabulated data. However, to be effective these techniques impose certain conditions on the data, one of which concerns minimum numbers of cellular observations – the data presented above, containing as they do a large number of cells with small numbers of observations, would not meet the requirements for powerful analysis.

An obvious solution to the problem of numbers is to increase the sample size. However, often this is not possible, especially in undergraduate research, so an alternative solution would be to reduce the number of subdivisions. In the above example, ignoring the regional differences would make more cases available for each cell (and more expected values, which is important from the point of view of further analysis), as would collapsing the occupational categories. Opting for two or three groups – such as managerial, white collar and blue collar – would considerably increase the pool of subjects available for each cell and might produce the added gain of achieving the requirements for statistical analysis. Of course, the disadvantage of taking this approach is that important distinctions among subjects can be lost and it is up to the individual how important this is in terms of the overall research issue.

A final point brings us back to the essential purpose of descriptive statistics: that they are intended to summarise, represent and illustrate. Unfortunately, contingency tables, while they do meet these requirements, sometimes fail to do so immediately and with clarity. They provide too much information for the 'at a glance' effect and often require close inspection for any patterns to emerge. Consider again the three tables above: there is no question that they contain all the relevant data, and in a precise format, but gaining an overall impression of how individuals are distributed across the various cells will not be immediate – this is true even of the most recent version of SPSS which, although neater in the presentation of output, still suffers from an overenthusiastic display of information. On the other hand, consider the figure below, a multiple line chart showing the same information as all three tables, except in a single presentation.

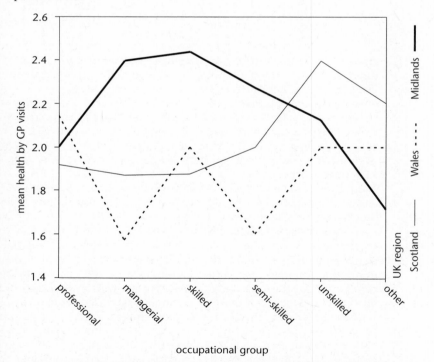

Inspection of the line chart instantly highlights the pattern of GP visits for each occupational class across the three regions. Of course, it lacks the precision of the tables, but charts of this kind are designed for impression and not precision. The bar chart below is another good example of this impressionistic function, whereby the combined data for all regions clearly identify those occupational groups who spend most time at their doctors.

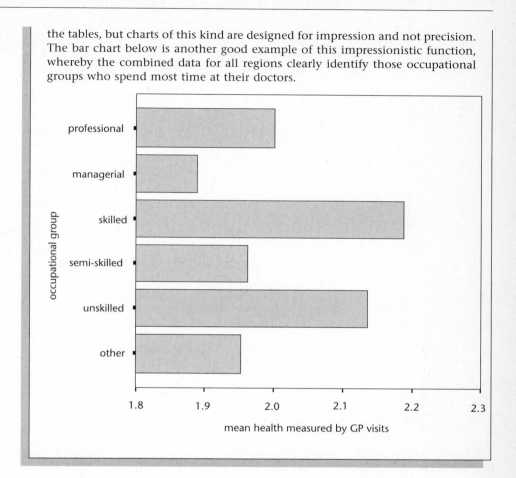

4.10 Interval data and correlation

4.10.1 Describing two continuous, interval variables

Much of the above discussion has concerned itself with the descriptive analysis of single continuous variables, single nominally-scaled variables and pairs of nominally-scaled variables. However, as we considered in Chapter 3, *Designing your study*, some research will involve exploring the relationship between two interval-scaled variables. Relating introversion scores to stress levels is an example of such an approach, since both measures can vary along their own continua. Matching measures of conservatism to authoritarianism is another and equating weight to different measures of blood pressure is a third. All these examples are similar in that they represent pairs of linked observations of continuous data, in a procedure termed correlation.

4.10.2 Correlation

Correlation refers to the relationship between two variables (co-relation). Specifically, the variation in one variable is said to be associated with the other in some way, as the following example shows.

Imagine we have observed that in Scotland, as the temperature rises the reported incidence of road rage also rises, i.e., we have two variables which appear to be related:

X	Temp	10	12	15	15	20	25	26	28	29	30
Y	Road rage	5	4	5	6	6	10	20	19	25	26

Merely by inspection we can see there is a relationship between the two, i.e., as X increases, Y also tends to increase.

This relationship can be seen more clearly in the following figure

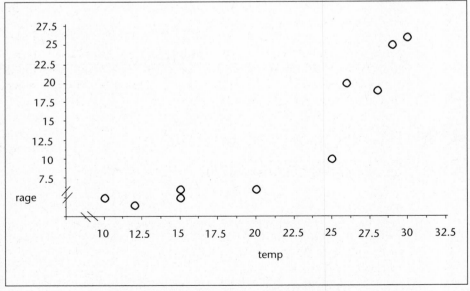

Figure 4.9   Incidence of road rage as a function of temperature

In our previous discussion of descriptive statistics we explained that there were three ways in which variables can be effectively described: by tables, by graphs and by statistics, and this is precisely the case with correlational studies. The twin columns of data for temperature and road rage represent the conventional tabular presentation of correlated variables, and it is important to realise that each pair of values actually represents a single observation, in which two measures were taken at the same time:

Observation	temperature	road rage
1	10 - - - - - - - - - - - 5	

Inspection of the tabulated data clearly suggests that some kind of relationship exists, for as scores on one variable (temperature) increase, so do scores on the other (incidents of road rage). As we have observed, however, trends are not always immediately apparent via tabulated data, sometimes requiring the simplified but more immediately illustrative effect of a chart or figure to identify pattern. Hence the scatterplot above demonstrates the general nature of the relationship: that as one variable increases, so does the other. Moreover, this pattern of change reflects a close link between the two variables since, for a given increase in temperature, there is a proportional – as opposed to a random or variable – increase in reported rage. (Note: these data are clearly hypothetical, as anyone who has lived in Scotland will appreciate; after all, when was the last time anyone in the frozen north experienced temperatures in the 30s?).

In the language of correlation, the above example demonstrates a **strong, positive correlation**: strong, because as one variable changes, the other changes by a similar amount, and positive since as one variable changes the other changes in the same direction (i.e., as one increases, the other variable also increases). Figure 4.10 further illustrates this point.

Given the language of correlation introduced so far (i.e., strong, positive) it can be rightly assumed that correlations can also be weak, and negative. Generally speaking we would expect that those who indulge in regular weekly study time will perform better come examinations than those of us whose idea of research is investigating how many pints of beer we can lift from a standard pub counter in a given evening. Compare the above figure with the next in the sequence:

In Figure 4.11 there is still a strong relationship between the two variables, insofar as when one variable changes the other changes by a similar amount. However, while one variable increases (social/pub time) the other one *decreases*. This will probably come as a great surprise to the majority of undergraduate students.

The final example, 4.12, shows a very poor, or weak relationship:

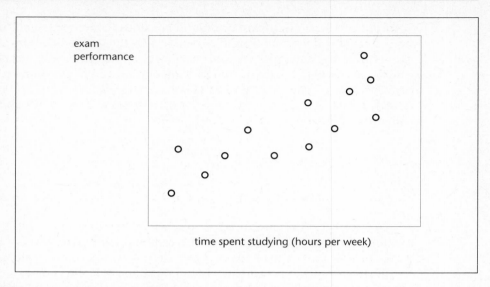

Figure 4.10   A positive correlation between exam performance and time spent in study (hours per week)

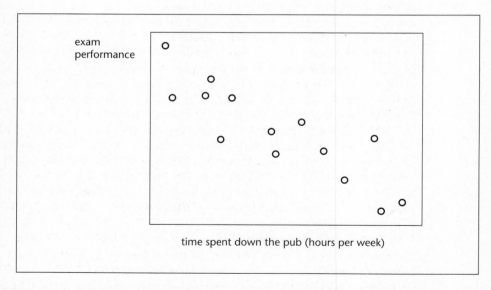

Figure 4.11   A negative correlation between exam performance and time in the pub (hours per week)

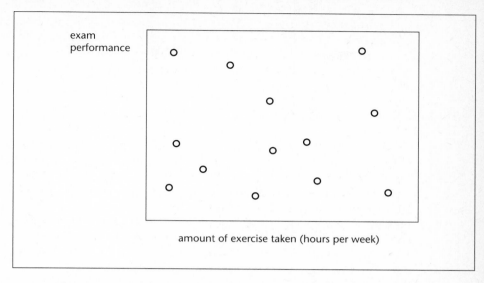

Figure 4.12 A weak correlation between exam performance and amount of exercise (hours per week)

Not surprisingly, taking varying amounts of exercise will have little or no effect on examination performance, indicated by the absence of any kind of pattern, or correlation above.

So far we have demonstrated two of the common methods for describing correlated data: tables and graphs. The third and final approach is that which attempts to represent and describe relationships through the use of symbols, and their related numerical values, in the form of statistics.

The most common version of representing the relationship between two variables statistically uses the symbol **r**, which is an expression for the **coefficient of correlation**, from Pearson. In numerical terms the coefficient of correlation is a value ranging from zero to 1, with the strength of a particular relationship indicated by how close the calculated value is to 1. Weak relationships will of course be indicated by values closer to zero.

Aside from providing a measure of the magnitude of a relationship, r also describes the direction of a relationship. If the calculated value for r is positive, this signifies that as one variable increases, so too does the other. Figure 4.10 is an example of a positive relationship. In fact, by inspecting the plots on the graph we can see that this is also a strong relationship, and the actual calculated value for r in this instance would be about +0.87.

Negative values for r indicate that, as one variable increases, the other decreases, as in Figure 4.11. Here, as the time spent on social indulgence increases, exam performance, as expected decreases. The actual value here could be −0.9.

The third chart above – Figure 4.12 – demonstrates a poor relationship: as one variable increases (exercise) the other variable seems to vary independently. The value of r here could well be + or −0.002, an extremely weak relationship in which the sign (+ or −) is largely irrelevant.

4.10.3 Cautions and correlation

In all of the above it is important to note that none of the relationships described necessarily imply causality. Certainly, study time and exam performance could well go together, but this relationship might be purely coincidental or even spurious; it is possible that studying in itself does not lead to an improvement in exam performance, but rather it is the type of person who studies a lot who does well in exams, which is not the same thing. In fact the danger is in assuming that just because we correlate two variables there must be some kind of relationship – when in reality, pairs of variables may easily be linked purely on the whim of the researcher, rather than in any logical expectation that they might be related. For instance, it would be perfectly feasible to correlate the number of frogs run over by careless cyclists on particular days with sunspot activity for the same periods, without anyone suggesting that any kind of causal relationship existed between the two, even if, by accident, a strong correlation coefficient could be demonstrated.

The problem is that many people assume that just because two sets of measures can be linked, that they *are* linked, and in more than simply a coincidental manner. However, this takes us into the realm of inferential statistics and goes beyond the scope of this particular chapter. A more detailed look at this issue is presented in Chapter 5.

A final point to be made here is a general caution about the use of statistics. So far in this chapter the impression has been given that tables, charts and statistics are alternative methods for describing data, each with its own particular strengths. While this statement is largely correct there will be instances in which reliance on purely statistical descriptive techniques can be misleading – as when a real relationship becomes obscured by the computational processes on which statistics are based. Box 4.15 makes the point.

4.11 Review

This concludes the section on describing data. The aim, as in all sections of this book, has been to introduce general principles and provide examples of those principles in operation. Moreover, this chapter has attempted to provide an introduction to one of the commonest statistical packages available to students. Students should now be able to create a data file in

Box 4.15   A relationship or not?

The figure below demonstrates a phenomenon understood by undergraduate students everywhere – the tendency for exam preparation to be closely linked to individual anxiety levels.

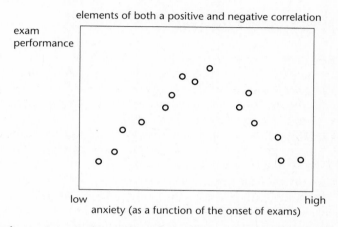

elements of both a positive and negative correlation

exam performance

low   high

anxiety (as a function of the onset of exams)

The typical experience is for studying behaviour to be minimal when exams are far in the mists of the future. However, with the onset of deadlines, most students can settle down to some studying: the odd book is read, journals might be applied for and, occasionally, a lecture might be attended. As exam pressure mounts, more and more time is spent in the library, studying at home and turning down social opportunities, reflecting growing anxiety levels and reflected in improved motivational levels. For each individual there will probably be an optimal distance from assessment periods which is associated with peak studying performance – for some it will be months, for some weeks, and for a few, possibly, only a few days prior to exams. However, if study is delayed beyond this optimal period and a hapless student doesn't open a book until the day before an examination, performance will seriously decline. Anxiety will be present of course, as will motivation, yet the consequences of too high levels of stress – fear, panic, frustration, anger – are likely to interfere with any attempt to concentrate on studies and performance will deteriorate.

This is precisely the case with the figure above: there is an initial rise in performance as anxiety increases, followed by a sharp decline when anxiety levels become extreme. Without doubt then there is a very strong relationship between these two variables, initially positive and subsequently negative. Yet, if the relationship were considered only statistically, the calculated coefficient of correlation would be misleading, since the positive elements in the calculation would be obscured by the negative ones. The moral to this illustration is that while statistics are often the most convenient method of exploring and describing data, they can be misleading; the wise researcher will always want to view the appearance of information.

SPSS, enter data correctly and perform elementary descriptive analyses. For an overview of what has been covered we suggest a review of the flowchart at the beginning of this chapter.

4.12   Explanation of terms

Boxplot   A type of graph used to represent interval-scaled data, emphasising the median, the IQR and the minimum and maximum values.

Central tendency   The frequently observed phenomenon whereby measurements of any trait or behaviour tend to cluster around some typical or central value, such as an average.

Coding   The process of transforming category information into a numerical value. Typically males might be identified by the value 1, and females by the value 2.

Confidence interval   The range of values within which we are confident that a population mean is likely to lie. Confidence is given as a probability, usually 95 per cent.

Correlation   A measure of the association between two variables. Expressed as a statistic r, which indicates both the strength and direction of a relationship.

Crosstabulation   A procedure in which the proportion of cases or observations falling across two nominal or ordinal variables is noted. The type of table in which the outcome of this procedure is presented is a contingency table.

Descriptive techniques   A series of procedures whose aim is to describe data in a manner which effectively summarises, simplifies and illustrates.

Dispersion   The tendency for scores in a distribution to vary around some middle value.

Frequency tables   A table in which the frequency of cases, subjects or observations are presented, either as a number, a percentage of the whole, or both. Such tables are useful for describing the distribution of cases across the categories of a single, nominal or ordinal variable.

Histogram   A type of graph, similar to a bargraph, used to represent interval-scaled data.

Interquartile range (IQR)   The difference between the values at the lower and upper quarter of an ordered array of values.

Kurtosis   A measure of the steepness or shallowness of the curve which forms part of the shape of a distribution.

Mean   The arithmetic average of an array of scores or measurements, calculated by summing all the scores and dividing by their number. This is the most powerful measure of central tendency because of its precision.

Median The middle value of an ordered array of scores. This statistic is sometimes used in preference to the mean when extreme scores are present.

Mode The most frequently occurring value in an array of scores.

Normal distribution A term describing the characteristic arrangement of observations on any variable, with most scores clustering around some central value and fewer and fewer observations occurring with the distance from this average measure.

Profile data (sometimes known as subject data) Descriptive information on the subjects who participate in a study. Typically the subject's sex, age group, social category, and so on.

Range A simple measure of dispersion, being merely the difference between the lowest and highest values.

Skew A measure of the extent to which a real distribution deviates from the normal distribution shape, as influenced by an unusual number of cases falling at one particular end of a distribution.

SPSS A modern statistical computer package developed to organise, describe and analyse research data.

Standard deviation The most powerful measure of dispersion, based on the extent to which each individual score in a distribution varies from the mean.

Standard error (of the mean) A statistic based on the standard deviation of a sample, which provides a measure of how close the sample mean might be to the population from which it has been drawn.

Standard normal distribution The term given to the theoretical distribution which serves as a model for all real, normal distributions.

Statistic A symbol, along with its numerical counterpart, which represents, summarises or defines important characteristics of a variable. The symbols themselves are usually taken from the Greek alphabet.

Value label Additional information used to describe and explain the coded values which represent the different categories in a variable. An SPSS element.

Variable label Additional information used to describe a named variable in SPSS.

Variable name The name used to identify a variable in SPSS.

z-scores The numerical values produced when actual scores in a distribution are transformed into the same scale and system of measurement as the standard deviation.

4.13 Reference

Terman, L.M. and Merrill, M.A. (1960). *Stanford-Binet Intelligence Scale*. New York: Houghton Mifflin.

4.14 Recommended reading

Howitt, D., and Cramer, D. (1997). *An Introduction to Statistics for Psychology*. London: Prentice Hall

Dometrius, N.C. (1992). *Social Statistics Using SPSS*. New York: Harper Collins

Kinnear, P.R. and Gray, C.D. (1994). *SPSS for Windows Made Simple*. Hillsdale, NJ: Lawrence Erlbaum.

Robson, C. (1993). *Real World Research*. Oxford: Blackwell

4.15 Sample data

Box 4.16 Recall data

Subject	Condition	Recall
1	control (no noise)	25
2	control (no noise)	22
3	control (no noise)	23
4	control (no noise)	26
5	control (no noise)	21
6	control (no noise)	18
7	control (no noise)	20
8	control (no noise)	19
9	control (no noise)	17
10	control (no noise)	22
11	control (no noise)	26
12	control (no noise)	17
13	control (no noise)	19
14	control (no noise)	22
15	control (no noise)	20
16	experimental (noise)	16
17	experimental (noise)	15
18	experimental (noise)	19
19	experimental (noise)	19
20	experimental (noise)	22
21	experimental (noise)	24
22	experimental (noise)	17
23	experimental (noise)	14
24	experimental (noise)	13
25	experimental (noise)	28
26	experimental (noise)	24
27	experimental (noise)	15
28	experimental (noise)	16
29	experimental (noise)	17
30	experimental (noise)	18

In a simple experiment to investigate the effects of noise on cognitive functioning, two groups of subjects attempted to memorise a list of common nouns under either a control condition of no noise, or an experimental condition of noise. In the experimental condition subjects wore headphones and were exposed to 'white noise' for the duration of the memorising period. After an interval of 24 hours subjects attempted to recall the original items. The results are shown alongside

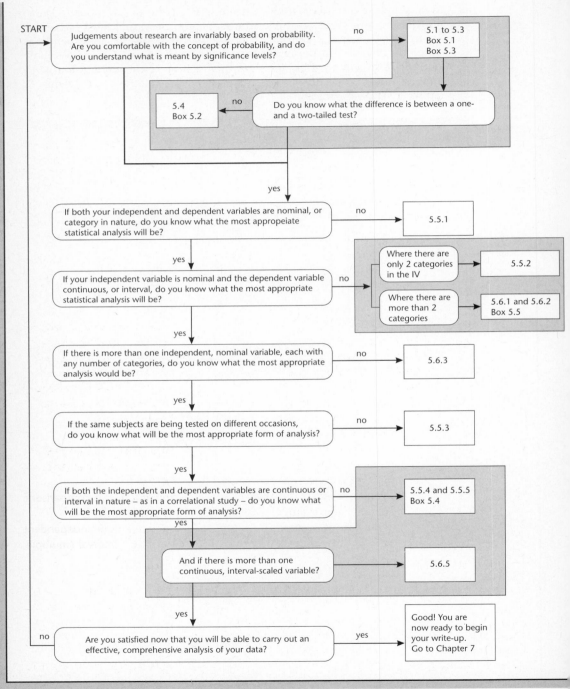

Flow Chart 5

START

Judgements about research are invariably based on probability. Are you comfortable with the concept of probability, and do you understand what is meant by significance levels?

no → 5.1 to 5.3 / Box 5.1 / Box 5.3

no → 5.4 / Box 5.2 ← Do you know what the difference is between a one- and a two-tailed test?

yes ↓

If both your independent and dependent variables are nominal, or category in nature, do you know what the most appropeiate statistical analysis will be?

no → 5.5.1

yes ↓

If your independent variable is nominal and the dependent variable continuous, or interval, do you know what the most appropriate statistical analysis will be?

no → Where there are only 2 categories in the IV → 5.5.2

→ Where there are more than 2 categories → 5.6.1 and 5.6.2 / Box 5.5

yes ↓

If there is more than one independent, nominal variable, each with any number of categories, do you know what the most appropriate analysis would be?

no → 5.6.3

yes ↓

If the same subjects are being tested on different occasions, do you know what will be the most appropriate form of analysis?

no → 5.5.3

yes ↓

If both the independent and dependent variables are continuous or interval in nature – as in a correlational study – do you know what will be the most appropriate form of analysis?

no → 5.5.4 and 5.5.5 / Box 5.4

yes ↓

And if there is more than one continuous, interval-scaled variable?

→ 5.6.5

yes ↓

Are you satisfied now that you will be able to carry out an effective, comprehensive analysis of your data?

no ←

yes → Good! You are now ready to begin your write-up. Go to Chapter 7

CHAPTER 5

Making inferences about research

'I've got two independent variables, six conditions and two outcome measures. Which test should I use?'

'All I want is a straightforward t-test. But what's this equal and unequal variances stuff?'

'I've got a probability of 0.5. Is this significant?'

'My ANOVA tells me I've got a significant effect – but it won't tell me where it is!'

'Help!'

Overview	
🗀 Inferential statistics	🗀 simple regression – predicting one variable from another
🗀 Probability explained	🗀 Complex analyses (analysis of variance and regression)
🗀 Scope for errors	
🗀 One- and two-tailed tests	🗀 more than two categories of an independent variable (ANOVA)
🗀 Statistical analysis	
🗀 nominal independent variables and nominal dependent variables (chi-square)	🗀 Analysis of variance
	🗀 more than one independent variable – nominal (two-way ANOVA)
🗀 nominal independent variables and interval dependent variables: between – group comparisons (independent t-test)	🗀 multiple group comparisons (*post hoc* tests)
	🗀 more than one independent variable – interval (multiple regression)
🗀 nominal independent variables and interval dependent variables: within – group comparisons (paired t-test)	🗀 Review
	🗀 Explanation of terms
🗀 interval independent variables and interval dependent variables (correlation)	🗀 Recommended reading

Chapter 5 goes beyond the description of data, which formed the basis of Chapter 4, and considers how these data can be used to make decisions: Did one group perform better than another? Do these observed differences signify a genuine difference? Do these results support my hypothesis? Was the theory correct? The major statistical tests will be demonstrated and the procedures for making statistical decisions explained. As with Chapter 4, examples and guidance for analysis will be given using modern computer software.

5.1   Inferential statistics

Descriptive statistics are in themselves an important means to understanding the characteristics of data. However, the parameters usually taken to describe variables – specifically, measures of spread and central tendency – can be further used to draw inferences. Comparing the means of two samples can be the first step in demonstrating that a genuine difference exists between two groups, or that a particular experimental treatment has a real effect on some outcome. And this is what inferential statistics are all about – making deductions and drawing conclusions. In the very first chapter of this book the purpose of research was defined as describing, explaining and predicting aspects of the world in which we live. Describing and, to some extent, explaining have been considered in the previous chapter on describing data. Understanding the world and the people in it, however, requires a more detailed appreciation of the information we gather and a sophisticated ability to manipulate it which goes beyond the purely descriptive. And if we ever hope to be able to predict behaviour, we need to demonstrate that events which we observe or effects we encounter during the course of a survey or experiment, are not mere chance occurrences. Not surprisingly then, inferential statistics rely heavily on the concept of probability.

5.2   Probability explained

Whenever researchers attempt to make a point, support an hypothesis or test a theory, they are trying to show that a particular set of observations is not merely a chance occurrence. This is not an easy task, due to the astonishing richness and variety of the countless elements which comprise human experience. No two people are ever alike – even identical twins, as we know, cannot share the same physical space and are therefore subjected to differing experiences and influences throughout their lives. Consequently, selecting any two people at random and looking for differences in measurable characteristics will produce a breathtaking lack of commonality. But this is normal – each of us inherits a unique genetic pattern, whose contribution to individual singularity is further enhanced by particular parental interactions, selective exposure to peer influences, attitudes, values, education, opportunities and cultural forces. The wonder of this is that there remains sufficient common ground within humanity for any form of intercourse whatsoever.

The point we are trying to make here is that whenever we look at any two individuals, or any two groups, we should *expect* there to be differences between them, and this is the researcher's problem. If we devise a study to demonstrate that a new form of learning strategy is more effective than traditional methods, how do we know that any differences between a sample using the new techniques and a sample using the traditional strategies is nothing more than a reflection of the very human tendency for variation? How do we know that the new approach had a *real* effect?

The answer lies in probability.

Every event in the world, every occurrence, happens with its own particular level of likelihood, or probability: the chances of someone having a puncture while driving home from work is pretty unlikely in these days of modern tyre technology, but it can happen (and often does, at the busiest junctions). Having two punctures is even less likely (less probable) while experiencing three flat tyres is unusual in the extreme. And if our hapless driver discovered four flats – and the spare – he could quite reasonably assume that something was going on.

Making decisions about the outcome of research operates in a similar manner. Comparing two groups of subjects on any measurable characteristic – be it height, shoe size or intelligence – will always produce differences. In fact, given what we have just said about human variability, we would *expect* differences. Moreover, we would be prepared to accept that such differences might reasonably range from the marginal to the moderate. Comparing the average heights of two groups of undergraduates for example could easily produce the heights of 1.9 metres and 1.8 metres respectively, showing a very slight difference between the two. We could however discover mean heights of 1.9 and 1.6 metres, and still not be too surprised. After all, while this difference of 0.3 metres is less likely than our previous finding, it is still possible, given this known tendency for variation in all things human. 1.9 and 1.4 might start us wondering though, while 1.9 and 1 would make us extremely suspicious – just like the driver with all the punctures. And this is how statistical – and subsequently research – decisions are made: when an event occurs which is so unlikely that, even within the bounds of human variability, it is remarkable, then we can claim that a discovery has been made or an effect demonstrated. Three simultaneous punctures might be possible, but four is a conspiracy. A difference in heights between 1.9 and 1.6 metres might be unusual, but that between 1.9 and 1 metre might suggest that our samples have not been drawn from the same population.

The question now to be addressed is 'How unusual is unusual?' Certainly we all have an intuitive idea of what is unusual but possible as opposed to what is downright impossible, but this is a subjective thing, based on feelings and, occasionally, misperceptions about the laws of chance. The example in Box 5.1 is a good illustration.

The rule, which has become the accepted norm for making statistical decisions, is that if an event occurs (a difference between groups, the outcome of a manipulation) when the chances of it occurring naturally are less than five times in a hundred, then this event is deemed too unusual to be plausible, or within the acceptable range of variability. The event is then given the status of being **statistically significant.**

This cut-off – known as the 5 per cent or 0.05 significance level – is deliberately far removed from high probability events (it will rain somewhere on any given November day in Britain for instance) to ensure as far as possible that when we decide an effect is present, a change has occurred or whatever, that we are not merely seeing an unusual but not completely out of the ordinary event. The astute reader though will have noticed the essential flaw in this approach – even an event so unlikely that we might expect to see it, naturally, only 5 per cent of the time, is still possible in an infinitely variable universe. And because of this, we can be led to false conclusions in our research, as the next section demonstrates.

Box 5.1   Probably improbable

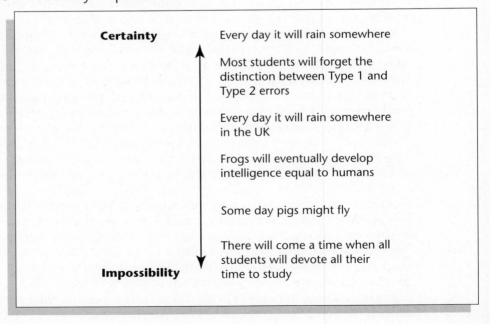

5.3   Scope for errors

Every event in the universe exists on an imaginary continuum running from certainty to impossibility, with the full range of probabilities in between (see Box 5.1). The convention is to view events as 'different' only when their probability of occurrence is as unlikely as 0.05 or less. However the danger here is that such events, though rare, could still occur by chance alone. In fact, according to the rules of probability, events of this rarity could actually occur by chance 5 per cent of the time. Or to put it another way, if we use this level of probability to identify events as significantly different from that which we might normally expect, we will be wrong approximately 5 per cent of the time. In research terminology this is known as a **Type 1 error** – the possibility that an apparently significant finding can actually be explained in terms of unusual but nonetheless valid variations and individual differences. Alternatively, a **Type 2 error** can occur when we wrongly accept that an unusual event is merely an extension of chance occurrences when in fact we have a significant finding. Expressed more simply, whatever we decide in research, there is always some chance that we will be wrong.

One solution to this problem of course would be to push our cut-off point further along the continuum of probability, not accepting a finding unless it is even less likely than the five times in a hundred level. (This is what our suspicious researcher did in the coin tossing example, being reluctant to end a friendship unless there was clear and unambiguous evidence of cheating (see Box 5.3).) And indeed, some researchers anxious to avoid Type 1 errors do just that, refusing to accept a finding as being significant unless its probability of occurrence is one in a hundred or less (known as the 1 per cent or 0.01 significance level). Unfortunately, while a finding significant at this extreme level is more robust, it will also be more difficult to demonstrate due to the need for a really clear-cut effect; a study in which an experimental and a control group are compared on some outcome measure would have to generate truly huge differences, or employ a large sample, before we could argue a statistically significant finding.

5.4   One- and two-tailed tests

An added complication to this problem of significance concerns whether or not our hypothesis and our test is one-tailed or two-tailed. This is a question which often causes difficulties in comprehension for those new to statistical analysis, but it needn't, once the principle is understood.

Suppose we were concerned with an industrial process of some kind, say the brewing of a particular variety of ale. To ensure that a new batch measures up to what we normally expect from this brew, we take a number of bottles off the production line and subject them to analysis – looking at flavour, strength, colour, and so on. We might even invite a few friends round to assist in the assessment process.

While modern production methods are now well controlled and the chances of a particular sample deviating from the norm are slim, this was not always the case. In the past it would have been quite likely in this kind of study to find samples deviating quite markedly from the expected norm. The point of this particular study would be to determine whether or not variation is within acceptable ranges, or whether the sample characteristics are so far removed from what would normally be expected of this brew that the batch would be recalled.

From the way this hypothetical example has been expressed, it should be clear that when we are comparing our sample to the expected characteristics of the population as a whole, we are prepared for differences to be in either direction: i.e., that the new batch will merely be different from our expectations; it might be stronger or weaker, it might be fuller flavoured, or insipid. The diagram below illustrates this.

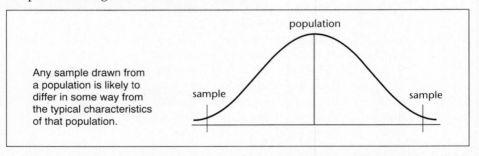

The figure above can be taken to represent the known characteristics of the particular brew we are interested in. There will be a mean for this population and variation about this mean. When we compare our sample statistics to these population parameters, we could find that our sample is placed somewhere beyond the mean (stronger, fuller flavoured, etc.). But equally, we could find our sample falling below the mean (weaker, less flavourful, etc.). Since the ends of this kind of distribution are known as 'tails', our sample could lie at either tail, and therefore any test which allows for this either-or case is termed a **two-tailed test**.

This allowance for observations to fall at either tail of a distribution requires further explanation in probability terms. So far we have argued that an event will be deemed statistically significant if it occurs with a probability of 0.05 (5 per cent) or less. However, if we try to test this in a two-tailed manner, we would be wrong to examine the 5 per cent cut-off point at each tail, since what we would be doing is checking for the occurrence of an event which appears only 5 per cent of the time in one direction and 5 per cent of the time in the other direction. In reality we end up using a 10 per cent significance level!

To ensure then that we evaluate an event in terms of only the 0.05 level, this measure of extremeness must be spread between the two ends of a distribution, meaning that the actual cut-off point of a two-tailed test is 2.5 per cent in either direction. See Box 5.2 for a fuller explanation.

Box 5.2 One- and two-tailed tests explained.

A quality control chemist with statistical leanings suspects that a current batch of dark ale will not be typical of the usual brew, due to a problem during the production process. Making a number of selections at random from the current production line, our closet statistician has colleagues rate the liquor on an index of taste. His expectation, and hence his hypothesis, is that the sample drawn from this current batch will be different from the known characteristics of this particular beer. However, he does not know in what way the sample will differ so he proposes an hypothesis which covers all eventualities: specifically, the sample could differ from the known characteristics of all previous batches (the population), but it could differ in either direction (i.e., stronger than or weaker than). This is a two-tailed hypothesis.

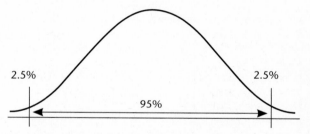

If our embryonic statistician selects the usual 0.05 cut-off for his test then he is proposing that the sample batch cannot be considered unusual unless it differs from the expected range of flavour in a way which would only ever happen 5 per cent of the time. Another way of looking at this is that 95 per cent of the time variations from the population average will be within an acceptable range. If the new batch however falls outside that 95 per cent limit, then it must be considered statistically different from the expected norm. The above diagram shows the range in which the sample must fall to be considered different – also apparent is the way in which the remaining 5 per cent of rare differences has to be divided between the two extremes of the distribution. In practical terms what this means is that to be considered significant within a two-tailed context, a particular event must be further out along the rarity continuum than we might have expected; it is almost *as if* we are using a 2.5 per cent cut-off level rather than the 5 per cent one, although in probability terms this is not the case.

All of the above is relevant only if the researcher is unsure of the way in which his sample might differ from the population. If on the other hand he was pretty sure that the new batch would not be so flavourful as the normal brew then in his comparison with the population he would only be looking at the lower end of the distribution, or at one tail.

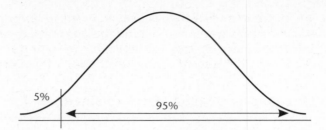

5%

95%

Clearly, while he is still working within his 5 per cent boundary, all of our researcher's scope for unusualness is at the same end of the continuum. Comparing this diagram with the previous one, it should be clear that betting only on one tail of a distribution is more likely to produce a result than if he had to consider both ends – but only if he gets the direction right. And this is the problem with one versus two-tailed tests: two-tailed tests are more difficult to prove, but will nonetheless pick up a significant finding no matter at which end of the continuum they fall. One-tailed tests on the other hand, while easier to produce a result, are only effective if the researcher has chosen the right direction to explore.

Returning to our beer tasting study now, on averaging judgements across 30 observations, a mean measure of 153.2667 is obtained. (Totally meaningless, but representing flavour for the purpose of this example!)

In the past, and using similar measures, this particular ale has produced a score of 156 on the same flavour index. Clearly the two averages are different, but what our researcher must now decide is whether or not the sample is too different from the population to be considered *really* different (a statistically significant difference).

An appropriate test here is the one-sample t-test, in which a sample statistic (sample mean) is compared with a known population parameter (population mean) and a formula applied to ascertain the likelihood that the sample comes from this population. (The precise formula for this calculation can be inspected in any standard statistics textbook.) Applying SPSS to the problem produces the following output:

One Sample t-test

Variable	Number of cases	Mean	SD	SE of Mean
SAMPLE	30	153.2667	8.913	1.627

Test Value = 156

Mean Difference	95% CI Lower	Upper	t-value	df	2-tail Sig
–2.73	–6.062	.595	–1.68	29	.104

The above SPSS output is fully explained at the end of this part, but for the purposes of our demonstration the important information is that, given all the other information about the sample (its size, the spread of scores around the mean), the observed difference of 153.2667 from the population mean of 156 would occur with a probability of 0.104 (or 10.4 per cent of the time). Large as this difference is, it is not large enough to be statistically significant: i.e., it does not fall at or beyond the conventional cut-off level, as the figure below demonstrates.

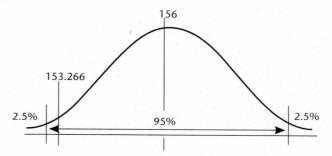

However, had our researcher been convinced that the new batch of ale would score lower on the index of flavour, then he could have applied a one-tailed test, whereby he could concentrate his attention only at one end of the continuum. In this instance, the observed difference suddenly approaches statistical significance:

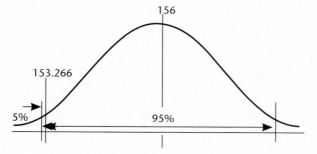

By way of a final demonstration, returning to the SPSS output, we observe that the two-tailed probability of obtaining this difference at either end of a distribution is 0.104. Converting this to a one-tailed probability is achieved simply, by halving the two-tailed value. Thus the probability of obtaining this observed difference, below the population mean, is 0.052.

(Note: this example is based, somewhat loosely, on the life of Gosset, employee of a well-known Irish brewing family and occasional statistician, known more familiarly as Student, originator of the t-test in its various forms.)

Hopefully by now the notion of events being evaluated in terms of their probability of occurrence is understood, but if there is still some puzzlement over this, Box 5.3 should illustrate the point.

Box 5.3　Taking a chance

Imagine you and a close friend are constantly disagreeing about what to do at weekends – where to go, who to go with and so on. To resolve these differences, a coin is usually tossed – your friend's 'lucky' coin, and invariably the fall is in her favour. She doesn't call it her lucky coin for nothing! However, you are now becoming suspicious that there might be something more sinister behind your friend's luck since you can no longer remember any occasion when you got to do what you wanted. In short, you suspect your friend is using a bent coin; you suspect your friend of cheating.

Stealing into her room one night you retrieve the questionable coin and prepare to carry out an experiment: you will toss this coin 100 times and observe the outcome. Your recollection is that in resolving differences your friend always calls Heads, and nearly always wins. Your expectation therefore is that in this experiment there will be an unusually high number of Heads, but what constitutes unusual?

If this coin were fair, then at each toss there would be two possible outcomes, Head or Tail, with each equally likely. In 100 tosses then, you might expect 50 Heads and 50 Tails. Of course, due to variations in a variety of factors (wind speed, hand used to flip coin, height of flip) you would accept some deviation from the expected distribution. For instance 55 Heads and 45 Tails might pass without remark, as might 60 Heads and 40 Tails. But what about 70 Heads and 30 Tails? Would this be unusual enough to convince you that your friend is a cheat? Would you risk a friendship of many years standing on a 70–30 distribution? Perhaps not – this is unusual but not impossible. But what about 90 Heads and 10 Tails? Surely this event is rare enough to prove our suspicions? This is how statistical decisions are made: we do not live in a perfect universe and so will always accept that actual events will vary somewhat from our expectations. However, when an event occurs which is so unusual that we might expect to witness it by chance only 5 per cent of the time, we argue that such an event is no longer within the accepted range of variability. This event, whether it be the extent to which a sample mean differs from a population parameter, or the observed choices on a questionnaire differ from what is expected, can be regarded as statistically significant. As with our surreptitious coin tosser there comes a point beyond which we will no longer accept events as being attributable to chance alone. In statistical terms this is known as the point of statistical significance. (In fact, in this particular example, a split of 60–40 would be rare enough in statistical terms to state that the coin was biased, although in defence of our friendship we would probably still make allowances for our friend and choose a much more remote event as our cut-off point.)

5.5 Statistical analysis

5.5.1 *Nominal independent variables and nominal dependent variables (chi-square)*

Many survey and questionnaire-based studies are of the nominal-nominal design. That is, the independent or causal variable comprises a number of categories, but the dependent or outcome measure is also composed of categories, as when the choice of response to an item (YES/NO) is determined by the sex of the respondent (male/female). (Note: while both these examples refer to nominally-scaled variables, the following discussion relates equally well to cases in which either, or both variables are ordinally-scaled.)

In this type of design the most appropriate form of analysis is by a combination of crosstabulation and chi-square (χ^2). The chi-square (pronounced ki-square) test of association, to give it its full title, compares actual observations with what would be expected were chance alone responsible for the distribution of events. As the difference between observations and expectations increases, this is reflected in the magnitude of the statistic. In the example above, if there were no sex effect in the choice of response to a particular item, we would expect a random, and more or less equal distribution of male and female responses in each of the yes/no categories. If this is not the case, then there will be evidence for a sex effect in choices.

A problem with this particular statistic is that it merely informs us that there is an effect of some kind within the associated variables, but not where. This is why a crosstabulation is useful, since inspection of the cells which comprise a contingency table can often identify the source of an effect. The example below provides an illustration:

A number of individuals classified as either Type A or Type B personality types respond to an item from a stress-proneness questionnaire. The particular item asks the question:

How often do you feel unsatisfied with the course your life is taking?
never   occasionally   all the time
A sample SPSS output is shown on the following page:

The following output is typical of SPSS – informative but hugely intimidating to anyone not totally familiar with this type of computerised analysis. However, there is a trick to dealing with any mass of information, and that is to take it a piece at a time.

The first part of the output which interests us is the information relating to the difference between actual observations and expectations: specifically, did

```
        P_TYPE (Personality type) by  SATIS (satisfaction with life)

                          SATIS                  Page 1 of 1
                Count |
                Exp Val |never  occasionally    all
                Residual|                      the time  Row
                        |    1.00|    2.00|    3.00| Total
        P_TYPE   ---------+--------+--------+--------+
                    1 |    7 |   24 |   44 |   75
        TypeA        | 25.0 | 20.5 | 29.5 | 50.0%
                     |-18.0 |  3.5 | 14.5 |
                  +--------+--------+--------+
                    2 |   43 |   17 |   15 |   75
        TypeB        | 25.0 | 20.5 | 29.5 | 50.0%
                     | 18.0 | -3.5 |-14.5 |
                  +--------+--------+--------+
              Column    50     41     59     150
              Total   33.3%  27.3%  39.3%  100.0%
```

Chi-Square	Value	DF	Significance
Pearson	41.36936	2	.00000
Likelihood Ratio	44.91151	2	.00000

Statistic		Value	ASE1	Val/ASE0	Approximate Significance
Lambda :					
symmetric		.38554	.06622	4.95702	
with P_TYPE	dependent	.48000	.06799	5.59773	
with SATIS	dependent	.30769	.06963	3.85435	

Type As and Type Bs make random choices among the three response categories?

Under the heading **Chi-square** are **Pearson** and **Likelihood Ratio**, which refer to two slightly different ways in which this statistic can be calculated. SPSS will actually print more than just these two but for most purposes the first is sufficient. Then two corresponding values are presented, with their degrees of freedom and, finally, a significance value. This last value is the one on which decisions will be made, since it represents the probability that the actual observations match our expectations, assuming chance were the only factor in determining our subjects' responses. In this instance the probability that observations and expectations are the same is so remote that the value actually drops off the end of the scale – and clearly well beyond the conventional 0.05 cut-off level. (Note: extremely low probability values, indicating hugely significant effects, are shown by SPSS as 0.0000.)

In our example chi-square tells us that the two personality types are not choosing randomly among the response alternatives. However, it does not tell us in what way actual choices are deviating from expectations – for this, inspection of the contingency table is necessary, which is why chi-square is rarely used on its own; the addition of a crosstabulation is needed to further explore the relationship between the two variables.

It is easy to appreciate how the contingency table shown can appear scary to the novice – there is a multitude of information on offer but again, provided it is considered a piece at a time, it becomes manageable.

At the top and to the left of the cells the numbers simply refer to the numerical values assigned to each category. To the right and at the bottom are the sums of all the observations in each row or column, along with the corresponding percentage of the whole which they represent. It is inside the cells though that the most useful information is to be found.

Each cell contains three values, the explanation for which can be found at the top left-hand corner of the table:

Count Exp Val Residual

Taking the first cell in the table, the Count is 7, representing the number of Type A individuals who chose the 'Never' response. The Expected Value however, if choice were a random event, is 25, producing a Residual of −18. In other words, there are 18 less observations in this cell than would be expected. (And how do we know what should be expected, if response to one variable were not influenced by the other? This is a simple matter of taking each cell in turn, multiplying the associated row and column totals and dividing by the total number of observations. For this current example, the expected number of observations in the very first cell is determined by:

$$\text{Row total } [75] * \text{Column total } [50]/\text{Grand total } [150] = 25$$

(Further examples of this procedure can be found in any of the statistically-oriented references at the end of this chapter).

Normally SPSS presents only the Count of observations in each cell, and additional information must be selected from a list of options when setting up the crosstabulation command. Of particular value is the Residuals option, permitting the speedy identification of particular cells in which actual observations vary dramatically from expected values. In our example, the category 'never' shows the greatest discrepancies, for both measures of personality.

The final important source of information is found under the heading **Statistic**, which is yet another table available through the general crosstabulation menu. In this section a number of measures of association are possible, describing the strength of the relationship between two variables. The particular statistic chosen in this example is Lambda (l), which indicates how much our independent variable (personality type) actually predicts the dependent (response). In our example the Lambda is given as 0.30769 when 'satisfaction' is taken as the dependent variable in the analysis. This tells us that there is a 30 per cent reduction in error in predicting the satisfaction response by knowing the personality type of the individual. If the two independent and dependent variables had been completely unrelated, the corresponding Lambda would have been 0.0. (Note: the Lambda table allows for either factor to be taken as the dependent variable, in addition to a 'symmetric' value, which is a compromise between the two; in the context of this example though 'satisfaction' is deemed to be the appropriate outcome measure.)

SPSS offers a number of similar statistics, each with their own particular strengths and weaknesses. However, although all are readily accessible as options, none should be selected unless its application is fully understood. The texts cited as recommended reading at the end of this chapter provide an excellent exploration of these most useful of statistics.

5.5.2 | *Nominal independent variables and interval dependent variables: between group comparisons (independent t-test)*

One of the most common experimental designs involves the exploration of the effects of a single category variable on some continuous measure. Comparing males and females on some measure of spatial ability might be one example, investigating the differences in neuroticism scores for Type A versus Type B personalities would be another (see Chapter 3). In both examples the independent variable is nominal, with Gender comprising the two categories of male and female on the one hand, and Personality made up of either the Type A or B categories on the other. Similarly, the dependent, or outcome measures are interval-scaled variables, with scores able to vary continuously on their respective scales.

Studies using this approach are often of the quasi-experimental variety, in which different groups are selected and compared on some measure, but the design is equally at home with the traditional experimental set-up in which the categories being compared are a control and an experimental group. As the following example illustrates:

A sample of male undergraduates is drawn from the student population and divided at random into two groups. Group 1 attends a presentation from a male 'nutritionist' extolling the gastronomic virtues of members of the genus Rana. In particular the legs, shallow fried in garlic and butter are supposed to be delicious. Meanwhile, Group 2 is attending an identical presentation though in this instance from an attractive female 'nutritionist'. Both presentations conclude with the information that this particular delicacy would be available that day in the campus dining hall (the result of an unfortunate earlier experiment involving cyclists). As part of a marketing exercise, the subjects in both groups are asked to rate how likely they would be to sample the new menu, on a 7-point scale running from 'No way' to 'Somebody stop me!'

This particular scenario is typical of the persuasive communication genre in which the covert purpose of the study is to investigate the impact of the source of a communication, rather than the communication itself. Specifically an experiment of this sort would be exploring the hypothesis that male subjects would respond differently to a message originating from an attractive female source than to the same message from a male source. The type of analysis ideally suited to a design of this nature, is the t-test.

The dedicated reader, interested in the historical development of statistical procedures, might recall that Gosset, in his guise of the statistician Student, developed an approach for comparing the characteristics of a sample with those of a population (known as the one-sample t-test). In particular he developed a formula for determining how far away a sample mean had to be from a population parameter to be able to say that this sample did not come from, or did not represent, that population. In an extension to this work, Student produced a variant of his t-test which could be applied to two samples, according to the following logic.

If two samples are drawn from a particular population, and measured on almost any variable, the first and most likely finding is that the means of both samples will be very similar. (Imagine selecting two groups of students at random and comparing their average heights.) However the second – and necessary – finding is that they will not be the same. This might appear a contradiction, but it is not; we are continually reminding ourselves that the scope for human variability is vast and that no two people can ever be truly identical since, even for identical twins, they cannot occupy the same space. Consequently, no two groups can ever be truly identical, even if drawn from a **homogeneous** population (one in which all individuals share similar characteristics). Therefore while we might expect any two samples to be similar in some measurable way, we would also expect them to be different.

Were we to take numerous pairs of samples from our population our expectation would be that, in the majority of cases, the differences between each pair would be minimal. However, because of what we know about human variability, we would also expect to find some instances where the differences between the pairs of samples were larger than marginal, but there would be fewer cases in which this occurred. Similarly, because the universe allows for considerable variety, we would encounter some cases in which the differences between pairs were moderate, but there would be still fewer of these. And just occasionally, we would expect to see a pair of samples between which differences were considerable. And this would be rare.

It is this rare finding which is the important one – if the difference between two sample means is so rare that it is only likely to ever occur 5 per cent of the time, we are in a position to argue that it is more likely that the two samples are not in fact drawn from the same population. Alternatively, if we draw two samples from a single, homogeneous population we might assume (without actually testing for it) that they will be similar on some key characteristic. If one group is subjected to an experimental treatment and then the groups are compared, any observed differences between them can be attributed to the treatment. This is the case with the above example on persuasive communications: initially both groups of male subjects – if properly sampled – might be expected to share similar views on the eating of frogs' legs. After the persuasive presentations from the different sources however (the experimental treatment), these views might have diverged. Which is the whole point of the study.

The **independent t-test** (unpaired t-test; independent samples t-test) compares the means of two samples and provides a probability that these means are the same (or that they come from the same population). SPSS output from our hypothetical frog-eating study is shown below:

```
t-tests for Independent Samples


                                Number
Variable                        of Cases      Mean        SD     SE of Mean
---------------------------------------------------------------------------
ATTITUDE   attitude to frogslegs

Male source                        75        2.8933      1.624       .188
Female source                      75        4.7200      1.721       .199
---------------------------------------------------------------------------


          Mean Difference = -1.8267

          Levene's Test for Equality of Variances: F= .137   P= .711


          t-test for Equality of Means                              95%
Variances  t-value      df     2-Tail Sig    SE of Diff        CI for Diff
---------------------------------------------------------------------------
Equal        -6.69     148        .000          .273       (-2.367, -1.287)
Unequal      -6.69  147.51        .000          .273       (-2.367, -1.287)
---------------------------------------------------------------------------
```

In true SPSS fashion, the t-test output above contains a great deal of information, yet again contributing to possible confusion, not to say intimidation, among novices.

There are in fact three distinct parts to the above table, the first containing simple descriptive statistics on the dependent variable, as a function of the independent variable. The most important data here relate to the mean measures on the attitude scale for each group: those with the male source producing a mean of 2.8933, and those with the female source producing a mean of 4.7200. Clearly these means are different, but it is the function of the t-test to determine whether or not this difference is sufficiently rare to be statistically significant.

One detail remains however before the test can be applied, and it has to do with variance (the extent to which individual observations in a sample vary around the mean). The t-test, while designed to test for differences between the means of two samples, nevertheless assumes that the distributions within each sample, and hence the average variation about the means are similar. If this is not the case – and this in itself can be an interesting finding – a modification to the t-test formula is necessary. The decision is made with relative ease, merely by comparing the variance within one sample with the variance within the other. Levene's test for the Equality of Variances does exactly that, and provides the probability that the two variances are equal. We can see that in our example a probability of 0.711 is shown, an indication that the distributions comprising each sample are similar. Indeed, even by inspecting the standard deviations of both samples we would have come to the same conclusion. Had the probability value dropped below 0.05 though, we would have had to accept that the variances were clearly unequal and apply the alternative formula.

The final part of the table relates to the t-test itself. Selecting the **Equal variances** option (based on the previous Levene's probability) we note the t value of −6.69 (which is merely a transformed measure of the difference between the sample means) and the associated significance value of 0.000. What this is telling us is that the likelihood of obtaining such a difference between two sample means by chance alone is so remote that the probability value falls off the end of the scale as it were – certainly well below our conventional 0.05 cut-off and less even than the more remote 0.005. (It is worth reminding ourselves that when the probability of an observed difference between means is so remote, SPSS prints the value 0.000. This does not mean that the probability of this particular occurrence is zero, nor does it mean that the observed difference was not significant, both common errors among undergraduates.) In other words, the source of the communication made a statistically significant difference to subjects' responses to the attitude item.

(Note: when working with t-tests there are two points to be appreciated. The first is that the value of t reflects the magnitude of the actual difference between the two sample means being compared. The bigger this difference, the bigger will be the t value and the more likely that this difference will be significant. The second point concerns the fact that t values can be both positive and negative, a possible source of anxiety for some students. In practice, the sign is unimportant, merely reflecting the difference between the sample means being compared. If the larger mean is subtracted from the smaller, the difference will of course be a negative value. It is the magnitude of the t value which is important, not its sign.)

5.5.3   *Nominal independent variables and interval dependent variables: within – group comparisons (paired t-test)*

In Chapter 3 a particular type of design was outlined which had some advantages over the conventional two-group comparison. Rather than use different individuals in each category (e.g., one set of subjects in a control group and another set in an experimental), the same people can be used in two or more conditions. The advantages of this approach are that fewer subjects are needed in a study, and the complicating effects of individual differences are minimised.

It is worth reminding ourselves that taking repeated measures on the same individuals requires a different approach to data entry than usual – or at least, that's how it appears. In Chapter 4, the rule for entering data into a conventional statistical programme was that cases or observations were identified first (by, for instance, a subject number) and then each associated piece of information in turn. For subjects tested on two different occasions, data entry into a package like SPSS would appear as follows:

Subject No.	Test 1	Test 2
1	score	score
2	score	score
3	score	score
4	score	score
.	.	.
.	.	.
.	.	.

Consider an experiment in which two forms of learning strategy were investigated. A group of 30 volunteers attempted to memorise a list of 20 common nouns using a rote learning procedure. A subsequent test measured the number of words correctly recalled by each subject. At a later date the same subjects participated in a second memory experiment, this time using a system of word association explained to them by the experimenter. Again, after an interval, recall of the word stimuli was measured. The relevant analytical information is shown below, comprising the output of a paired t-test (known also as a correlated t-test; a dependent t-test; a related t-test; a within-subjects t-test).

```
t-tests for Paired Samples

                 Number of           2-tail
Variable           pairs     Corr     Sig        Mean         SD      SE of Mean
----------------------------------------------------------------------------------
ASSOC    learning by association                10.4667      3.224      .589
                   30        .079     .679
ROTE     learning by rote                        9.1000      3.881      .708
----------------------------------------------------------------------------------


          Paired Differences         |
    Mean         SD    SE of Mean    |     t-value          df        2-tail Sig
----------------------------------------|-------------------------------------------
   1.3667      4.846      .885       |       1.54           29           .133
95% CI (-.443, 3.176)                |
```

Note the means of both measurement periods: 9.1000 for the learning by rote condition, and 10.4667 for the learning by association condition; the t-value is 1.54, which reflects the magnitude of the difference between the two means, and the significance value is 0.133, which is the probability that these two means are derived from the same population (that they are the same, in other words, with any differences being attributable to chance factors).

The decision made in this example is that learning strategy did not significantly affect recall. However, since this is a counter-intuitive finding (a large body of research comfortably demonstrates the effectiveness of many mnemonic strategies) we would probably want to look closely at the way in which this particular study was carried out: at the precise nature of the training provided by the experimenter; at particular characteristics of the subjects which might have confounded a real experimental effect; at the time interval between learning and recall; at the possibility of a repetition, or order effect; and at the size of the sample, to see if this was sufficiently large to compare the two learning conditions. (See Chapter 2, Section 2.4.3 for a fuller review of within-subjects designs and associated problems.)

5.5.4 Interval independent variables and interval dependent variables (correlation)

When both major elements in a design are continuous, interval-scaled in nature (as in relating variations in road rage incidents to changes in temperature), the type of study being described is correlational. This particular methodology has been considered in some detail in Chapter 3, and it is worth reminding ourselves of the main characteristics of the approach.

1. Correlation simply describes a relationship between two variables.
2. The correlation statistic (r) demonstrates whether or not this relationship is strong or weak, and identifies the direction of the relationship.
3. The correlation statistic is a positive or negative value ranging from 0 to 1.

The most important of these is the reminder that, at its simplest level, correlation is purely a descriptive device. It informs us that two things may vary together in a particular way, but it does not allow us to say much more than that. It certainly doesn't allow us to say that one variable causes changes in the other, although many researchers – even experienced ones – often mistakenly argue that it does. Certainly the temptation to do this is strong; we are all used to making assumptions about our world and about things which go together. In many instances though such assumptions are unwarranted, reflecting more our unsophisticated perception of the world than any real cause and effect relationships.

Consider the widely held view among undergraduates that ratings in a test will be directly related to the number of hours spent in study. A perfectly reasonable assumption one might think, except for the occasional appearance of the individual – much loved by their fellow students – who seems to spend minimal time in study yet consistently outperforms all others in their class.

The explanation here is quite straightforward, for the relationship between study and performance in assessments is not simply a matter of time but of comprehension. The student who spends several hours every night preparing for an exam but who ultimately fails to understand key concepts will not perform effectively, whereas the person who quickly grasps important principles and understands how they are applied will probably do well, even with less studying. This is not to say that there will be no relationship between study time and exam performance, since in many cases the time spent on a topic will often result in an improved understanding of that topic. The point is that the relationship between the two variables is not as straightforward as most people think. And this is the problem with correlations – we can readily demonstrate relationships between pairs of variables, but understanding the nature of such relationships is often more tricky. Box 5.4 further explores this issue.

While it is important to recognise the dangers in reading too much into the relationship between two variables, it is also useful to appreciate that correlation is often merely the first step in what can become a number of extremely sophisticated forms of analysis.

One of the simplest features of a correlation can be found in the **coefficient of determination**, a statistic which allows us to state the

Box 5.4   As we always suspected . . .

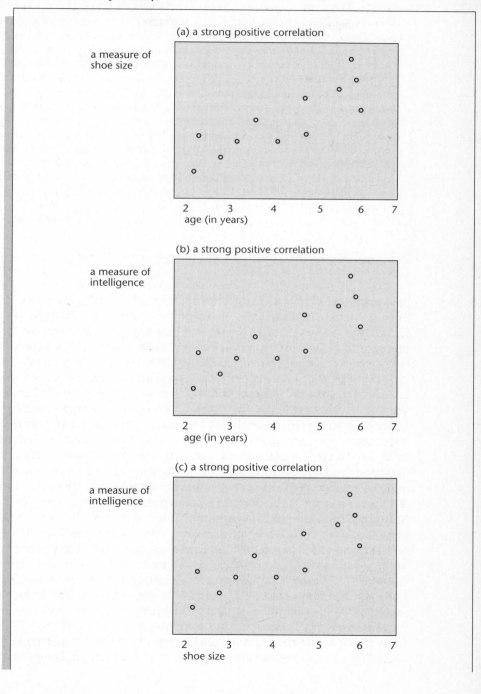

The relationships expressed in both (a) and (b) are much as we would expect, reflecting the often intuitive nature of correlations. However, the relationship shown in (c) is clearly – and the authors are being in no way footist about this – nonsense. Yet because both shoe size and intelligence correlate with age it becomes inevitable that they will correlate highly with one another. The difference is that while we happily accept the first two, along with the implication that age is acting as a causal factor, the third relationship we perceive as purely spurious. And this is the problem with correlations – the relationships between the twinned factors in (a) and (b) seem perfectly reasonable yet we laugh at any implication that (c) demonstrates anything more than coincidence. However, if one considers the nature of both intelligence and shoe size we quickly realise that mere age changes are not in themselves sufficient explanations: the real factors responsible for physical and intellectual growth are the complex maturational processes responsible for human development from birth into adulthood. As expressions of these fundamental influences then, both intelligence and shoe size will be related but not in any causal manner – both are simply expressions of underlying processes which affect many things.

proportion of variation in one variable which can be predicted by another. This particular statistic can be readily obtained by squaring the relevant correlation value. Hence if we had found that the correlation between temperature levels and road rage incidents in the west of Scotland was 0.902 we could further state that 0.815 (0.902*0.902), or 81 per cent of the variability in rage incidents could be predicted by temperature levels. This is an extremely useful piece of information and moves correlation away from the purely descriptive into the realm of inference. We are now in a position to argue that temperatures probably have a strong causal effect on incidents of road rage. However, even with a correlation of 0.9 the relationship is not clear-cut since, depending on the r-squared value, about 20 per cent of variation in road rage is caused by some other factor, or factors. Or to put it another way, 20 per cent of the variation in road rage incidents – a substantial amount – cannot be predicted by temperature.

In Chapter 1 one of the important functions of research was identified as prediction, yet correlation on its own is not a good predictor. If we take our temperature and rage example we could suggest, within a range of values, the likely number of rage incidents for a particular temperature. However, this would only ever be a vague approximation since the related observations do not form a straight line. In the figure below, based on the temperature and rage example in Chapter 4 (4.10.2), there is clearly a relationship between the two variables; however selecting a temperature value of, say, 22° does not allow us to predict the exact number of people likely to be charged for hurling abuse (or worse) at other road users. If though we could replace the information on our graph with a straight line which best fitted the observations, we could make a more precise estimate of one variable from the other. This is exactly what simple regression allows us to do.

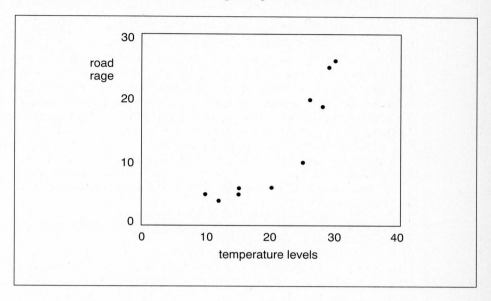

5.5.5 | *Simple regression – predicting one variable from another*

In the previous section the value of replacing the plotted observations in a correlation with a single line were outlined. Providing the line is a good fit of the data we should be able to read the value of one variable corresponding to the other simply by inspecting the line. The trick of course is to ensure that our line is a good fit.

One way of generating a line to symbolise our data would be to draw one using only our judgement of what looks appropriate. However, any two people performing the same task would invariably produce very different drawings. Fortunately there is a more precise method for achieving the best fitting line, based on the mathematical formula: $\mathbf{y} = \mathbf{a} + \mathbf{bx}$.

Many of you will recall coming across this formula as part of the standard school maths curriculum – it is the formula for a straight line. In plain English, what this formula does is identify the corresponding value on the y variable for any given value on the x variable. As a formula for a straight line, then, this is clearly misleading since to draw any line we need two points – a starting point and another point to join up with. In days gone by students would be expected to calculate the values for a and b from the original correlated data, and most current statistics texts still provide the means to carry out these calculations. For the modern student though, computer packages are more than happy to do this for them, as the next illustration shows.

Continuing with our temperature and road rage example, the regression command in SPSS produces the following output. It is worth noting that, while the analysis of interest is a simple regression, this is presented as a special case of a much more complex procedure, that of multiple regression. Consequently, much of the content is designed to explain the effects of several (multiple) independent variables on a single outcome variable, and because of this some of the information below is redundant for our one predictor variable case.

```
            * * * *  M U L T I P L E   R E G R E S S I O N  * *
    * *
Listwise Deletion of Missing Data

Equation Number 1
Dependent Variable..  RAGE

Block Number 1. Method: Enter     TEMP

Variable(s) Entered on Step Number
  1..  TEMP      temperature levels

Multiple R          .90251
R Square            .81452
Adjusted R Square   .79134
Standard Error     4.06407

Analysis of Variance
                DF    Sum of Squares    Mean Square
Regression       1       580.26667       580.26667
Residual         8       132.13333        16.51667

F =    35.13219     Signif F =  .0004


------------------ Variables in the Equation ------------------

Variable        B       SE B      Beta      T Sig T

TEMP        1.066667   .179960   .902510   5.927  .0004
(Constant)  -9.800000  3.991707           -2.455  .0396
```

As usual SPSS offers a wealth of information which is of considerable interest to statisticians. The average researcher though can be more selective and the relevant parts of the above output are as follows:

1. The correlation between the two variables is shown by the **Multiple R** statistic of .90251 (remember that this procedure has been established to evaluate the relationship between multiple independent variables and an outcome measure – even though there is only one IV SPSS still describes it as a multiple element).
2. The **coefficient of determination** is given by the **R Square** value of .81452. This is the proportion of the variance in the outcome measure which is explained by the predictor variable.
3. The values required to interpret our y = a + bx equation are shown in the **Variables in the Equation** section. Specifically, the value for **b**, which is a measure of the slope of our regression line (how steep or shallow this line is) is given in the column headed **B** and adjoining the variable name. Thus **b** in the equation is 1.066667. The value for **a**, known as the y-intercept, and representing the point on the y-axis which is cut by the regression line, is given in the same column and identified as the Constant. In this case **a** is given as −9.8.

We now have all the information we need to create our best fitting line and by substituting the regression values for the symbols in the straight line equation, y = a + bx becomes : y = −9.8 + 1.07x.

Armed with this information we can now do two useful things. First, we can draw our best fitting line: by selecting any two values of x we can apply the formula to identify the corresponding y values – giving us the two points needed for any line. For example:

> For x = 0;   y = −9.8 + 1.07(0); = −9.8
> For x = 30; y = −9.8 + 1.07(30); = 22.3

We can now produce our best fitting line, as shown in the figure below:

The second application of our newly developed formula is that for any one measure of the independent variable we can now predict a corresponding dependent value. Thus, if temperature was 20° our estimate of road rage incidents would be 11.4.

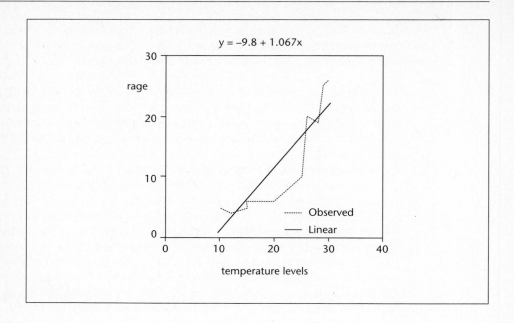

$$y = -9.8 + 1.067x$$

5.6 Complex analyses (analysis of variance and regression)

5.6.1 *More than two categories in an independent variable (ANOVA)*

In Chapter 2, Designing a study, it was explained that while the two-category independent variable was typical of research designs (control group vs experimental group; male vs female) there were many instances in which a causal factor would comprise a number of components (see Box 2.7). Comparing the general health of the five different occupational classes is one example previously cited; measuring the personal incomes of people born under the 12 different star signs would be another. In fact there are many situations in which an independent variable will not fit conveniently into the two-group scenario, and this has particular implications when it comes to analysing the data from such a study. In Section 5.5.2 of this chapter the t-test was offered as a powerful group comparison test. However, its application is limited to the two-group case and the t-test is really unsuitable here. For more complex comparisons of the kind described, what is needed is **analysis of variance**.

Developed by Sir Ronald Fisher, **ANOVA**, as it is more commonly termed, is an extremely sophisticated analytical tool. As such it is ideally suited to the many category case. However, the procedure is also complex and requires a little explanation, although for a fuller review one of the many statistical texts recommended here should be consulted.

5.6.2 *Analysis of variance*

In the previous section (5.6.1) it was shown that real life investigations don't always fall neatly into the two-group comparison outcome. The social class example for instance contained five groups while the independent variable in the astrological sign case comprised 12 categories. These are all merely extensions of the two-sample situation however: they still involve only one independent variable (class, star sign, or whatever) and differ only in the number of elements into which the independent variable can be subdivided.

In ANOVA terminology, the independent variable is usually called a Factor, and the various subdivisions, Levels. The above examples would be called Single-factor or One-way ANOVAs (one independent variable). Furthermore, if different subjects are used for each condition or level, they would be termed **Unrelated** or **Between-groups ANOVAs**; had a repeated measures design been used, they would be **Related** or **Within-groups ANOVAs.** (In case anyone has forgotten the difference between repeated measures and different subjects designs, a review of Chapter 2, 'Designing a study', will help, especially Sections 2.4.2 and 2.4.3.)

The next question most newcomers to advanced statistics ask is, apart from the opportunity to learn new jargon, what advantage does ANOVA have over t-tests? Why not just carry out a series of t-tests on all the various pairs of condition? The following example shows why not:

personal incomes as a function of a star sign	
Aries vs Taurus	Aries vs Gemini
Aries vs Cancer	Aries vs Leo
Aries vs Virgo	Aries vs Libra
Aries vs Scorpio	Aries vs Sagitarius
Aries vs Capricorn	Aries vs Aquarius
Aries vs Pisces	
etc	

For one thing, ANOVA explores all these relationships in a single step, rather than in the multiple repetitions which would be required by the t-test. For another, in a situation in which lots of t-tests are carried out, chance alone would throw up the occasional significant finding and lead to a misplaced interpretation of the data. And finally, the single-factor ANOVA is merely the beginning of what this sophisticated technique can do.

Unfortunately there is a cost: ANOVA will only tell us that a difference exists *somewhere* among the various comparisons being made, not necessarily where. However, since there are ways round this, it is a small price to pay.

So why analysis of *variance*?

We already know that when data are collected from some sample on an outcome measure, the mean provides the most common descriptive statistic. However, we also know that scores vary around this mean, a variance which is due to two things:

1.   Individual differences among subjects.
2.   Error (mistakes in measurement; misclassification of subjects; random occurrences, etc.).

This variance within a sample and around the sample mean is known as the **within-group variance** and is one of the key ANOVA measures.

Consider an example in which we hypothesise that the general psychological wellbeing of a number of experimental subjects will be determined by the amount of physical exercise they take (based on the healthy body–healthy mind notion). If three groups are compared, one taking no exercise, one taking occasional exercise and one taking regular exercise, we might observe the distributions as shown in the figure below.

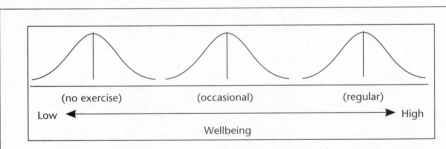

The distributions of response on a wellbeing questionnaire for groups taking no exercise, occasional exercise and regular exercise. Mean scores are positioned for each group on a wellbeing scale running from 'low' to 'high'.

Here we can see that each of the groups is represented by a mean score somewhere along our well-being continuum. We also observe that, within each group, there is variation about the respective means – there is within-group variance for each sample. Moreover, because the sample distributions are different, there will also be variance between the subjects in one group and subjects in another group. This is known as **between-group variance**, another important ANOVA measure, and attributable to three things:

1. Individual differences.
2. Error.
3. A real difference, or Treatment Effect.

Such between-group variance can be considerable, as in the above example (where the samples are clearly scoring at different levels on the outcome measure), or negligible, as in the example below:

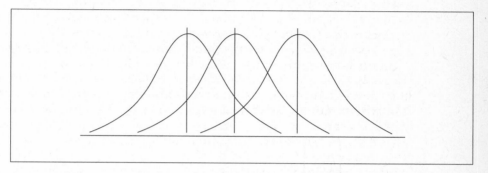

What ANOVA aims to do is determine whether or not the observed differences among these distributions are significant, or perfectly acceptable, given the effects individual differences and errors have on measurement. More specifically, if subjects were in different groups, would the differences between them be greater than if they were in the same group? The significance of these differences is tested using Fisher's F-statistic:

$$\frac{\text{Between-group variance}}{\text{Within-group variance}}$$

The logic of this is that when we compare individuals, whether in the same group or in different groups, much of the variation between them is due to the same things: individual differences and error. Applying the F-ratio procedure then we have:

$$\frac{\text{Individual differences; Error; Treatment effect}}{\text{Individual differences; Error}}$$

Once the common sources of variance are eliminated from both the numerator and the denominator, anything left over must be attributable to the treatment effect. If this is small (expressed as a small F-value) then assigning subjects to one group or another has little impact on the variability among subjects. If this is large however (expressed as a large F-value), then this signifies that belonging to one group as opposed to another makes a real difference, and one which cannot be attributable to either individual differences or error (since these common elements have now cancelled one another out).

There is a third measure of variance used in ANOVA, and this is termed the total variance. This is obtained by treating individual subjects as if they belong to one single distribution as opposed to their own particular group. A **grand mean** can be calculated for all subjects, irrespective of sample, and the measure of variance for the combined subjects provides the total variance.

In the language of ANOVA, variance is given as the average of the **sums of squares**, or SS (the sum of the squared deviations from the mean), such that the within-group variance is known as MSwithin, between-group variance as MSbetween and the total variance, SStotal. Box 5.5 illustrates the derivation of these terms.

Box 5.5   The language of ANOVA

The measurement of any variable generally produces a conventional type of distribution:

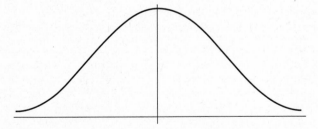

This typical arrangement of scores is usually expressed in terms of a measure of central tendency, such as the mean, but it is clear that this is an artificial measure since all the scores which comprise this distribution vary to a greater or lesser degree from this middle value. Moreover, while many forms of analysis rely heavily on the mean, Analysis of Variance, as the term suggests, is more concerned with how scores vary or deviate from the mean. This is calculated as follows:

1. Once the mean has been established, each individual score in a distribution is compared with this central value:

Mean	Score	Difference (Mean − Score)
50	25	+25
50	60	−10
50	48	+2
50	55	−5
.	.	.
.	.	.
.	.	.

2. In order to eliminate negative values from our calculations, each score is squared:

Mean	Score	Difference (Mean − Score)	Difference^2
50	25	+25	625
50	60	−10	100
50	48	+2	4
50	55	−5	25
.	.	.	.
.	.	.	.
.	.	.	.

3. Adding up all these values gives us a measure of the total variation (squared) within a distribution. Another way of expressing this is that we now have a Sum of the Squares (sum of the squared deviations) or, as ANOVA terminology prefers it, SS.

To compute the F-statistic, which tells us whether or not a manipulation or treatment has had an effect, we need to generate a number of different measures of variation. We need to know the amount of variation within each group – SSwithin; we need to know the variation between the groups – SSbetween, and we also need to know the total variation for the combined groups – SSTotal.

However, just when we think we have got the hang of ANOVA, there is one additional step required before calculation of Fisher's F-statistic can be carried out. Specifically, Analysis of Variance is concerned not with the total variation for each of the within and the between conditions, rather it is based on measures of *average* variation (for which the statistical term is **variance**). Hence, the within variance used in calculations is based on within/df (the within-group variation divided by the appropriate degrees of freedom for each sample); the between-group measure is based on between/df (between-group variation divided by the number of groups-1); the total variances measure is based on total/n-1.

This may appear complex but all this does is provide a measure of average variation for each component. At the end of this exercise we would be left with:

Mean Squares within (Mean SS within or MSwithin)
Mean Squares between (Mean SS between or MSbetween)

The Oneway ANOVA output presented in this chapter demonstrates the application of the Analysis of Variance terminology.

Continuing with our exercise and wellbeing example, the SPSS output for such a study is shown below. (Note: SPSS allows for oneway ANOVA calculations via the **Compare means** menu, and not just under the ANOVA heading, which is normally reserved for more complex designs.)

```
- - - - - O N E W A Y - - - - -


    Variable   WELLBEING  a measure of psychological health
  By Variable  EXERCISE

                              Analysis of Variance


                              Sum of        Mean         F     F
           Source      D.F.   Squares       Squares    Ratio  Prob.

Between Groups           2    152.7600      76.3800    4.8302  .0093
Within Groups          147    2324.5000     15.8129
Total                  149    2477.2600
```

The information most relevant to the researcher, and the one which is usually inspected before anything else, is the F probability value. This is a measure of the likelihood that there is no difference in wellbeing scores between any of the three groups. In this case the probability value is 0.0093, which is well below our 0.05 cut-off value, pointing to a significant difference somewhere in the comparison. (See Section 5.6.4 on multiple group comparisons for further discussion on this topic.)

The rest of the ANOVA table might appear complicated but if the reader would take a moment to consult Box 5.5, the terms and their meaning will soon become clear.

All ANOVA tables begin with a description of the analysis being carried out – in this case we see that the dependent variable 'wellbeing' is being explored in terms of the independent factor of 'exercise'.

In the analysis itself, each of the sources of variance are presented – 152.76 (between); 2324.5 (within); 2477.26 (total), with each value representing the sum of the squared deviations from the relevant mean. Degrees of freedom (df) for each source of variance are presented next: 2 in the between variances case (df for categories are given as $k - 1$, or the number of groups less 1. There are three exercise levels, hence df = 2).

Mean squares are shown next, being merely the sums of squares for each source of variance divided by the appropriate degrees of freedom.

Finally, the F-statistic itself is shown, a calculation which requires that the mean squares (between) is divided by the mean squares (within). The more ambitious student might wish to attempt this, and the other calculations manually to confirm the SPSS version. (In which case it would be useful to know that there were 50 subjects in each condition, giving a total of 150 who participated in the experiment.)

On a practical note, when inspecting the output from an ANOVA, special attention should be paid to the degrees of freedom (df). In an analysis comprised of three groups, the particular degrees of freedom would be $(k - 1) = 2$, as in the current example. Similarly, if a sample comprised 150 subjects, the relevant degrees of freedom would be $(n - 1) = 149$. In ANOVA, inspection of the between-group df is to be strongly recommended: it would not be the first time that, in the setting up of the data for analysis, one of the groups to be compared is omitted. The only clue that this has occurred would be in the degrees of freedom, which in the between-group case would be one less than it ought to be. Unfortunately this is often overlooked in our eagerness to get to the F-statistic.

5.6.3 | *More than one independent variable – nominal (two-way ANOVA)*

Just as it is common for independent variables to comprise more than two categories, so it is often the case that a study comprises more than one independent variable. In Chapter 3, Designing a study, considerable discussion was offered on this issue, with particular attention paid to the problem of whether the existence of several independent variables should be dealt with by controls, or by incorporating them into the design. In the event that we decide that more than one factor is having an effect on some outcome measure, and providing these factors are nominal in character, we are led once again towards Analysis of Variance.

In the case of more than one causal factor, successive one-way ANOVAs are as inappropriate as repeated t-tests would have been to test a single factor containing more than two categories, and for the same reasons; sooner or later, successive tests will throw up an apparent significant finding which is really a naturally occurring though rare event (Type 1 error). Moreover, when two or more factors are impinging on a dependent variable, it will often be the case that they will not do so independently, having rather an interactive effect. Once again, the notion of interacting factors is discussed in Chapter 2 and ought to be reviewed if this idea is causing confusion.

If our design is of this more complex variety, the type of ANOVA required is termed a two-way ANOVA, or sometimes factorial or multi-factor Analysis of Variance. An example follows.

Assume that in the study previously outlined, in which psychological wellbeing is thought to be related to particular levels of exercise, we are subsequently led to suspect the existence of a second factor which might affect wellbeing – a personality variable encountered previously is the Type A/ Type B distinction. Now the hypothesis might be that the competitive element in the Type A personality would interact with exercise to have an effect on wellbeing scores, in a way that Type B would not. Or stated more simply, the effects of exercise on wellbeing are not the same for Type As as they are for Type Bs.

The ANOVA logic is the same as in the oneway case, with multiple conditions being compared in terms of variance. The output of such a study is shown below.

```
* * *   A N A L Y S I S   O F   V A R I A N C E   * * *

        WELLBEING a measure of psychological health
    by   EXERCISE
         TYPE      personality type
```

Source of Variation	Sum of Squares	DF	Mean Square	F	Sig of F
Main Effects	155.700	3	51.900	3.318	.022
EXERCISE	152.760	2	76.380	4.883	.009
TYPE	2.940	1	2.940	.188	.665
2-Way Interactions	69.160	2	34.580	2.211	.113
EXERCISE TYPE	69.160	2	34.580	2.211	.113
Explained	224.860	5	44.972	2.875	.017
Residual	2252.400	144	15.642		
Total	2477.260	149	16.626		

The multifactor output is similar to that from the oneway analysis, except there is more of it, as one might expect. The key difference is that there are two elements to the more sophisticated output. The first deals with **Main Effects**, which describe the impact of each factor, or independent variable, on its own. In this case, the table informs us that there is a significant main effect somewhere in the analysis (significance value of 0.022). Closer inspection of the table identifies the variable 'Exercise' as being almost solely responsible for this effect (0.009) with 'Personality Type' having almost no impact whatsoever on wellbeing scores (0.665).

The second major element in the multifactor output examines interactions. In this case however we can see that the effect of exercise on wellbeing is not modified by the personality type of subjects. Exercise on its own is the key determinant of psychological wellbeing, at least, according to this particular study.

5.6.4 *Multiple group comparisons (post hoc* tests)

In the earlier section which introduced Analysis of Variance (5.6.2) it was explained that ANOVA will determine that a significant effect exists among a number of comparisons, but not where this effect is. In the example which formed the basis of this introduction, wellbeing scores were compared across three different exercise regimes producing an F-ratio of 4.8302 with a corresponding probability of 0.0093. What this indicated was that a significant difference in wellbeing measures was detected somewhere among the three different exercise categories. What we really want to know however, is which of these groups was significantly different from another to produce the highly significant probability value. If there had been only two groups in our analysis there would be no problem – as with the t-test, a significant finding is easily explained simply in terms of the difference between the two means. In the case of three or more groups however, it is not so easy.

Consulting a table of means is one way of trying to locate effects, and indeed many undergraduates do this in order to explain an ANOVA finding. But this is not enough – just by looking at how the means of different groups differ will not tell us if the significant difference was, say, between groups 1 and 2, or 2 and 3, or 1 and 3. Or indeed if all three comparisons were significant. What we need to do is compare the measures under each condition with measures under every other condition using an appropriate statistical test. This brings us back to a problem encountered earlier – when we carry out multiple tests the chances of Type 1 errors increase. To reduce this possibility a variety of tests have been developed for making multiple comparisons. (Note: these are known as *post hoc* tests, since they are applied *after* the ANOVA has been carried out.)

The simplest of these involves nothing more complex than carrying out a series of t-tests on all possible pairs of group means while applying a technique known as the **Bonferroni procedure**. What this does is to modify the level of significance used to decide whether or not a particular pairwise comparison is significant, in the following manner.

Normally we use the 0.05 level as our cut-off point for a single test. If we were to apply t-tests to each of the possible comparison pairs of exercise groups (i.e., three comparisons) the Bonferroni procedure requires merely that we share our 0.05 level among all three tests. Thus, in any one comparison, for a difference to be significant it would have to fall on or below 0.016.(0.05/3).

The straightforward t-test with a Bonferroni correction is one method of identifying where, among a multiple group analysis, an effect is occurring, but there are others, which try to deal with the Type 1 issue in different ways. Opinion is divided among researchers as to which approach is the best, a problem intensified by the fact that not all the available group comparison tests are suitable in all situations. Moreover, some theorists will argue that, rather than wait until after an ANOVA has implied a significant effect, group comparison tests should be planned *in advance*, as an extension of hypothesised outcomes. Needless to say, the issues are complex and, while fascinating, beyond the introductory nature of this book. However, any student intending to use an ANOVA should be aware that on its own the procedure will only provide part of the story; sound advice would suggest consultation with supervisors on the most appropriate form of group comparison. Alternatively, each of the references at the end of this chapter discusses multiple comparison tests in varying degrees of complexity.

5.6.5 | *More than one independent variable – interval (multiple regression)*

The previous sections have been devoted to situations in which the independent variables in a study are nominal, or category variables. However, we have already seen that often a causal factor can comprise measures on a continuous, interval scale. Section 5.5.4 in this chapter provided several examples.

Conventionally, when the variables in a study comprise continuous data, the mode of analysis is correlation, with inferences being made via regression analysis. The same holds true when several independent variables are involved, except we now talk about multiple correlations and multiple regression. The example which follows illustrates the procedure.

Without apology the authors decided that the final example in this section had to involve their favourite small, green amphibians once more. Consequently, in a study investigating the number of frogs squished by cyclists (denoted by the variable name 'OOPS') three variables were considered as possible influencing factors. They were the AGE of the subjects, the EXTRAVERSION scores of the subjects and the cycling EXPERIENCE of the subjects. Each of these potential causal factors was selected on the basis of arguments that they would all in some way relate to the levels of coordination required to circumnavigate hordes of hopping and leaping frogs across a standard cycle route. The output from a multiple regression analysis is both complex and considerable, and the table below represents only a part of what is available with this analysis. In the interests of clarity some elements of the typical output have been omitted.

The standard information available is initially descriptive, telling us what variables were involved in this particular analysis. The dependent variable is identified as 'OOPS' and the various independent variables are listed in turn.

```
        * * * *   M U L T I P L E   R E G R E S S I O N   * * * *


Listwise Deletion of Missing Data

Equation Number 1   Dependent Variable..OOPS no of frogs run
over

Block Number  1.  Method:  Enter  EXTRAV   EXPERIEN AGE


Variable(s) Entered on Step Number
   1..     AGE
   2..     EXTRAV    extraversion
   3..     EXPERIEN  cycling experience (years)


Multiple R             .29635
R Square               .08782
Adjusted R Square      .06908
Standard Error         2.39370

        * * * *   M U L T I P L E   R E G R E S S I O N   * * * *

Equation Number 1    Dependent Variable..   OOPS   no of frogs
run over


------ Variables in the Equation -------

Variable            B          SE B        Beta         T   Sig T

EXTRAV          .036284     .052201     .056395      .695   .4881
EXPERIEN       -.085801     .023254    -.299381    -3.690   .0003
AGE             .011726     .020323     .045621      .577   .5648
(Constant)     4.956523     .954764                 5.191   .0000


End Block Number    1   All requested variables entered.
```

(Note: in later versions of SPSS, while the statistical output remains unchanged, the presentation can vary. By example, the variables in the equation table above will appear as follows in version 8).

	Coefficients[a]				
	Unstandardized Coefficients		Standardized Coefficients		
Model	B	Std Error	Beta	t	Sig.

a. Dependent Variable: OOPS no of frogs run over

Following on from this is the correlational information, the most important of which is the R Square value. Standing at only 0.08 the implication is that a mere 8 per cent of the variance in frogs run over can be explained by a combination of the various causal factors. However, since these factors *are* acting in combination it is quite possible that the effects of one particular factor are being obscured by the effects of others – therefore it is still possible that one or more of the independent variables is having a significant impact on the decline of the frog population.

Looking at the 'variables in the equation' section, we observe a number of columns of data. The first of these simply identifies the various variables in the analysis. The second column, headed 'B', refers to the value b in our old friend $Y = a + bx$, where b is a measure of the slope of the regression line or, alternatively, the amount of change in the y (outcome) variable for every unit change in the x (independent) variable. Hence, for every increase on the Extraversion scale of 1, there is a corresponding change to the number of frogs squished of 0.03, and so on.

The next important section here is found under the BETA column heading, the values here being the correlation between each independent variable and the outcome variable with all the other 'causal' factors controlled for, or held constant. As a general rule of thumb, the larger the value, the more important is the variable in predicting or determining the dependent variable. The final two columns describe t-values and their associated probabilities. The information given here measures the improvement in the predictive power of the independent factor as each variable is added to the equation. Thus, adding EXTRAVERSION to all the other variables produces a t-value of only 0.695, with an equally insignificant probability of 0.4881 (the probability that the inclusion of this variable made a difference), while adding EXPERIENCE as a predictor produces a much larger t-value of −3.690, with a significance value of 0.0003. Therefore we can state here that of all the independent variables which could be included in an attempt to predict the number of frogs run over, EXPERIENCE was the only one which made a significant difference. In other words, when it comes to accounting for the decline in the frog population, experience is the dominant factor.

5.7 Review

In Chapter 5 we have discussed a number of methods for analysing data which go beyond the descriptive, allowing us to make inferences and predictions. In so doing we have merely introduced these techniques while avoiding all but the most basic of computations. Moreover the analytical methods offered comprise only the beginnings of a range of sophisticated statistical procedures. And here a note of caution is necessary: some of the advanced procedures outlined carry with them various restrictions in their application which should be understood before they are to be used for purposes beyond the straightforward examples offered in their explanation. The authors can think of no better exhortation for further reading than that.

5.8 Explanation of terms

ANOVA The common expression of the technique of Analysis of Variance.

Between-group variance A measure of the variation among individual scores when subjects are compared across two or more groups.

Bonferroni procedure A technique for reducing the possibility of a Type 1 error when multiple comparisons are made among a number of group means. This is part of the process of identifying exactly where an effect has occurred in an Analysis of Variance.

Chi-square A procedure for comparing the observed frequency of response with expected frequencies in a nominal-nominal study, i.e., when both the independent and dependent variables comprise categories. The difference between what is observed and what is expected is evaluated in terms of the likelihood of obtaining particular discrepancies by chance. This test is used in between-subjects designs.

Coefficient of determination A statistic which describes the proportion of variance in one variable which can be predicted from another. Based on the correlation coefficient which is squared to provide this value.

Homogeneous A description applied to a population in which the members share consistent and similar characteristics.

Independent t-test A test which compares the means of two different groups measured on some outcome variable. The magnitude of the observed difference is evaluated in terms of probability. This test is used in between-subjects designs and is also known as: unrelated t-test; unpaired t-test; between-groups t-test; independent samples t-test.

Inferential statistics Forms of statistical analysis whose purpose is to allow predictions to be made and hypotheses to be accepted or rejected.

Main effect The effect on an outcome variable of a series of independent variables, each treated on its own and without the influence of any other.

Paired t-test This test compares the means of two different measures on a single outcome variable taken from a single group, usually on two different occasions. The test is commonly applied to within-subjects designs in which comparisons are made on a before treatment and after treatment basis, or in a no treatment treatment study, or a treatment 1 treatment 2 study. Related terminology is: correlated t-test; within-groups t-test; related t-test; repeated measures t-test; dependent samples t-test.

***Post hoc* tests** A term applied to tests made after an Analysis of Variance, the purpose of which is to identify the exact source of a significant effect. See also 'Bonferroni procedure'.

Statistically significant A term applied to an event when its likelihood of occurrence is so rare as to exceed a pre-determined probability level, usually taken as the 5 per cent or 0.05 level.

Type 1 error Said to occur when an observation or event is deemed to be statistically significant, when in reality it falls within the bounds of acceptability. An example might be when we accept that an observed difference between the means of two groups is significant, when in fact what we are observing is a naturally occurring, if extremely unusual event.

Type 2 error Said to occur when an observation or event is deemed to be only rare but within the bounds of acceptability, when it is in fact significant. An example might be when we accept that an observed difference between the means of two groups is a naturally occurring, if unusual event, when in reality we are observing a significant difference.

1-tailed test An analysis based on a specific, or directional prediction of the outcome of a study, e.g. that the mean of one group will be greater than or less than the mean of another.

2-tailed test An analysis based on a non-specific, or non-directional prediction of the outcome of a study, e.g. that the mean of one group will be different from the mean of another.

Within-group variance A measure of the total variation among individual scores within a group or sample.

5.9 Recommended reading

Diekhoff, G. (1992). *Statistics for the Social and Behavioural Sciences: Univariate, Bivariate, Multivariate.* Dubuque, IA: Wm. C. Brown Publishers.

Dometrius, N.C. (1992). *Social Statistics Using SPSS.* New York: Harper Collins.

Howell, D. (1987). *Statistical Methods for Psychology.* Boston: Duxbury Press.

Howitt, D and Cramer, D. (1997). *An Introduction to Statistics for Psychology*. London: Prentice Hall.

Huck, S.W. and Cormier, W.H. (1996). *Reading Statistics and Research*. New York: Harper Collins.

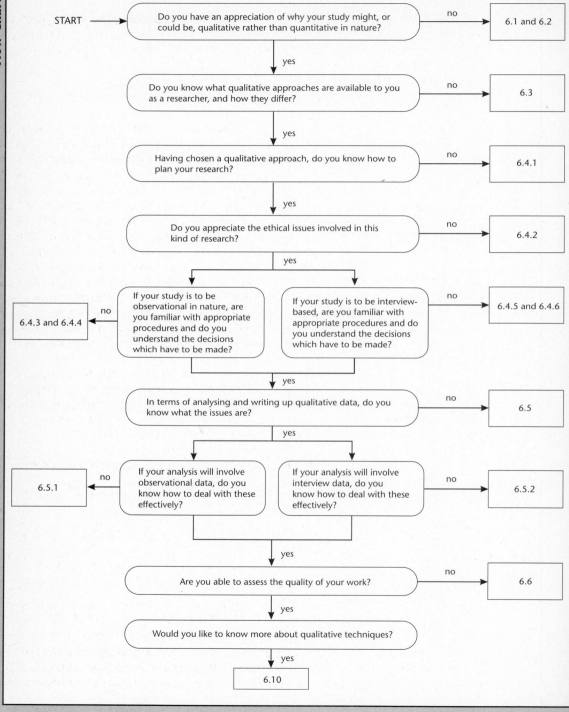

START → Do you have an appreciation of why your study might, or could be, qualitative rather than quantitative in nature? —no→ 6.1 and 6.2

yes ↓

Do you know what qualitative approaches are available to you as a researcher, and how they differ? —no→ 6.3

yes ↓

Having chosen a qualitative approach, do you know how to plan your research? —no→ 6.4.1

yes ↓

Do you appreciate the ethical issues involved in this kind of research? —no→ 6.4.2

yes ↓

6.4.3 and 6.4.4 ←no— If your study is to be observational in nature, are you familiar with appropriate procedures and do you understand the decisions which have to be made?

If your study is to be interview-based, are you familiar with appropriate procedures and do you understand the decisions which have to be made? —no→ 6.4.5 and 6.4.6

yes ↓

In terms of analysing and writing up qualitative data, do you know what the issues are? —no→ 6.5

yes ↓

6.5.1 ←no— If your analysis will involve observational data, do you know how to deal with these effectively?

If your analysis will involve interview data, do you know how to deal with these effectively? —no→ 6.5.2

yes ↓

Are you able to assess the quality of your work? —no→ 6.6

yes ↓

Would you like to know more about qualitative techniques?

yes ↓

6.10

6

Qualitative research

'I want to find out what these people are really experiencing, not just hand out a questionnaire.'

'I'm no good at statistics: perhaps I should do something qualitative.'

'What do I do with all these interviews?'

'I have no numbers!'

Chapter 6 offers an introduction to qualitative research, with the reservation that it is not possible to cover such a broad and potentially controversial topic in a single chapter in more than the most general of terms: the aim is merely to introduce readers who are new to qualitative research to the major issues and to point them in the direction of more detailed texts. The main approaches are briefly described and two typical methods of data collection – observation and interviewing – are considered. Guidelines are offered on the planning and conduct of qualitative research; issues pertaining to analysis and writing up are discussed; and recommended reading is provided.

The reader will note that, unlike earlier sections, Chapter 6 is extensively referenced and supported by a lengthy recommended reading section. This departure from the typical format of the book has been based upon the authors' judgement that qualitative approaches will be relatively new to undergraduate programmes. Consequently, although we provide a broad introduction to the topic here, students adopting a qualitative strategy are strongly advised to pursue the recommended reading which concludes this chapter.

6.1 What is qualitative research?

Qualitative research is often introduced in terms of the way in which it differs from quantitative research: that it involves transcripts, for example, or that it does not involve statistics. However, while such distinctions are true up to a point, they are overly simplistic and do neither form of research justice. First of all, there are many different forms of qualitative research, encompassing quite distinct approaches and methodologies. Secondly, quantitative and qualitative approaches need not be in direct opposition; they can happily coexist or even overlap, and often within the same study. However, there is a crucial difference between the two forms of research: a qualitative study relies on the skills and personal qualities of the researcher in a way that is not normally acknowledged or expected in quantitative research. This aspect of qualitative work is made clear in Parker's (1994) definition of the term: he defined it as 'the interpretative study of a specified issue or problem in which the researcher is central to the sense that is made' (p. 2). This means that researchers are often faced with the task of finding themes, patterns and associations from the ground up, and the development of theory will often occur as a consequence of the intensive interaction between researcher and subject. This can be very time-consuming. It can also be emotionally draining, as the need to appreciate the participant's point of view can require a full and sometimes painful understanding of the problems and burdens they face. Qualitative research demands an extra level of involvement on the part of the researcher and although this can be difficult, it can also be rewarding and exhilarating.

6.2 Deciding to do a qualitative study

A qualitative approach can be particularly useful in describing the experiences of a group of individuals, especially if it is not large in number. Qualitative data, such as quotes or comments or selected responses to open-ended questions, can also help both the researcher and the reader understand the findings of quantitative research – a description, in words, of what was actually happening in a situation, or how people claimed they were feeling, will often clarify or illustrate the results of a statistical analysis. In the field of psychology, qualitative studies are often concerned with social or health-related issues, but qualitative data can also help illuminate issues from the 'harder' end of the field, such as learning and memory. There are no set boundaries: most topics can be studied using quantitative and qualitative techniques and in an ideal world the two approaches would be used in a complementary, rather than oppositional, way. Sometimes the two approaches merge into each other, particularly when conducting and analysing observations. This need not be a problem for researchers as long as they are clear about what is being done.

For the undergraduate, the decision to adopt a qualitative approach will be based on many considerations: sample size will be one, the complexity and subtlety of a situation will be another.

However, the decision will often reduce to a philosophical issue based on perception of the world and personal preference. On a practical note, given the existence of different philosophies, it is in the interests of any student contemplating a qualitative study to explore the views of potential supervisors at the outset.

6.3 An overview of the main approaches

6.3.1 Ethnographic research

Ethnography is one of the classic qualitative approaches. It is concerned with describing social groups or situations and delineating behaviours and shared beliefs or understandings of particular groups of people. Typically, the researcher or ethnographer joins a group for a period of time to find out as much as possible about the way the participants live. The aim is to understand something of their lives from the inside (as opposed to observing from afar), to find out and describe what goes on and why, and all with reference to the social context.

An ethnographic approach might be taken to find out what happens in well-defined environments such as a classroom, a hospital ward, or a factory; or in a group of people with a common purpose, such as a football team, a town council, or a local action group. The approach is essentially phenomenological in that the aim is to represent the 'world view' of the target group. Typically, theories and hypotheses are generated and explored *during* the research process and there is an assumption that researchers will put aside their own beliefs and values before exploring those of their target group.

The research starts as soon as the researcher goes into the new situation and the methods used to collect data will often vary over the course of study: for example, researchers may initially read available documents, observe what appears to be happening and talk to the people involved both formally and informally, while later they may use more structured methods, such as observations and interviews, to explore issues, theories or hypotheses which have arisen – always gathering extensive amounts of descriptive information.

The study described in Box 6.1, of computers in a classroom setting, might well be undertaken using an ethnographic approach. The researchers would spend some time before the introduction of the computers getting to know the context, by visiting the school at different times and on different days and spending time in the staffroom and classroom, and by sitting in on formal and informal discussions. They would take notes during visits and write up detailed field notes following visits, noting not just what had happened but also their own reactions. Such notes provide important data, enabling researchers to track changes over time and to untangle their own feelings from those of their participants.

It is not always possible to identify the key factors or events at the outset of a study: in this example we might notice a number of features which seem to relate to the use of the computers and the software but only at the end of the study will the full patterns have emerged. We might observe, for example, that computers have to be locked away every night in cupboards because of the risk of theft and that this discourages some teachers from using them; that in some classrooms children are allowed individual access to the computers while in other classrooms the children always use them in groups of three or four; that some children seem eager to use computers while others avoid them; that some teachers are confident in their use of the technology while others are not. Our aim in all of this would be to understand the causes and implications of these observations, and the ways in which the various factors interrelate over time. To facilitate this, we might subsequently focus

Box 6.1   A suitable case for computation?

A primary school is to be provided with a set of new computers for use in the classroom, together with software which can be used by the children to create narratives. While it has been assumed that the children will automatically benefit from this, the evidence from earlier quantitative studies suggests that children do not always achieve higher marks or standards when this new software is used than they would do otherwise. It is not clear whether this is due to inadequacies in the software or the ways in which the computers and software are used in the classroom.

on a few key or representative individuals at certain stages of the study, repeatedly observing or interviewing them.

Ethnographic research such as this is necessarily lengthy and therefore expensive. However, many researchers willingly adopt some of the techniques and ideas from the ethnographic tradition to suit their own purposes – after all, adopting a qualitative philosophy does not require the rejection of pragmatism. However, by the same token, not all researchers are able to accept the proscriptions of the pure ethnographer: for instance, it is not always reasonable to assume that researchers can discard their own ideas and values during their research: psychology students studying other psychology students, or nurses studying other nurses, do not approach their subject as neutral observers. Needless to say, different points of view are held on this issue, but at least some of those writing in the area suggest that it is perfectly acceptable to adopt some strategies and discard others to develop a methodology which exactly suits a particular research topic (e.g., Tesch, 1990).

6.3.2 | *Action research*

In broad terms, action research involves identifying problems in particular settings, generating hypotheses about the causes and 'cures', and, most importantly, acting on these and evaluating the impact. It differs from ethnographic research, therefore, in that changes are implemented and their effects evaluated during the period of research. Similar methods of data collection may be used, although action research may make greater use of questionnaires, focus groups and meetings among participants.

In action research, the extent to which the researcher exerts control over the target group in order to effect change can vary considerably, depending on the extent to which the participants are involved in generating ideas and implementing strategies for change themselves. Many factors will be relevant here, including the extent to which group members are of one mind, the power structure within the group and the organisational constraints upon it. For example, nurses wishing to make changes to a particular ward may be constrained by a lack of unanimity amongst themselves, by the actions of the charge nurses, by the hospital management, and by the nature of the ward itself. Although ideally the role of the researcher would be more observational or collaborative than coercive, sometimes people need more structured assistance in effecting change, particularly if the existing routines are long-standing. It is also often the case in action research that the researcher provides emotional and motivational support for the participants. Again, this can be time-consuming and draining, but the process can be deeply satisfying if the action leads to positive changes.

Action research could be appropriate in the scenario outlined in Box 6.2, the problems faced by ex-residents of a long-stay institution. The first stage

Box 6.2   A healthy option?

> A local long-stay institution has closed and the residents have been relocated in various settings within the community. Some of the ex-residents appear to be showing signs of distress or unhappiness. Families and carers have expressed a great deal of concern about this, but their ideas about the causes and remedies appear to vary considerably. Research is required to find out about the various causes of distress in both the ex-residents and their families and carers so that appropriate interventions can be put in place.

would centre on obtaining a full understanding of the problems from the various points of view (management, staff, residents, family, etc.). The researchers might start by collecting any available documentation to find out what had happened to residents and their families before and after discharge from the institution. They could organise meetings of ex-residents, ex-staff, carers and families to gain an understanding of the extent to which participants' perceptions of events were consistent with those embodied within official documents, participants' views on the causes of problems, and their views on possible remedies. Other points would probably emerge through such meetings or informal conversations: for example, the researchers might uncover resentments, fears and sorrows among families regarding what had happened to their relatives and the impact that events had had upon their own lives. They would interview and observe the ex-residents in different settings to find out what they thought and felt about what had happened to them, and to identify problems which had arisen. The intervention used in this research could emerge from any one group of participants or from the researchers with the co-operation of participants, but the focus of the intervention would be the wellbeing of the ex-residents. Changes could be evaluated through interviews, meetings, reports, conversations and observations. If it was judged that more could be done (and if resources were available), another intervention could be planned, implemented and evaluated, contributing even more to the wellbeing of the target group. However, in this kind of study, it is always possible that one group benefits from an intervention at the expense of another. There is no simple answer to such a problem, but it helps to clarify the objectives of the study at the onset to all groups of participants.

6.3.3   Grounded theory

Grounded theory is an approach to research whereby a theory, any theory, is grounded in actual data rather than imposed *a priori* (i.e., in advance of the study). Grounded theory was first described by Glaser and Strauss (1967) and it represented a reaction within sociology against the unwarranted or haphazard imposition of existing theories upon new situations or contexts. It has its roots in symbolic interactionism, so that the emphasis within this approach is on the symbolic meanings which people attribute to events and the ways in which these meanings interact with the social roles that people fill. Data are gathered in much the same way as in other qualitative approaches, including examination of documents, observations and interviews. The analysis, however, is focused on the search for the kind of patterns and relationships which can generate theories and hypotheses, with processing continuing until adequate explanations emerge to explain the phenomenon under investigation.

The grounded theory approach is probably most appropriate in situations that are bounded in some way and to which the participants have given some thought. For example, it could be useful in the study described below (Box 6.3) of the use of medication among people with asthma. The researcher would interview participants to learn about the meanings of taking medication in different contexts, when participants were filling different roles. A person can be comfortable using an inhaler as a patient, at the asthma clinic or when in hospital, because it will help him or her to recover, one of the responsibilities of the role of patient. However, that person may be far less comfortable using inhalers at work, at a club or among friends: the meaning of the action varies according to the social role.

The grounded theory approach is less useful when the issues to be researched are not particularly salient or important to the participants: individuals lacking in involvement may generate ideas or thoughts during the research process to appease the needs of the researchers who may then find themselves in the position of reproducing, in a painstaking manner, the participants' 'off the cuff' theories. In addition, the approach is not suitable for studies in which the researcher is an 'insider' because it is assumed that the researcher has no preconceived theories about the issue.

Box 6.3 Breathing space

People with asthma do not always comply with the regime of medication prescribed for them by their doctors. Some people therefore experience more problems with asthma than in theory they need do. Doctors at a local asthma clinic, keen to find out more about non-compliance, have used self-report questionnaires and diaries. However, they suspect that some of their patients overestimate the extent to which they comply with instructions and they feel that the results of their study have not produced data which can help them promote compliance in their patients.

6.3.4   *Discourse analytic research*

The problems with defining discourse analysis are similar to those with defining qualitative research in general: 'it is a field in which it is perfectly possible to have two books on discourse analysis with no overlap in content at all' (Potter and Wetherell, 1987, p. 6). The discourse can include anything written or spoken, conversations, and the underlying social structures embodied in the words used. There are many different approaches to discourse analytic research, many underlying philosophies, and many possible units of analysis, which goes some way towards explaining the contemporary debate about the nature and scope of the technique.

Broadly speaking, a researcher adopting this approach is concerned with what is said or written in terms of the conditions, assumptions and views of the world embodied in the words. Through this the researcher aims to understand something about the speakers or writers: perhaps their self-categorisations and the ideas, constructs or conditions that influence this; perhaps their views of other people; perhaps the barriers to change or personal growth. The approach can also be used to understand such things as the power relationships between people who occupy complementary social roles and the constraints imposed by different forms or repertoires of discourse.

Analysis itself is carried out using either a piece of text or a transcript of spoken words, and it can be combined with other qualitative methods. Within an ethnographic study, documents and speech can be subject to discourse analysis, and this analysis can aid understanding of the actions of participants within the social context. For example, do teachers use language in a way which indicates alliance with management or the children? Do they see themselves as subject to the whims of an educational authority, or do they feel part of a decision-making process? Are the different factions among the children made apparent in their speech? Do the teachers use different ways of speaking to or about some children than they do to or about others? It is possible, for example, that the ways in which teachers talk to children have some bearing on the ways in which computers are used by children in the classroom, or that different factions among the children use the computers in different ways or to different effects.

A discourse analytic approach could be applied to the study of non-compliance among people with asthma. The phenomenon under investigation is in itself allied to a particular form of medical discourse: the word *compliance* comes from a domain in which one group of people (doctors) tells another group of people (patients) what to do. Some people with asthma may not understand their use of medication in those terms and may in fact be complying with a different set of norms, according to the people with whom they identify. One possible line to follow would be the extent to which the discourse (language) used by people with asthma was medical: for example, medication could be described in 'technical' terms (e.g. salbutamol, fluticasone); by trade names (Ventolin, Flixotide); in the current patient-friendly terms fostered by practice nurses and drug companies (reliever, preventer); or in particular lay terms (blue puffer, orange puffer). Similarly, the researcher could examine the ways used to describe the asthma clinic: the words could suggest a foreign or alien place; a safe place; a place of punishment or retribution; a place in which one was powerless; or as a place in which negotiation was possible. The words used to describe interactions with health professionals could also be considered: the words could suggest confrontation, alienation, fear, dependence, inequality, or misunderstanding. In short, analysis of the type of language used by participants in such a study could say a great deal about attitudes, perceptions and relationships, and could provide an explanation of the complex and subtle behaviours relating to the use of medication.

The starting point for discourse analysis is the transcript or document in which language has been expressed. Various ways of systematising transcripts have been developed which take account of pauses, inflections, intonations and stresses (e.g. Jefferson, 1985). It does of course take a long time to transcribe interactions in this way but it promotes a true involvement with the material. The process of analysis then varies according to the focus of the study: 'there is no mechanical procedure for producing findings from an archive of transcript' (Potter and Wetherell, 1987, p. 168). The analysis could, among other things, focus on the different types of discourse used (either by different individuals or by the one individual at different times); on the ways in which different types of discourse are used to explain behaviours, feelings or reactions; or on the ways in which discourses are used to construct a narrative. It is a demanding process and requires skills which take time to develop. However, there is an advantage to taking this approach in that transcripts and documents can be made available to other researchers, and can be reproduced in reports to support the adequacy of interpretation. There are many useful accounts of the various forms of discourse analysis; some of these are provided in the recommended reading list.

6.3.5 Hermeneutics

Hermeneutics is concerned with language, or rather the process of using language to make experience understandable or comprehensible. Within this approach, it is assumed that the researcher's own background will have a bearing on the investigation and interpretation. Thus there is an assumption of consciousness and awareness of the phenomenon or situation under investigation and in this respect hermeneutics differs from phenomenology, in which the researcher is required to lay aside their own values and knowledge before the investigation.

Within the hermeneutic interview, themes are introduced by the researcher but the participant's views and responses are not constrained in any way by the researcher. Reflexivity is central, in terms of conscious and conscientious reflection on the process and on one's own role within that process. Interpretation depends upon the insight, openness and patience of the researcher: again, the emphasis is very much on the personal qualities of the researchers rather than on the objectivity that they might bring to bear. The assumptions, knowledge and insights of the researchers are made explicit as they continue a circular or spiralling process of analysis and interpretation. Starting with global perceptions, the researcher follows and interprets emerging themes, attempting to capture meaning at different levels. All three of the example studies shown in Boxes 6.1, 6.2 and 6.3 could involve hermeneutic interviews and analysis, particularly if the researchers have prior knowledge or experience of the topic under investigation.

6.3.6 │ *Participatory or emancipatory research*

With this approach, the research population, or the participants themselves, take a central role. Participants are involved to a greater or lesser extent in setting the research agenda, designing the study, and collecting the data. The named researcher, therefore, acts more as a facilitator, helping the participants in effect to conduct their own study. The extent to which research is participatory can, of course, vary. For example, people with asthma could be consulted about the issues they would like to see addressed in the research, they could design the interview, and they could act as the interviewers. Similarly, using the other research examples described above, teachers, pupils, ex-residents and carers, could all be centrally involved in the research.

This approach has a number of benefits: participants dictate the agenda and are therefore unlikely to be exploited in any way. It ensures that the questions or issues that are most important to the participants are those which are addressed. It also gives the research the kind of credibility and face validity (see Chapter 3, Section 3.3.5) which is vital to ensure co-operation and involvement, and the quality of the data may be greatly enhanced as a result. On the other hand, participatory research can be difficult to set up if the research population consists of different factions with different agendas: there may not be a single or central way of viewing the issue or topic. For example the subjective experiences or views of people who join a support group for asthmatics may be very different from those who passionately avoid such groups. In addition, it may not always be straightforward to steer subjects away from 'unresearchable' topics; the researcher's role here can demand more tact and diplomacy than is usually required.

6.4 Conducting a qualitative study

6.4.1 Planning the research

At the outset, the researcher has to consider the time and resources available to collect, analyse and interpret data, and to maintain involvement with participants – issues of primary importance to the undergraduate who may only have a single semester to implement and write up a study. While qualitative studies are not designed in the ways understood of quantitative studies, they do demand deliberation and preparation. There is, of course, much argument about the extent to which the researcher should go into the field with preconceived ideas or even questions, but the inexperienced qualitative researcher should probably have an idea about the boundaries of the project: researchers working on their own to a tight time schedule (such as date by which the work must be handed in) may only be able to collect data from some of the relevant people on some of the relevant topics.

Having clarified as far as possible the research domain and the likely constraints on the study, researchers then must consider the relevant factors: for example, the extent to which they have prior knowledge of a setting and the implications of that knowledge; or the extent to which the impact of change is of interest; or the extent to which the focus of study should be the perceptions or understandings of individual participants. Ways of collecting data or information should also be considered ahead of time. Sometimes researchers have to exclude methodologies, and therefore approaches, because of various limitations: for example, there is no point in attempting a discourse analysis of interactions if it is not possible to make recordings of the interactions.

Miles and Huberman (1994) suggested a useful series of steps to help plan a study. The first is to map out a conceptual framework; drawing boxes or 'bins' which encompass the issues of interest. This may be problematic for researchers wishing to limit the imposition of their own preconceptions, but it can help mark the scope of a project. The second step is to formulate some research questions which are consistent with the conceptual framework. This may be a rather circular process involving a redrawing of the framework as the questions emerge. The research questions may of necessity be rather vague, but formulating the questions can help researchers to understand their own preconceptions and biases; these can then be made explicit, a crucial underpinning to much qualitative research. More pragmatically, the process of formulation can highlight problems: some questions may not in fact be 'researchable' and although it is not always possible to spot this at an early stage, the more thought and deliberation that goes into planning the less likely it is that the study will fail. (It might be useful at this point to review our general introduction to research in Chapter 1, particularly under the Sections 1.4 and 1.5.)

The third step is that of clarifying the boundaries of the research, perhaps in terms of time, participants, location and possible constraints. Finally, the ways in which information might be gathered and recorded should be considered, taking into account all of the previous steps. Again, the decisions might be quite vague at first, but they will serve to point the researcher in at least one direction before piloting the methods.

Piloting, in whatever form, is as important in qualitative research as it is in quantitative, although it is often the case that methods will be tried out during the study rather than beforehand. It may not even be described as piloting, but at some stage most researchers have to find out whether or not their chosen methods actually produce data or information which can be used. This applies as much to the more open-ended or unstructured methods as well as to the structured. For example, it may be that sitting in on meetings provides the researcher with information about the relationships among the various members of a group but not about the ways in which decisions are implemented (particularly if one person is responsible for the implementation). The piloting issues involved in the use of observation and interviews are discussed below; in all forms of piloting, however, it is crucial to keep detailed notes, to record all of the factors, both situational and personal, which inform the decisions about methodology.

6.4.2 | Ethical issues

As with all forms of research, it is essential that ethical issues are addressed at the planning stage of a qualitative study and that the ethical guidelines published by the British Psychological Society are adhered to. (See Chapter 3, Section 3.6 for a general review of ethical considerations in research.)

Generally speaking, it is good practice, and often a requirement, to provide potential participants with written information about the research and to ask them to read and sign consent forms. There is an art to writing these and it is worth getting representatives of the target population to read early versions. They can point out ambiguities, jargon and omissions. Information and consent forms should be as clear and straightforward as possible while being honest about the demands that will be placed on participants, such as the main topics to be covered in an interview and the time it will take. Sensitivity should be used here because not everyone can read or write: in this case, the researcher should explain the study to potential participants in a relatively neutral way, allowing them to ask questions and accepting their response.

A number of points should be considered before observing or interviewing participants, or before delving into archive material. These include the extent to which people should be observed without their knowledge, the extent to which stored information should be accessed without consent, confidentiality, and feedback on results to participants. While it may seem relatively harmless to make video recordings of children's use of computers in the classroom, it may not seem so to the people involved. Advice should be sought not only from ethical committees but also from representatives of participants. Sometimes researchers wish to observe people's behaviour in settings where knowledge of being observed might change the behaviour. In such cases, the researcher should consider the extent to which this might cause embarrassment or distress to the unwitting participants; it may not be necessary to take video recordings, for example.

Interviewing raises some specific ethical issues. In a sense, an interview is based on a contract between the researcher and the interviewee and this should be negotiated explicitly. Even if someone agrees to be interviewed, they should be given the opportunity to terminate the interview at any point. The interviewee should also be told about access to the record of the interview and the methods used to ensure anonymity and confidentiality. If the researcher intends to use quotes in the final report, this should be negotiated with the interviewee even if names are not to be assigned. These issues are important: it is necessary to ensure that interviewees are not exploited, and also that there is trust between researchers and interviewees.

6.4.3 | Observation

Observation is used in both qualitative and quantitative research in a number of different ways. It can be used to establish what actually happens in various settings, to generate hypotheses and theories, to illuminate findings or examine situations more closely, and to evaluate the impact of interventions. It is in some ways a straightforward and easily understood way of collecting data, but it requires as much preparatory thought as any other method. Decisions must be made before beginning the observations and the nature and causes of these decisions should be made explicit. The example of observing children's use of computers in the classroom provides a means of illustrating these decisions, as shown in Box 6.4 (on the following page).

6.4.4 | Conducting observations – practicalities

A number of useful guidelines can be offered, covering the conduct of an observational study, and these are as follows:

Consider the ethical issues surrounding your proposed observation. Make contact with the relevant committees and official organisations, and also discuss your plans with representatives of those you wish to observe.

Box 6.4   Observational decisions

The following reviews the types of decisions which must be made during the planning stages of an observational study. The examples are based on the scenario outlined in Box 6.1.

Whom is to be observed?

A classroom may contain 20 to 30 children. Are particular children to be targeted? If so, why?

Where are they to be observed?

The researcher can focus on the use of a particular computer, or can observe the actions of target children using any of the available computers. Such decisions will be partly dependent upon the observational method chosen and the resources available to the researchers.

What is to be observed?

This is a crucial question. What does the researcher mean by 'using the computer'? Is it sufficient or necessary for children to be sitting in front of the computer? Must the computer be switched on and operational? Must the keyboard be used or the mouse moved? If a child observes others using the computer but does not speak or touch the computer, are they 'using' it? Must the software of interest be used, and must it be used 'correctly'? Such issues should be addressed at an early stage. The target acts must be clearly defined and these definitions must be justified.

When and how to observe?

These are essentially sampling issues. If the researcher is interested in specific behaviours, **time sampling** or **event sampling** can be used. Time sampling involves choosing different periods of time during which to observe, and recording all behaviours or events that occur during that period. This is useful if the researcher is interested in commonly occurring behaviours, or in what happens in a particular situation at different times of day. It would be less useful if the target events or behaviours did not occur frequently. Event sampling, on the other hand, involves recording the relevant details about a target event, although this clearly requires that the researcher knows at least roughly when and where this event is likely to take place (e.g., when the children attempt to open a new application on the computer). The methods chosen to record the observation should be consistent with the aims, but there may be situational and other constraints. Video or audio recording may seem ideal, but may provide an incomplete record of events – for example, people might move about and obscure the behaviours of others, and voices might not be audible. Checklists, notes, stopwatches and event recorders can all be used; none will provide a perfect record of everything that happens.

Do a number of 'informal' observations to begin with. Use these to make decisions about whom, where and what you are going to observe (see Box 6.4). Think about where you should position yourself or where to position equipment. If you are going to use a video recorder, try it out: can you clearly see the behaviours or events that you are interested in? These activities will also make your presence (and that of your equipment) more familiar to the people to be observed. Always carry spare batteries – there can be nothing more frustrating than to set up an observation and recording session only to discover that your recorder has died.

Prepare detailed descriptions or definitions of the events or behaviours that are to be observed. These may be refined later but it is important to be as clear as possible from the outset.

Conduct a pilot study. Is the equipment reliable? Are you observing what you planned to observe? Can you record all of the necessary details in the time allowed? If you are conducting the study alone, you can enlist the help of colleagues to investigate the reliability of your interpretations: if another person interprets the events or behaviours in different ways then your descriptions of behaviour or events should be reconsidered. If you are working with another person, spend time at this stage in establishing agreement and make full records of the decisions made.

Keep records of observations. Make these as detailed as possible, including details of times, the situation and context, the potential range of participants, and anything else that was going on at the time of the observation. Also keep records of your own reflections about what happened. For example, the behaviour of children in a classroom might be affected by such things as the weather, television programmes that were on the night before, the prevalence of minor illnesses, or visits by representatives of the educational authority. If you think that something was influencing the situation under observation, talk to the people concerned: there may be an explanation.

Finally, start your analysis or interpretation of observations as soon as possible – you may wish to check out specific hypotheses which emerge from the early observations by making some changes to later observations. You may become aware of flaws in your approach which could be remedied before it is too late.

6.4.5 Interviewing

The term interview is used here to describe anything from informal chats with someone to highly structured question and answer sessions. In qualitative research, interviews are generally semi-structured at most, meaning that while interviewers may well have a pre-prepared set of questions or topics they go into the interview ready to deviate from that set. As with observation, the researcher must decide whom to interview, what the topics of discussion are to be, where to interview, how to conduct the interview and how to record it. Obviously the aims of the interview will dictate the structure: for example, preliminary interviews to find out more about the organisational structure of a hospital will be different in nature from interviews with patients to find out about their experiences.

All interviews are social events, interactions between two or more people. Consequently, there are questions to be addressed about the sharing of intimacy and power between the interviewer and interviewee. Certain qualitative approaches, particularly participatory research, call for a more equal distribution of power between interviewer and interviewee than might have been customary in the past, such as the right of the interviewee to ask the interviewer questions. Typically, the interviewee will look to the interviewer for some guidance on this, at least initially, and will expect them to begin the interview. The interviewer can do much to establish the tone of the interview in the first few minutes, in terms of seating, posture, appearance and language. While informality and equality might seem ideal (and may indeed be so for many people) some interviewees may be more comfortable with a more formal approach, and their wishes should be respected.

The researcher should consider beforehand the issue of disclosing personal information within the interviewing setting. Self-disclosure can help establish a comfortable and open relationship between interviewer and interviewee and it can facilitate certain topics: for example, if the interviewee with asthma learns that the interviewer also has asthma the conversation may open up considerably. However, personal information can also be intrusive and off-putting to the interviewee. Interviewers who express their own points of view or experiences at every turn can inhibit the flow of the interview, particularly if the interviewer and interviewee do not share common values or experiences. Some interviewees will not want to know anything about the person who is interviewing them. Although decisions such as these cannot always be made in advance, the issues should be considered before interviewing commences.

If the topic of the interview is a sensitive one, the interviewer should be prepared to offer support. This might be in the form of addresses and telephone numbers of support organisations, or relevant leaflets or information. Sometimes unforeseen problems arise during interviews. In this case, the interviewer should be as helpful as possible while respecting the wishes of the interviewee, offering to contact an agency on behalf of the interviewee, for example. There are no simple answers to this but preparation helps. Interviewers should also consider their own wellbeing, ensuring that there is someone to talk to, in confidence, about difficult interviews. Finally, interviewers should consider their personal safety, particularly when interviewing people in their own homes. Common sense should be used, but many institutions now have policies and guidelines about this. Box 6.5

Box 6.5   Interview decisions

A number of decisions must be made before interviews are conducted. The example used here is based on the scenario outlined in Box 6.2, that of interviewing people with asthma, although the issues will be relevant to any interview-based study.

Whom is to be interviewed?

A representative sample of the people who have attended the asthma clinic (possibly taken from medical records)? Those who attend the clinic on a specific day? Those who respond to a notice posted in the asthma clinic? The decision will depend upon the resources and time available and the extent to which access to medical records is permitted or thought appropriate. The researcher should decide on the extent to which the sample should be representative and on the appropriate criteria to use to select the sample.

What is the purpose of the interview?

This leads on to consideration of other issues, such as the topics or themes to be explored and the format or structure of the interview. Interviews can be highly structured, using set questions to be phrased in exact terms and in an exact order; semi-structured, where the researcher has some set questions or topics and an idea about the order in which they could be covered, but is prepared to deviate from the order according to the flow of the interview; or loosely structured, where the researcher introduces a topic in general terms and then follows the lead of the interviewee. The format or structure of the interview should reflect the general aims and ethos of the research, but decisions should be made and justified before beginning the interviews. Clearly it is important to pilot the interview. This helps establish the most appropriate ordering of questions or topics, the ways in which questions should be phrased, and whether or not the interview actually elicits the information required.

A semi-structured format would probably be the most suitable approach to take with the asthma study. The researcher wants to find out about the person's use of medication and their feelings about this, and to understand more fully what it means to that individual to have asthma: some interviewees will need prompting to discuss these topics. The researcher could therefore delineate a list of open-ended questions, starting out with the more factual questions about the person's experience of asthma and moving on to the more delicate issue of non-compliance after some trust or rapport has been established. However, people's feelings about asthma could emerge at any point during the interview: the researcher has to decide whether or not to follow up on such disclosures as they are made, abandoning the structure in favour of the disclosures.

Where to interview?

It is probably best to start out with the intention of interviewing people in private, although this can be difficult if interviews are conducted in people's homes. These decisions should be discussed with interviewees beforehand – they may prefer to be interviewed at home or they may wish a more neutral setting, depending upon the topics to be covered.

How is the interview to be recorded?

As with observation, there is no one perfect method. Audio or video recorders can be used but this must be negotiated with the interviewee. Alternatively, the interviewee's responses can be recorded on paper during the interview. While this is less intrusive it can interfere with the process of the interview, since the researcher has to interrupt contact occasionally. It also limits the analysis to one which is essentially thematic because a full transcript will not be available for more detailed analysis. Finally, it introduces a source of bias in that the notes made will be those that strike the interviewer as relevant or important at the time.

which follows this section, provides a review of the decisions to be made as part of the interview process.

6.4.6 | Conducting interviews – practicalities

As with the section on observation, a number of guidelines are now offered on conducting an interview-based study, and these are as follows.

Decide whom is to be interviewed. Consider how many interviews you would like to do and how many you are actually able to do. Decide on the criteria to be used in selecting your interviewees. Consider the ways in which you can gain access to the names of potential interviewees and negotiate these as soon as possible – ethics committees and decision-making boards can take a while to grant permission.

Draw up information sheets and consent forms. Indicate the nature and purpose of the research, and the broad aims of the interview. Give a contact name, address and telephone number. Indicate the process of recruitment. If information sheets and consent forms are to be mailed to potential interviewees, enclose a stamped addressed envelope.

Consider the ethics of your study, and the steps you should take to ensure that you do not cause unnecessary upset or distress to your interviewees. Consider confidentiality and anonymity: for example, you should ensure that tapes or transcripts are identified by number only, that they are stored in a safe place with a lock, and that the documentation linking name to subject number is stored elsewhere (also in a locked place). Consult representatives of your target group as well as any relevant ethics committees.

Make sure that you have done your preparatory work. Draw up a provisional interview schedule with any topics or questions that you wish to explore. Pilot this and continue to adapt or change your interview schedule until it easily elicits the information you are looking for. Make sure that at least some of your pilot interviews are with people representative of your target group. Use these pilot interviews to establish a style of interviewing which suits the purpose of your research, and with which you and your interviewees are comfortable. By interviewing people in situations similar to those you are interested in, you will discover problems and difficulties with the way in which you have structured your questions, and you should be able to establish a convenient way of recording people's responses. You will also gain a sense of the time required of the interviewee: this is important when fixing up a time for the interview. Consider the issues associated with power and intimacy within an interview. Try out your audio or video recorder if you intend to use one, and make sure that it works. Record all the decisions you make during this phase of your research and provide justification for the decisions.

Plan a timetable for interviewing and begin to contact your potential interviewees. At this stage you can tell them how long the interview is likely to last and can negotiate a place in which to interview them. If you are interviewing in a particular setting, you could try to find a private room in which to interview people. However, you should respect the wishes of the interviewee: they may prefer to be interviewed at home.

At the start of the interview, do what you can to make a person comfortable. Explain the research again and ensure that the interviewee knows that the interview can be stopped at any time. Negotiate the use of recording equipment and respect the interviewee's wishes. If the interviewee initially agrees to the use of a tape-recorder but then seems uncomfortable with that decision, offer to switch it off. If the interview becomes difficult, or if the interviewee becomes upset, switch off the tape-recorder and take some 'time out'. You may both decide to terminate the interview at this stage but the interviewee may in fact wish to continue. Take time at the end of the interview to address any issues that have arisen and to allow the interviewee to ask questions of you.

When you are doing your interviews, keep records of where and when the interview was conducted and how long it took. As soon as possible after the interview, check that your tapes are audible or that your notes are legible, and write out full notes, including your own thoughts and reflections about the interview. If your recording equipment failed in some way, you may still be able to salvage something from the interview if you do this quickly enough.

6.5 Dealing with qualitative data

6.5.1 Analysis and writing up

The analysis of qualitative data is an ongoing process that is best begun early, as soon as the data collection begins in fact. Writing up should also be started early on: analysis and writing up are closely intertwined in qualitative studies. Typically the process of analysis is very arduous and the researcher often goes through a phase of feeling disheartened in one way or another. Although this might not seem like a particularly helpful comment, it is worth knowing that it is a common experience and that it does not signify failure. Perseverance usually pays off.

All sources of data can be subject to analysis, including documents, handwritten or typed field notes, tape recordings of interviews or conversations, and observations. Field notes are very important at this stage – these are the notes made (or scribbled) during and immediately after visits to the location and they cover events, information and the thoughts and reflections of the researcher. The best way to approach the analysis of field notes is to write them up in some structured way; the most useful structure will depend upon the focus and orientation of the research (see Miles and Huberman, 1994). One way to go about this would be to start with a description of the contact with participants on that day, giving details of the people involved and the events or situations that were witnessed. Following this, details would be given of the main themes or issues that emerged. The researchers would then indicate their own part in the activities, reflections, and any other potentially relevant observations. If the researcher has conducted a recorded interview, the field notes should include reflective remarks on the process which can be added to the interview transcript when it becomes available. These remarks might cover the researcher's perceptions of the relationship formed with the interviewee, thoughts on what was said and how it was said, thoughts on the quality of the interview, and reactions and 'mental notes'. When the remarks are added to the transcript they can be made available to other researchers for scrutiny.

6.5.2 Observational data

Observational data can be analysed in different ways. If the observations include discrete behaviours or events then it might be possible to create categories. For example, if the observation was focused on interactions between people it would be possible to discriminate between different forms of interaction. It would then be possible to examine the frequencies of these different forms of interaction, as well as considering the situations in which they occurred, and the outcomes and implications for those concerned.

Categorisation is generally a process during which the researcher has to consider the extent to which new events or behaviours can be slotted into existing categories or whether it is necessary to create a new category. Categories should be meaningful in terms of the aims of the research: it becomes difficult to deal with a large number of categories, but collapsing events into a small number of categories can mean that important or relevant variation is missed. A large 'miscellaneous' category usually means that the category system is flawed in some way. It is important to keep clear and detailed records of the process of categorising: the criteria used to select categories and to assign events should be made explicit in the final report.

Categorisation is the point at which the overlap between a quantitative and qualitative approach can become apparent: frequencies can be reported, numbers can be applied, and analyses undertaken. Some qualitative researchers prefer not to submit their observations to strict categorisation for this reason, since quantitative techniques may run counter to their personal philosophy of research. Others will be more interested in sequences of events or behaviours, choosing to describe what happens rather than to categorise. In any event it should be borne in mind that the categorisation of people and social situations is essentially a flawed and subjective process: for example, mistakes can be made when categorising people according to social class or ethnic origin, and it is better to describe people rather than to ascribe labels which may not be accurate. The whole issue concerning the use of numbers to describe events can be reviewed in Chapter 4, Sections 4.1 and 4.2.

6.5.3 | Interview data

Burman (1994) pointed out that researchers dealing with interviews have to decide on the precise source of their 'raw data': is the analysis to be conducted on the transcript (such that the transcript becomes the source) or on the interview, including the social context in which the interview was conducted? This is not always an easy distinction (or decision) to make but it may be helpful to consider the extent to which the major focus is on the language used by the interviewee or on the interaction between interviewee and interviewer. Important decisions have to be made, therefore, about the way in which interviews should be transcribed, including the extent to which pauses and other speech acts should be represented. A full transcription may be a necessary condition for certain forms of analysis and it makes other forms of analysis much easier to undertake. It is, however, very time-consuming and therefore expensive. Sometimes the necessary information can be extracted by listening to audio-tapes; however, this may leave the analysis open to criticism.

As with observations, some responses to interview questions can be categorised according to the aims of the research. However, most qualitative research rests upon different forms of analysis and these depend very much on familiarity with the material. Generally speaking, analysis will involve a search for consistencies on the one hand and variations on the other. The level at which these qualities are sought will vary and it is common for the researcher to consider different levels within the same analysis. Thus the analysis might focus on the use of particular words or phrases, or a response to a particular question, or a narrative on a particular issue. In addition, the researcher might be looking for both individual and group consistencies and variations, moving between the different levels in an effort to find meaning.

One way to begin the process is to focus on a particular question: how do people with asthma feel about their condition, for example, or how do ex-residents feel about their experiences of leaving a long-stay institution? What kinds of expressions are used during the interviews? Are there ways to link these expressions together, or to distinguish one form of expression from another? Some researchers find that metaphors help them at this stage, although there is a danger that the metaphors will gain an unwarranted 'reality'. With the asthma study, metaphors capturing isolation, loneliness and death might be appropriate, or those describing different ways of understanding health. However, the researcher has to be vigilant and systematic in noting aspects of the interviews which are inconsistent with the metaphors.

As mentioned above, the units of analysis can vary. Some researchers prefer to take several copies of transcripts and then to impose order in different ways: using, for example, different highlighters, or cutting up the transcripts and sorting them into different piles according to the question being addressed. Computer software is now available to help with this process: different units of text can be tagged and assigned to any number of different files which can represent themes or categories. While this may be a more tidy way of doing things and can certainly help with the management of the analytical process, the researcher still has the task of ascribing labels and therefore meaning to the material. Having said this, software can be extremely useful. Detailed advice about the use of software in the analysis of qualitative data can be found in the text by Miles and Huberman (1994).

6.5.4 | *Points to consider when writing up*

There is no one 'correct' way of writing up a qualitative study and many different formats can be used to impart the relevant details to the reader. For example, it may make more sense to discuss the findings as they emerge rather than to have a separate discussion section, so that the reader can understand the process of interpretation more clearly. Some researchers write up their work almost as a narrative, telling the story of the study from its inception, including details of methodology and of key decisions in chronological order. Whatever the format, a number of points should be covered.

The process by which key decisions were made should be described in some detail. These would include the decisions made about the research agenda and the approach taken, the inclusion of participants, the methodologies used, and the ways in which analysis and interpretation were undertaken. Observation and interview situations should also be described in some detail. Given the central role of the researcher in a qualitative study, the researcher's thoughts, reflections, feelings and reactions are relevant and they should be included in the report. All of this will help the reader to understand and evaluate the findings and conclusions.

6.6 The quality of the research

There is much debate around the question of judging the quality of qualitative work. Some authors have argued that the criteria used to judge quantitative research are not always appropriate here (e.g., Tindall, 1994). This does not mean, however, that the quality of the work is unimportant. In fact, many qualitative researchers are committed to improving and maintaining the quality of their work, not only for their own peace of mind but also because of the responsibility they feel towards their participants. It is a crucial issue and it requires vigilance and honesty on the part of the researcher.

As with any research, the final report should be adequately referenced and should take the work of other authors in the area into account. However, because each qualitative study is unique in some way, extra care should be taken to justify and explain both the theoretical stance taken and the choice of methodology. In addition, the role of the researcher should be clearly and fully described, so that the reader is made aware of the extent to which the researcher, for example, imposed the agenda, interfered with existing routines, or co-operated with participants.

The procedures used to analyse the data should be carefully explained. In the same vein, sufficient original data should be provided to enable the reader to evaluate the interpretation. For example, if 18 out of 20 interviews produced similar responses, the researcher should present a good number of examples (e.g., quotes) from those that were similar and also examples from the two that were different. Finally, the quality of the research might be judged on the extent to which the findings would be meaningful or comprehensible to participants, particularly if a participatory approach had been adopted.

One of the problems faced by qualitative researchers is that they are subject to the same biases as everyone else. For example, a particularly vivid event or description tends to be remembered and recalled more easily than the more mundane (the availability heuristic; see Kahnemann and Tversky, 1973). This is a problem when the vivid description is not particularly representative of the remainder. Researchers should take the time to pull back and consider the extent to which they are reporting the whole picture and not just the aspect to which they are attracted. Miles and Huberman (1994) stressed the importance of considering outliers, or cases which appear to disconfirm interpretations;

they should be discussed rather than ignored. Similarly, alternative explanations and interpretations should be fully explored in the report.

Since qualitative research typically centres on a particular context, event or situation, and since each researcher brings to the study their own orientations, qualities and skills, there are no grounds for expecting consistencies across studies. There is much less emphasis on generalisability, therefore, in the qualitative field than in other forms of research. However, there are grounds for expecting the researcher to provide sufficient information about the process to permit others to evaluate the interpretation.

Triangulation is the term used to describe the ways in which the reliability and validity of a qualitative study can be assessed. The term reflects the way in which a second point of view on a phenomenon creates a triangle. Triangulation can be used in different ways: to assess the extent to which different participants or sources provide the same information; the extent to which different researchers perceive the phenomenon in the same way; the extent to which different methods, such as observations and interviews, provide consistent information; and the extent to which different theories or explanations provide adequate accounts of the same data. Useful accounts of the ways in which triangulation can be used are provided by Miles and Huberman (1994) and Tindall (1994).

While triangulation is important, it does not mean that all participants, or all researchers, have to agree: it is quite possible for different groups of participants to see a situation in different ways, for example. Where inconsistencies are found, however, they should be honestly reported. If two colleagues disagree about the interpretation of a phenomenon then this disagreement should be presented to the reader; it does not automatically mean that the study was a failure and in fact it might lead the researchers into new areas of debate.

6.7　Review

This chapter has attempted to introduce the qualitative approach to research. In it we have discussed the general philosophy behind the approach, outlined a number of typical methodologies and offered practical guidance on carrying out a qualitative study. In addition, because both the qualitative philosophy and associated techniques will be new to many readers, we have referred extensively to related work in the area to allow the motivated reader to pursue their interest further. By the same token, we are also providing an extensive list of recommended reading at the end of this chapter.

6.8   Explanation of terms

Action research   Research in which changes are implemented and evaluated during the course of a study.

Discourse analysis   Analysis of written or spoken text.

Ethnography   An approach seeking to describe or reconstruct social groups or scenarios.

Grounded theory   Theory emerging from, or originating in, the data.

Hermeneutics   An approach centring on understanding or empathising with participants' views of a phenomenon.

Triangulation   The use of different sources or point of view to enhance the interpretation of data.

6.9   References

Burman, E. (1994). Interviewing. In P. Banister, E. Burman, I. Parker, M. Taylor and C. Tindall, (eds), *Qualitative Methods in Psychology: A Research Guide*. Buckingham: Open University Press.

Glaser, B.G. and Strauss, A.L. (1967). *The Discovery of Grounded Theory*. Chicago: Aldine.

Jefferson, G. (1985). An exercise in the transcription and analysis of laughter. In T.A. van Dijk (ed.), *Handbook of Discourse Analysis*, Vol 3. London: Academic Press.

Kahneman, D and Tversky, A. (1973). Availability: A heuristic for judging frequency and probability. *Cognitive Psychology*, **5**, 207–232.

Miles, M.B. and Huberman, A.M. (1994). *Qualitative Data Analysis*, 2nd edition. Thousand Oaks, CA and London: Sage Publications.

Parker, I. (1994). Qualitative research. In P. Banister, E. Burman, I. Parker, M. Taylor and C. Tindall (eds), *Qualitative Methods in Psychology: A Research Guide*. Buckingham: Open University Press.

Potter, J. and Wetherell, M. (1987). *Discourse and Social Psychology: Beyond Attitudes and Behaviour*. London: Sage Publications.

Tesch, R. (1990). *Qualitative Research – Analysis, Types and Software Tools*. New York: Falmer Press.

Tindall, C. (1994). Issues of evaluation. In P. Banister, E. Burman, I. Parker, M. Taylor and C. Tindall, *Qualitative Methods in Psychology: A Research Guide*. Buckingham: Open University Press.

6.10   Recommended reading

Banister, P., Burman, E., Parker, I., Taylor, M. and Tindall, C. (eds) (1994). *Qualitative Methods in Psychology: A Research Guide*. Buckingham, UK: Open University Press.

Bryman, A. (1988). *Quantity and Quality in Social Research*. London: Unwin Hyman.

Bulmer, M. (ed.) (1982). *Social Research Ethics*. London: Macmillan.

Burman, E. and Parker, I. (eds) (1993). *Discourse Analytic Research: Repertoires and Readings of Texts in Action*. London: Routledge.

Charmaz, K. (1995). Grounded theory. In J.A. Smith, R. Harré and L. Van Langenhove, *Rethinking Methods in Psychology*. Thousand Oaks, CA and London: Sage Publications.

Dex, S. (ed.) (1991). *Life and Work History Analysis*. London: Routledge.

Edwards, D. and Potter, J. (1992). *Discursive Psychology*. Thousand Oaks, CA and London: Sage Publications.

Hammersley, M. (ed.) (1993). *Social Research: Philosophy, Politics and Practice*. London: Sage Publications.

Hammersley, M. and Atkinson, P. (1995). *Ethnography: Principles in Practice*, 2nd edition. London: Routledge.

Henwood, K. and Pidgeon, N. (1992). Qualitative research and psychological theorizing. *British Journal of Psychology*, **83**, 97–111.

Kvale, S. (1983). The qualitative research interview: A phenomenological and hermeneutical mode of understanding. *Journal of Phenomenological Psychology,* **14**, 171–196.

LeCompte, M.D. and Goetz, J.P. (1982). Ethnographic data collection in evaluation research. *Educational Evaluation and Policy Analysis*, **4**, 387–400.

Leonard, V. (1989). A Heideggerian phenomenological perspective on the concept of the person. *Advances in Nursing Science*, **11**, 40–55.

McIntyre, R. (1996). Nursing support for relatives of dying cancer patients in hospital: Improving standards by research. Unpublished PhD thesis, Department of Nursing and Community Health, Glasgow Caledonian University.

Nikander, P. (1995). The turn to the text: The critical potential of discursive social psychology. *Nordiske Udkast*, **2**, 3–15.

Pidgeon, N. and Henwood, K. (1996). Grounded theory: Practical implementation. In J.T.E. Richardson (ed.), *Handbook of Qualitative Research Methods for Psychology and the Social Sciences*. Leicester: British Psychological Society.

Rheinharz, S. (1992). Phenomenology as a dynamic process. *Phenomenology and Pedagogy*, **1**, 77–79.

Richardson, J.T.E. (ed.), (1996). *Handbook of Qualitative Research Methods for Psychology and the Social Sciences*. Leicester: British Psychological Society.

Shaughnessy, J.J. and Zechmeister, E.B. (1994). *Research Methods in Psychology,* 3rd edition. New York: McGraw-Hill.

Silverman, D. (1993). *Interpreting Qualitative Data: Methods for Analysing Talk, Text and Interaction*. London: Sage Publications.

Tappen, R. (1989). *Nursing Leadership and Management: Concepts and Practice*. Philadelphia, PA: F.A. Davis.

Whyte, W.F. (1984). *Learning From the Field*. London: Sage Publications.

 Notes

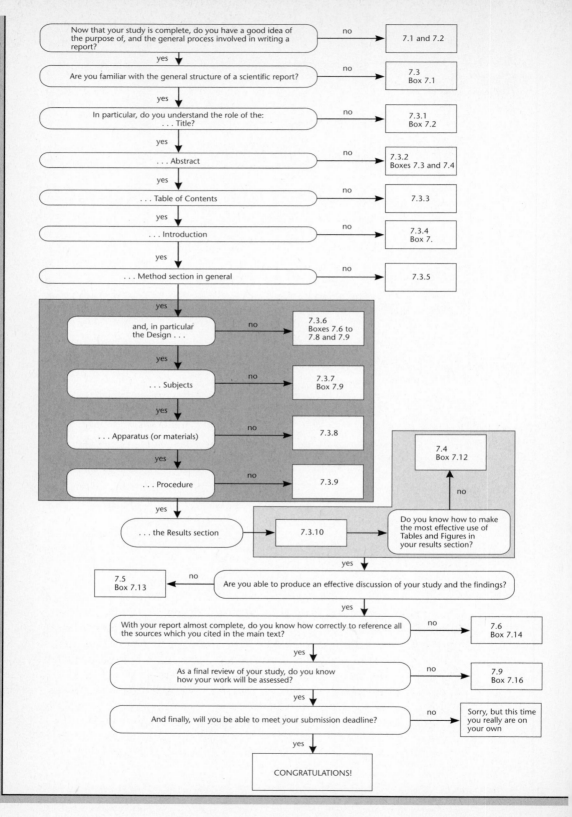

Now that your study is complete, do you have a good idea of the purpose of, and the general process involved in writing a report? — no → 7.1 and 7.2

yes ↓

Are you familiar with the general structure of a scientific report? — no → 7.3 Box 7.1

yes ↓

In particular, do you understand the role of the: . . . Title? — no → 7.3.1 Box 7.2

yes ↓

. . . Abstract — no → 7.3.2 Boxes 7.3 and 7.4

yes ↓

. . . Table of Contents — no → 7.3.3

yes ↓

. . . Introduction — no → 7.3.4 Box 7.

yes ↓

. . . Method section in general — no → 7.3.5

yes ↓

and, in particular the Design . . . — no → 7.3.6 Boxes 7.6 to 7.8 and 7.9

yes ↓

. . . Subjects — no → 7.3.7 Box 7.9

yes ↓

. . . Apparatus (or materials) — no → 7.3.8

yes ↓

. . . Procedure — no → 7.3.9

yes ↓

. . . the Results section → 7.3.10 → Do you know how to make the most effective use of Tables and Figures in your results section? — no → 7.4 Box 7.12

yes ↓

Are you able to produce an effective discussion of your study and the findings? — no → 7.5 Box 7.13

yes ↓

With your report almost complete, do you know how correctly to reference all the sources which you cited in the main text? — no → 7.6 Box 7.14

yes ↓

As a final review of your study, do you know how your work will be assessed? — no → 7.9 Box 7.16

yes ↓

And finally, will you be able to meet your submission deadline? — no → Sorry, but this time you really are on your own

yes ↓

CONGRATULATIONS!

CHAPTER 7

Writing a report

'What's an abstract?'

'How does a design differ from a methodology?'

'What do I do with all this raw data?'

'Which is the independent variable again?'

Overview

- The purpose of a report
- Writing guidelines
- The structure of a report
  - title
  - abstract
  - contents
  - introduction
  - method
  - design
  - subjects
  - apparatus
  - procedure
- results
- Tables and figures
- Discussion
- References
- Appendices
- Presentation and style
- Presenting a report
  - oral presentation
  - practicalities: giving a presentation
- Review
- Recommended reading

This chapter considers all the important elements which comprise a proper scientific report and offers guidance on clear and concise methods for writing up the various activities involved in any piece of research. Included are what should go into a report, why it should be there and where it should go. Issues of style are discussed and various ways of reporting results are considered, along with the perennial problem of referencing. For students of psychology and the social sciences everywhere, the procedures outlined here represent the final stage in a lengthy process of research. Moreover, because what is being presented is of a much more practical nature than the material covered in previous chapters, a great deal of what follows is of the *what to do – what not to do* variety. It is hoped that the inclusion of a number of checklists will be of particular use to everyone about to write up their research.

A flowchart is provided to direct your reading through this chapter although, as with all previous chapters of this book, if the entire process of writing up a report is new to you, you might wish to start at the beginning and take each section in order.

7.1   The purpose of a report

You may have conducted a brilliant study (or at least, this is your belief). However, other people can only know of the brilliance of this research by being told about it in some way, usually through a written report, which will offer details on what you've done, why it was done and what the outcomes were. For an undergraduate, a large proportion of marks is likely to be assigned to the final report, and success will depend almost entirely on the quality of the writing and presentation. It is therefore important to consider the way in which this work will be presented from the earliest stages.

7.2   Writing guidelines

Ideally, a study should be written up as it progresses (it really is easier this way, rather than trying to remember what you did after the fact). Mapping out the main points of the literature review as you do it will often serve as a guide in the formulation of hypotheses and will clarify design and methodological issues – points made right at the beginning of this book in Chapter 1 (see especially Sections 1.5.1 to 1.7.1). Writing up the methodology section while it is still fresh in your mind will save you hours of work at a later stage, as will keeping a strict record of your references from the beginning (this goes for a bibliography as well, though note that a bibliography is quite different from a reference section. See Section 7.6 near the end of this chapter). The point here is that, if you are going to (or might) cite material in the body of your report, this must be properly referenced (see Box 7.14), with authors, year and journal. Noting this information at an early stage will avoid frantic scrabbling through scores of journals when it comes to writing up. One of the commonest mutterings overheard in university libraries everywhere is 'Where was that reference?'

Another area where it is important to keep a track of what you are doing is in the results section: writing up your results as you conduct the analysis will identify any significant gaps while there is still sufficient time to fill them. Alternatively, this might also help you to recognise when further analysis is unnecessary – a common problem with many undergraduate reports is overanalysis of data – which creates needless work for both the student and the supervisor. However, even the most conscientious of researchers may have to make amendments to their report at the last minute, and it is only when discussions and conclusions have been written that the overall structure may be assessed (this is the reason why you should always write the abstract *last*). It is important to allow yourself the time to read your work critically before it has to be submitted, to reflect on its contents and to make any necessary changes. This is why it is important to make notes as you go along, and the following should serve as a guide:

1. Full references of articles or books that you have read, with details of the main points of studies or theories.
2. The arguments behind your hypotheses;
3. The ways in which you recruited subjects, with details of the numbers agreeing or refusing to participate.
4. Changes that you may have made to any questionnaires or other instruments, and the arguments behind the changes.
5. Details of pilot studies, and any modifications made as a result of those studies.
6. The exact procedures you employed, with appropriate justification.
7. Details of coding procedures.
8. Details of analyses.

Keeping research notes like this can take many forms, although perhaps a diary or lab-book format is the simplest; keeping up with reading, meetings with supervisors and notes needs a certain amount of self-discipline, and it is surprising how often one simply cannot remember such details at a later stage. You really will be saving yourself time and trouble if you keep an accurate running record of your research activities in some organised format. Relying on memory alone, or random scraps of paper will not be effective; your supervisor will (or should) keep a diary of your progress and it is very much in your own interests to do the same.

7.3 The structure of a report

The basic structure of your report should normally follow the familiar layout of a standard laboratory report, i.e., it should consist of the four major sections: Introduction, Method, Results and Discussion, in that order, headed by the title and abstract and followed by the reference list and any appendices. Part of the reason for keeping to this conventional format is that the reader will know just where to find each piece of essential information about your research. You should therefore make sure that your report conforms to this layout as much as possible, and that relevant information is where it should be.

The report on a substantial research project is obviously likely to be more weighty than the average laboratory report. A common question from undergraduates though is 'How long should the report be?' The answer however, no matter how unsatisfactory, must be: *whatever it takes to report the research concisely, but clearly, accurately and completely*. Having said this, most student researchers will probably have some sort of length indication specified by their department or tutor (e.g., 'about 10,000 words'). This is always a rough indication, since an assessor is not actually going to count the words, but any such limit is worth bearing in mind and a report should always endeavour to end up somewhere within the recommended range. One of the most annoying aspects of undergraduate reports for supervisors is unnecessary length – a product of overwriting and a sense that every concept, theory or piece of previous research must be explained in great detail, especially in the introduction. In most cases this is not necessary and a general overview is sufficient, except when a particular study or issue forms the basis for the current piece of research, in which case detail is essential.

7.3.1   Title

This should be concise but informative, and should give a clear indication of what the project is about, e.g., 'Individual differences in the perception of embedded figures'. Readers should be able to tell, from the title alone, whether a report is of interest to them. A title that is too concise may be at best uninformative and at worst, misleading: for example, the title 'Gender differences in memory' gives no indication of which aspects of memory were investigated. If a report is likely to be placed on library access, or in other ways made available to a broader readership, it is important that the title contains the relevant keywords that any interested readers would be likely to use in their literature search (e.g., 'individual differences', 'perception', or 'embedded figures').

7.3.2   Abstract

The abstract is a short summary of the main information contained in the report as a whole. It should ideally be about 100 or 150 words in length. Although the abstract is positioned at the beginning of the report, it is often the last part to be actually written – it will certainly be easier to write the summary when the report is finished than the other way around. The abstract should – very briefly: identify the problem studied; the hypotheses tested; the method employed, including the number and kind of subjects; the results obtained; and the main conclusions drawn. Statistical details should usually be excluded, unless you have used a novel type of analysis, or have departed

Box 7.1   The structure of a typical project report

Title
Brief, clear, accurate, don't try to be funny or whimsical (10–12 words at most).

Abstract
Approximately 100-150 word summary. Say briefly what it's about, what was done, and what was found. Write this last!

Introduction
What was this research all about? What relevant previous work was there? What did they find? Is there a central theory, or a debate about different theories? Was the present experiment the same (a replication) – if not, how was it different? In either case, what was expected to happen (the hypotheses)?

Method
Four sub-headings, setting out the structure of the study, as follows:
Design   What sort of study was it (e.g., an experiment, a survey, a case-study)? Repeated measures design, independent groups, or a mixed design?
What were the dependent variables (what was measured)?
What were the independent variables (what varied across different subjects)?
What was the subjects' task?
Subjects   How many? Any *relevant* description.
Apparatus   What materials or equipment did the experiment need? What changes were made, and why?
Procedure   Briefly describe what happened. Quote the instructions given to the subjects.

Results
A written presentation of summary results, not individual subject's data. For example, give the mean and standard deviation for the dependent variable for each different condition. If any graphs or tables help to clarify the results, put them in here but don't merely duplicate tabular data – figures are only useful if they clarify or highlight data in a manner not possible with tables. Report the statistics used, and say briefly whether the results supported the hypotheses or not.

Discussion
An examination of your results, comparing them with previous findings. What conclusions do they point to? How do you interpret your findings? You could also suggest improvements or variations in the experimental design, or further hypotheses which might be tested.

References
Only list references actually cited earlier in the report. If it is important to mention other sources used though not explicitly cited, these should be given in a separate bibliography.

Appendices
This is the location for the raw materials used in the study: stimuli, examples of questionnaires, and so on. Raw data and computer printouts are not recommended, unless there is a case for inclusion. Supervisors will normally inform you of their expectations here.

Box 7.2   Common errors in the title

Some authors try to apply snappy titles to their work, incorporating puns, innuendo or otherwise playing on words, e.g.,

Sex and the single hemisphere . . .

or

Psychoanalysis? Dream on . . .

Amusing as these may be, they don't actually offer much information about the studies and would be likely to be overlooked in the early stages of a literature review for this reason.

Box 7.3   Common errors in the abstract

In the search for brevity some writers reduce the information content of an abstract to the point where it becomes impossible to judge the nature of a study without reading the entire report. This is a particularly common problem among undergraduate students, but is not exclusive to them.

A study on consumerism among a stratified sample failed to demonstrate significant differences between any of the comparison groups on any of the fifteen differentiating behaviours. In all cases the null hypotheses were accepted.

An abstract of this nature is virtually useless – there is no real indication what the study was about, which aspects of consumerism were being studied, or who the subjects were. Nor is there any indication as to what kind of statistical analysis was carried out in order to test the hypotheses – whatever they happened to be.

Equally unhelpful is the two-page abstract in which the writer is incapable of summarising the important elements of the study:

In a study carried out over five days between 1 April and 5 April 100 subjects participated in a between-groups experiment on reaction time. The subjects were initially drawn from a local population comprising primarily university undergraduates, all of whom lived within the campus area, except for a small group who commuted from a neighbouring district. Of these, the population was known to comprise 80 per cent males and 20 per cent females, with an age distribution roughly . . . blah! blah! blah! . . .

This amount of detail, if extended to the rest of the study, would provide an abstract almost as long as the report itself, which is as counter productive as the previous, minimal example. A look back at Chapter 1, Box 1.7, will provide an illustration of what is appropriate.

from the norm in any other important way (e.g., used a non-standard significance level, etc.). In short, an abstract should be like an extremely condensed version of the full report providing key information from the introduction, method, results and discussion sections (see Box 7.3).

Writing a good abstract (one that conveys key information clearly and accurately, without exceeding the length limit) is difficult, but it is important. Like the title, the abstract may be accessed by on-line search systems, so it should contain enough specific information to enable a researcher to find the work in the first place, and then to decide whether to read the whole thing. This is becoming increasingly important with the advent of modern databases since the abstract (and the title) will often be the first point of contact others will have with a researcher's work. It is therefore important to get it right (see Box 7.4).

7.3.3   Contents

If the purpose of a write-up is a final report rather than an article intended for publication (which, alas, is something few undergraduates actually consider), a list of contents could be provided, based on section or chapter headings. This is particularly important if more than one experiment is being reported,

Box 7.4   Abstract: checklist

A good abstract should contain the following information:

1. The research issue being explored – this would comprise the research question, or the theory being investigated in the study.
2. The hypotheses being tested – the specific predictions which form the bases of the study.
3. The design of the study – the way in which it has been set up to explore the hypotheses, expressed in the language of design (e.g., repeated measures; counterbalanced).
4. The key characteristics of the subjects, in so far as this information is relevant; for example, there is little point in offering detail on subjects' ages unless age influenced, or explained, the findings in some way.
5. The key characteristics of any apparatus used, again only insofar as this may be relevant – if findings can only be explained by reference to the specifics of apparatus, or if replication could not take place without this particular information.
6. The outcome of the study, in terms of whether or not hypotheses were accepted or rejected.
7. A comment on any unusual features of the study, if appropriate.

or if a project moves forward through a number of successive stages. Also included here should be details of any appendices, and this is probably an appropriate point at which to remind you to number the pages, something often forgotten by keen (or late) students.

7.3.4   Introduction

This is the first major section of the report. A good introduction should provide the reader with the essential background to the project, starting out with a broad description of the particular research topic that is being dealt with, and moving on through a clear and accurate account of the previous research which has led up to the project. You should be able to show that your particular study is a natural development of this previous work, and that it adds something – even if that something is only that an effect is (or is not) replicated with a different sample. It is also important to show that you are aware of current or recent work which is relevant to the study, and that the important theoretical issues are understood.

There is no one correct way to begin an introduction, but it is probably a good idea to start off with a brief overview of the area of study to set the scene for what is to follow. For example, if a study concerns the relationship between exercise and mental health, one could begin by describing the general assumptions made about this relationship, followed by a delineation of the aspects of exercise and mental health to be considered in further detail in the report. If a study concerns ways of coping with a particular illness, you could begin by describing the aspects of the illness which may be found stressful, followed by an outline of the model of stress and coping which it is intended to use as a framework for analysis. The introductory paragraphs should therefore outline, in a general way, what the study is about and which aspects of a particular issue you are exploring.

The central part of an introduction should cover the relevant research which forms a background to the project. If the research is based on one particular published study, describe this in some detail, including number and type of subjects, design, measures, analysis and results. Then you should comment on the study, taking into account such issues as the adequacy of the subjects, measures, design and analysis used, the extent to which the results may be generalised to other populations, and any theoretical implications of the results. You can then describe other studies in the area using this framework, although unless they relate directly to the research issue, or provide a further basis, in their specifics, for what you are going to do, these should not be presented in anything like this amount of detail. In this way, the major concerns, related issues and matters pertaining to the particular approach you are taking, can be clarified as you proceed. Consequently, hypotheses or research questions should not come as a surprise to the reader:

every aspect of the hypotheses should have been mentioned at an earlier point in the introduction and follow on naturally and logically from what has gone before.

The introduction should normally lead towards an overview of what the study will actually do (but saving the details for the next section) and should conclude with a statement of the hypotheses that the study actually tested. It is often useful to state these twice: first, as a general prediction of outcomes (e.g., that a certain experimental treatment will enhance performance, but only for women); and then as a precise experimental hypothesis (e.g., 'it was therefore hypothesised that a significant condition-by-sex interaction would be observed, in which female subjects in the experimental condition would gain significantly higher scores than controls, while males would not'). It is also useful at this stage to identify (as much for your own benefit as the reader's) the independent and dependent variables. The more precise hypotheses can be, the more straightforward will be the conduct of the study itself.

Pilot studies may also be mentioned in the introduction if they have contributed to the development of hypotheses or research questions.

Box 7.5   Common errors in the introduction

1. Writing an anecdotal, subjective background which is based more on personal opinion than a sound knowledge of the field.
2. Trying to cover the entire history of research in the field: be selective, and review only what is directly relevant to your own study – this is especially important in areas which have proved popular among researchers (imagine trying to review the last 50 years of research into personality and you will get the point).
3. Explaining too much: you may assume some psychological knowledge on the part of your reader. You should not have to define common terms – unless, of course, you are using them in a specialised way. (It is worth considering the nature of your readership here – a report for publication in a scientific journal will not have to spell out the characteristics of standardised tests. A presentation to undergraduates on the other hand might require that the structure of a particular personality questionnaire be explained.)
4. Explaining too little: we are not all expert in your field, so write as if for the intelligent (but interested) non-specialist. In practical terms a balance will have to be struck between this and the previous point.
5. Failing to show how your review of the relevant literature leads up to, and provides a rationale for, your particular study.
6. Failing to state just what it is that your study is seeking to accomplish. A frequent form of this error is failing to state your hypotheses at the end of the introduction.

Otherwise, the convention is that details of pilot studies are given in the method section, especially where they relate to developing questionnaire items or strategies for data gathering.

7.3.5   Method

The method section is the next major part of a research write-up in so far as it presents all the information about how the research was actually carried out. Its purpose is to explain the study in such a way that the reader can follow the logical development presented by the writer, from general introduction, through specific hypotheses to actual testing and data gathering. Even with a sound literature review and a logical set of hypotheses, a study will fail to impress if it is not clear what was actually done: Who participated? How were subjects assigned to groups? How were experimental treatments imposed? What checks were made on extraneous factors? These are typical questions posed by anyone reviewing or assessing a report and the answers should be readily available in this section.

There will be times when a researcher will feel that there is reason to replicate previous work, and this can only be done if there exists sufficient detail on how the original research was carried out. To facilitate this, the method section normally comprises four major divisions, as the following sections demonstrate.

7.3.6   Design

This, the initial part of the method section, presents the formal description of the study. It is usually brief and concise, but lacking in specific details about subjects and procedure, and it is generally couched in the technical language of research design (between-subjects; repeated measures; counterbalanced, etc.). First, you must specify what kind of investigation has been carried out (e.g., was it an experiment, an observational study, a survey, a case study, and so on.). You should then define the variables either measured or manipulated in the study, making the distinction between independent variables (or predictors) and dependent variables (or outcome measures). This ought to be a straightforward task, since these matters will have been sorted out in the early stages of a study. However, supervisors are often surprised at the confusions which appear over the description of variables present in a study, even in cases where the rest of the work is of a high standard. (If this is still a problem, a review of Chapter 2, Sections 2.3.6 through 2.3.8 will be helpful.)

This difficulty of correctly identifying variables can sometimes be aggravated in correlational studies where characterisation is sometimes less clear, but you should usually be able to distinguish between the variables that you want to find out about, and the variables that you are just using to get there. You should also specify any important extraneous variables: i.e., factors which, under other circumstances, might be considered independent variables in their own right, but which in this case might have to be controlled for.

Another important design element is whether you have used repeated measures (within-subjects design), independent groups (between-subjects design), or a combination of the two (mixed design) (see Chapter 2, Sections 2.4.2 through 2.5.5). This should be accurately reported, especially in experimental studies (note that correlational designs by definition use repeated measures). The factor levels which combine to form the experimental conditions should be described if appropriate, as should the method by which the subjects were assigned to groups. Box 7.6 provides an example of the information expected in a typical design.

A common mistake made by undergraduates is to confuse the Design with procedural matters. It must be remembered that the design of a study is the plan of campaign, formulated before the study proper is implemented. Consequently when decisions are made it isn't possible to know how many subjects would actually respond to your questionnaire, or that your particular experimental manipulation would produce a revolt among one of your groups. This is why the design is a formal statement of intent, expressed in general terms and using the language of experimentation. If still in any doubt about this, the whole of Chapter 2, Designing a study, should be reviewed. Box 7.7 also illustrates this point.

If your project is at the more qualitative end of the spectrum, you should still try to give a formal and objective description of your project under this heading. Thus you should clarify the method (e.g., observation, or semi-structured interview), the main variables or factors under consideration, corresponding to dependent variables (e.g., types of non-verbal behaviours, expressed sources of stress at work), other variables or factors corresponding

Box 7.6   Design section: an example:

A mixed design 2 × 3 factorial experiment was carried out, in which subjects performed a rotary pursuit task at several levels of delay following the ingestion of either alcohol or water. The dependent variable was *number of errors* per trial. The within-subjects factor was *time since ingestion*, at three levels (i.e., 1 minute, 10 minutes, and 20 minutes). The between-subjects factor was *treatment*, i.e., either alcohol (experimental group) or water (control group). Measures of subject age and handedness were taken, to be considered as covariates in subsequent statistical analysis.

Box 7.7   Common errors in the design

Many people, and especially those new to the scientific report, readily confuse procedural elements with the design. By way of example, what follows is an outline of procedural matters:

Eighty subjects were used in the study, 40 males and 40 females, of varying ages and backgrounds. Both groups were treated identically, being shown a video, prior to the experimental manipulation, in which the procedural details were explained. The manipulation itself comprised a small parts assembly exercise in which a number of rivets, washers and bolts were assembled in a predetermined order and then inserted into a pegboard. On completion of the experiment each subject completed a questionnaire which rated various attitudinal factors on a 1–5 scale . . .

The key point about a design is that it should serve almost as a schematic map or diagram of a study in which the major elements – and only those – are illustrated.

Box 7.8   Design checklist

Your design should contain the following information:

1. The nature of the study (e.g., experimental; survey; case study; etc.).
2. The structure of the design (e.g., repeated measures; independent groups; etc.).
3. The independent and dependent variables.
4. Extraneous variables and any controls used to reduce their effect.

to independent variables and covariates (e.g., gender, age, employment status), and time factors, such as the frequency of repeated observations.

The final element in this section is shown in Box 7.8, comprising a checklist of key points which you should review before you consider any other developments in your study. It is worth remembering that if you have come up with an inappropriate design, or if you are unclear about key design elements, everything which follows will be affected.

7.3.7   Subjects

Give *relevant* details of subjects, including number of subjects used, age and gender, and on what basis they were allocated to subgroups. Any subject characteristics which might have affected their responses should be mentioned, and you should explain how these were dealt with. You should also state how the subjects were obtained, and give refusal rates if appropriate. You should aim to give sufficient detail to enable you and the reader to decide the extent to which your subjects were representative of the population. For example, if you recruited subjects through a self-help group or through a newsletter, you may have distributed 100 questionnaires but had only 40 returns. This should be stated, since it may imply that your results are applicable only to a subsection of the target population. While this may be a limitation of your project it is not something to be hidden, or indeed to be ashamed of. In this case, the possible limitations of your results should be considered in the discussion section (see Box 7.9).

Box 7.9   Subjects section: an example

> The subjects, all members of a university subject panel, were 60 undergraduate volunteers (30M, 30F), who performed the experiment individually. The median age was 19 years (range 17–23). Subjects were assigned to either the control group or the experimental group on a quasi-random basis, with the constraint that equal numbers of male and female subjects were included in either group. Given the nature of the task, the subjects were screened to ensure that their eyesight was normal or corrected to normal.

7.3.8 *Apparatus (or materials)*

Give full details of all equipment, apparatus and materials used. Trade names and model numbers of pieces of equipment should be given. The full names of published tests should be given, with references. Details of pilot studies may be given here, if they confirmed the utility of apparatus or materials or, alternatively, if they indicated the need for changes or alterations. If questionnaires or other test materials have been changed in any way, give full details and a rationale for the changes made. For example, you may have changed the wording on a test item originating in the USA to make it more suitable for a UK population, or you may have omitted an item because it was unethical within the context of your project.

If you have used a fairly lengthy test instrument, you may wish to give some representative examples of items in this section, and refer the reader to an appendix where the entire list can be found. If your test instrument or questionnaire incorporates a number of different sections or subscales, make it clear what these are and how they are to be calculated. If you have written a computer program for your study, give a careful explanation of what it actually does. The program itself can be listed in full in an appendix.

You may have devised an interview schedule for your project. In this case, describe the main areas covered in the interview and indicate the sources of any particular questions or wording. Give the interview schedule in full in an appendix.

7.3.9   Procedure

Describe exactly what was done, and include verbal instructions given to subjects. If instructions were provided in handouts or with test materials, include these in an appendix. Bear in mind that the function of this section is to give the reader sufficient detail to repeat the study. Indicate the circumstances under which the subjects responded (e.g., in a designated room on their own, in groups, in their own homes, in the library), the order in which test items were completed (e.g., whether the order was randomised or fixed, and if fixed, what the order was), and the approximate length of time required by subjects. You should also clarify here the extent to which subjects were offered anonymity, the instructions subjects were given with regard to terminating their involvement in the project, any payment offered, and debriefing or feedback procedures. You may have given some of this information in earlier sections. However, it is important to provide a full and clear description of procedure in this section, even at the risk of repeating yourself.

The method is the second major section of the report, but is often the first to be written. The reason for this is that most of the technical details, the structure, and the 'nuts and bolts' of the study have to be decided in advance. The method section is also the easiest to write, since you do not have to invent anything or be creative in any way: you are simply reporting factual information about your study.

7.3.10   Results

This section contains all the objective outcomes of your study, i.e., the factual results, as generated from analyses and without any theoretical interpretation, inference, or speculation, and it should be presented in conventional text format, as in the rest of the report. The temptation to expand and speculate here is admittedly huge – after all, this represents the point at which you have finally learned whether or not your predictions have been upheld. However, the discussion is the place to argue implications, not the results section. (The names given to these different parts of a report by the way ought to be something of a giveaway!) At this stage, what is needed are, first, the descriptive statistics, which summarise your data in a standard form, and second, inferential statistics, which test whether your results can be distinguished from chance and hence whether your hypotheses have been upheld. It's not usually appropriate to report individual subjects' raw data unless your study requires it, e.g., in a case study, or any argument as to what your findings might imply. Keep this section as cool, numerical, and objective as possible, while ensuring that the reader understands the results of your study.

Descriptive statistics should normally consist of the means and standard deviations of your main outcome variables (which may be compared with any available published norms), both overall and for any appropriate subgroups or conditions. For example, you may wish to give separate means and standard deviations for males and females, or those in different age groups. The descriptive statistics can often be conveniently presented in a table (see Table 7.1), or alternatively in a figure (see Figure 7.1), if the nature of tabulated data is potentially misleading, or if there is so much of it that the information to be expressed is obscured. (It is worth noting though that tables and figures should be used as either-or alternatives – it is not appropriate to present the same data twice, once in each format.) If you are using a test or materials that other authors have used, compare your results with theirs at this stage. Thus you should show that your sample has provided data that fall within an expected range (or not), and that these data are suitable for further statistical analysis. Both of these points may be raised in the discussion.

If your sample seems to be different from other samples in some important way (e.g., they gain markedly higher or lower scores on particular tests), you may still be able to undertake further analysis, but you should indicate the nature of the difference and show that necessary steps (e.g., data transformation, re-coding) have been taken. The presentation of descriptive statistics is important, and forms the logical starting point of further analysis. For this reason it is worth checking and recording them before moving on to the main analysis.

The results of the statistical analysis should then be presented in a clear and logical way. The most obvious approach is to deal with each hypothesis in turn, in the order given at the end of your introduction. The aim is to show clearly what your data say about each one, and then to state simply whether this evidence supports it or not. Generally speaking this requires you to report the appropriate significance test, giving the value of the statistic, the degrees of freedom, and the associated probability. You should then help the reader by translating (briefly) what the test is telling you into a straightforward verbal statement, while avoiding the temptation to expand or speculate (see Box 7.10).

Always bear in mind that you must clarify your results for the reader. It is tempting to use shorthand when describing certain variables, particularly in

Box 7.10 An example

> A significant positive correlation was found between age and scores on the measure of attitudes ($r = .43$, df = 29, $p < 0.01$), indicating that older subjects tended to express more positive attitudes.'
>
> (Note: $r_{(29)} = 0.43$, $p < 0.01$ is an alternative format for the above.)

tables. Tables derived from computer print-out usually bear the abbreviated labels used to code variables rather than the full variable name. If you do have to use shortened names in tables, provide a key underneath the table. When you are presenting results, describe relationships as fully as possible to avoid confusion: for example, it is clearer, if more lengthy, to say 'scores on the measure of neuroticism were significantly correlated with scores on the "wishful thinking" coping scale' than to say 'neuroticism and wishful thinking were significantly correlated'.

Although the results section often contains a large amount of numerical and statistical information, it is nevertheless part of the text of your report and should be written in English. It is not acceptable simply to present a series of tables or diagrams, unless there is also a clear accompanying text which explains the logic of your analysis. Even less appropriate would be to base this section on computer print-outs.

If you have lengthy or complex results, clarity is often greatly helped by including illustrative tables or figures. These can be a real help to the reader in understanding the overall pattern of your results, and therefore in following the argument. Sometimes, however, they can simply be confusing and counterproductive, or irrelevant and annoying. Box 7.11 gives a results checklist, which is a useful guide to what ought to be covered in this section.

Box 7.11 Results checklist

1. Have you presented descriptive statistics which represent the data fairly and adequately?
2. Do the results as shown deal with each hypothesis stated at the end of the introduction?
3. Are all the results of your analysis presented appropriately?
4. Are all tables and figures correctly labelled?
5. Is it possible to assess the outcome of the study by consulting the results alone, without the need to refer to other sections of the report?
6. Have you included results that are not relevant to the research issue in general or the hypotheses in particular, or to which you do not refer again?

7.4 Tables and figures

Tables are easily produced by a word-processor, and usually consist of summary numerical data (e.g., means and standard deviations, correlation coefficients, etc.), presented within a system of rows and columns representing various categories (e.g., experimental conditions, subject groups, etc.) (see Table 7.1).

Table 7.1 Mean reaction time (RT) in milliseconds (with standard deviation) for six age groups.

	Mean age	Mean RT	SD
Group 1	21	679.73	95.42
Group 2	24	588.66	76.32
Group 3	28	624.29	59.45
Group 4	30	696.75	64.77
Group 5	36	701.61	122.50
Group 6	45	828.03	101.45

Figures usually involve a more pictorial mode of presenting the data (e.g., bar-charts, histograms, scatterplots, etc.), and are either produced directly by your statistics package or indirectly by means of specialist software for diagrams and graphics. Increasingly also, many integrated word-processing/spreadsheet/drawing packages offer this facility bringing the opportunity to create effective illustrations within everyone's grasp. Generally speaking, the data contained in tabular form are precise (actual numerical values are used) whereas figures offer a less exact though often more immediate impression. Figures 7.1 and 7.2 demonstrate the point.

All tables and figures must be numbered (e.g., Table 1; Figure 1) and should be given captions which are self-explanatory. The reader should be able to understand what a table or figure is all about without digging through the text to find out. At the same time, the information displayed in tables or figures should not be mysteriously independent of the text: it *must* be discussed, explained, or otherwise used in some relevant way.

The whole point of using graphs, figures and tables is to report, accurately and clearly, the outcome of a study. However, this section of any written report is often the main source of misleading, inaccurate and inappropriate information. Figure 7.3 shows a typical example. Here the researcher is guilty of two errors. On the one hand, there is simply too much information offered on the line graph and it becomes almost impossible to identify any trend

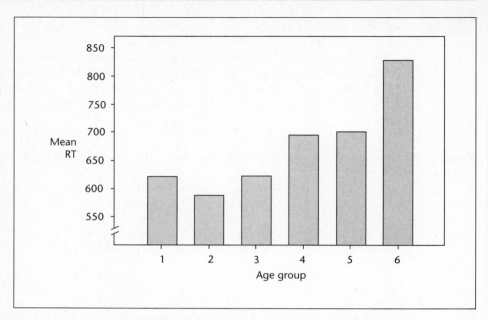

Figure 7.1   Mean reaction time (RT) in milliseconds for six age groups (n=36)

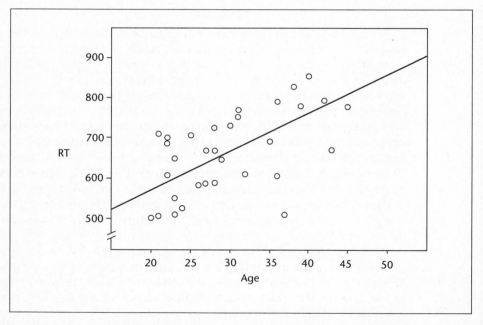

Figure 7.2   Reaction time (RT) in milliseconds as a function of age with the least squares line of regression shown

or pattern in the data. On the other, there is no information on what each of the plotted lines is measuring: the legend for the graph is missing. Furthermore, this particular researcher seems to have lost the ability to count, as can be observed by closer inspection of the figure in question.

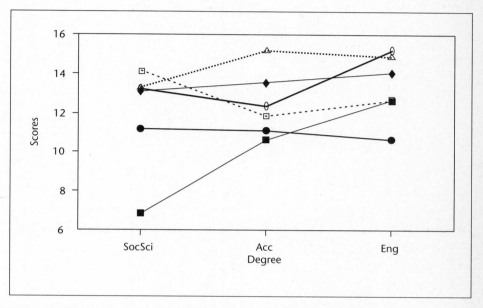

Figure 7.3 Scores on five personality dimensions across three degrees

In the next example, Figure 7.4 demonstrates how a sneaky researcher can manipulate the vertical and horizontal axes of a figure to maximise an effect. Presenting data in this form suggests that there are indeed huge differences between the sexes, when measured on a social supportive scalar instrument. Compare this with the final illustration in this section, Figure 7.5, in which the axes have been manipulated in a different, but equally misleading way. The data are the same as for the previous figure, but the impression created is totally different.

This kind of manipulation is not recommended and the sophisticated reader is likely to pick up on such attempts to deceive quite quickly. If in any doubt how best to present data fairly and objectively, most current statistical software packages use a recognised format for graphs which provide an acceptable standard. If still in doubt, there is an old adage beloved of statisticians long gone now, that the vertical axis should always be 3/4 the length of the horizontal!

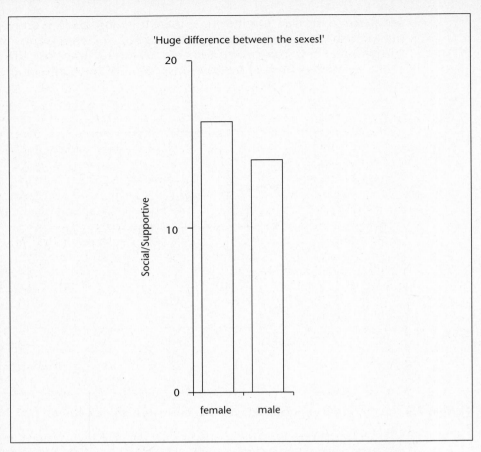

Figure 7.4   Scores on a social supportive measure for both males and females

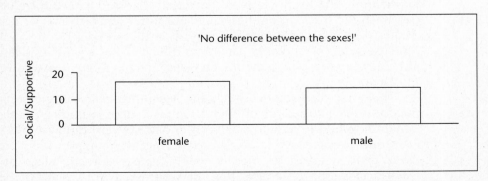

Figure 7.5   Scores on a social supportive measure for both males and females

The above discussion on tables and figures is relevant to most research you might undertake. However, a qualitative project might well require a different format. You will probably have undertaken quite complex coding procedures during your analysis, and details should be given in this section. Any other transformations should be presented here. Indicate the range of responses given with regard to each of your main questions or areas of interest, and describe how and why responses were categorised. As with more quantitative studies, you might compare the range of responses resulting from your study with those found by other researchers. In some instances the results of a qualitative study might be better presented within a rather different discussion format, in which the results and discussion sections are combined. It is worth considering all of your options at this stage. The most important consideration is to ensure that the reader understands as fully as possible what you found and what it means, whatever format you choose to present your findings (The reader is directed to Chapter 6 on qualitative techniques for a fuller account of how to deal with this type of research.)

This section concludes with a checklist to serve as a reminder of what tables and figures are supposed to be doing. This is shown in Box 7.12.

Box 7.12 Tables and figures checklist

1. All data which are relevant to the study must be shown, either as a table or a figure.
2. All tables and figures must be clearly labelled and numbered. Axes should show the appropriate units of measurement and the variables represented on them.
3. Table and figure labels should state clearly what is being presented, in general terms. Specific information about the content of a figure or table can be presented in the form of column headings for a table, or the legend for a graph.
4. The numbering of tables and figures must be logical and sequential so they can be readily referred to in any discussion.
5. Duplication should be avoided – data should be presented in one format only. If a table offers a clear presentation of data, an additional figure on the same data is of little value.
6. Overcomplexity should be avoided. If a table or figure cannot present findings in a clear and unambiguous manner, the data must be reorganised or a different mode of presentation sought.

7.5   Discussion

This is the section that demands the most from your creativity. The discussion should review your hypotheses in the light of the results. Start off by repeating, in simple terms, the main results of your study, and indicating the implications of these results for your hypotheses. Then you can draw on the main points of your introduction: for example, you can indicate whether your results are consistent or inconsistent with the findings of other researchers, or whether they support one theory rather than another.

You have to present some explanations for your results – this may be straightforward if your results are entirely in the expected directions and all of your hypotheses were supported. It may be less straightforward (although more interesting) if your results were not consistent with the results of other researchers. Under these circumstances, you have to review all of the potentially relevant points made earlier in the report: you may have used a different subject pool, used a slightly different procedure, changed the test materials in some way, and all of these may have affected your results. You should not attempt to hide any such discrepancies between your study and those of others: rather the effects of discrepancies and variations should be highlighted, since they tell you something very important about the strength or robustness of any predicted effects. Moreover, being honest and 'up-front' like this also indicates that you appreciate the scientific limitations of your study, which in itself is commendable.

Overall, you should ensure that you cover all of the main points raised in your introduction. Thus if you mentioned the possibility of gender differences in the introduction, you should raise this issue again in your discussion, even if you were not able to examine gender differences, although you should be able to explain why not (e.g., limitations within the subject pool). One of the aims of the discussion is to highlight the limitations of your project and areas worthy of further investigation. You are not expected to conduct a study which covers every option; on the other hand, you are expected to discuss the strengths, weaknesses and limitations of your work in a clear and objective tone. You should also consider ways in which your project might have been improved, and the direction of any future work which may be profitably undertaken in this area.

A very important point to note is that the failure to uphold your hypotheses does not mean that the study has 'failed'. To show that something is *not* the case can be as important as showing that is *is* the case: a null result does not mean that the discussion has nothing to say. You should not, therefore, write your discussion of a null outcome in an apologetic way; yes, we all like to get a 'significant result', but the rejection of a hypothesis can be equally informative, and may lead to new ideas.

The discussion should end with a paragraph or two of conclusions. It may be tempting at this stage to make rather sweeping statements. Remember the

Box 7.13 Discussion checklist

1. Have you discussed all the important issues raised in your introduction?
2. Have ideas crept in to the discussion which are not really related to the study?
3. Does the discussion concentrate purely on the findings, or does it consider broader issues?
4. Conversely: does your discussion take sufficient note of the actual findings?
5. Are there any findings which you have not discussed?
6. Have you considered whether your data might support another explanation other than the one you prefer?
7. Does the discussion point to original thinking?
8. Are your conclusions clear?

limitations of your study and try not to go beyond your own results. A useful checklist which can be applied to the discussion section appears in Box 7.13.

7.6 References

The References section of a report offers an alphabetical listing (by first author's surname) of all the sources mentioned, or referred to in the main text of the report, research by others, book chapters, commentaries and quotations – any material in fact to which you have made reference in the body of a report must be cited. An important point here, and one which is a traditional source of confusion to many undergraduates, concerns the difference between a reference section and a **bibliography**. References, as already mentioned, relate to work actually cited. A bibliography, on the other hand, is a listing (again alphabetically, by first author) of any work which was consulted, browsed or which in some way contributed to the background, formulation and conduct of your study. For instance, in reviewing the type of research carried out in a particular area you might have read several journal articles and book reviews, none of which provided specific material to which you referred in your report. However, in so far as they did contribute to the overall foundations of your work, they are still worth mentioning. This is the function of a bibliography – an opportunity for you to provide an overview of your own research into a topic.

The format for presenting references tends to vary slightly from publication to publication, but the majority of psychology journals conform to the format set out in the *Publication Manual of the American Psychological Association*. The BPS also issues standard guidelines, which differ from the APA only slightly. When in doubt, the best advice is to get hold of a mainstream publication such as the *British Journal of Psychology* or the *Annual Review of Psychology* and model your references accordingly.

Citations in the text itself should be by the author's surname and date *only* – which is the minimum information needed to correctly identify the full reference where it appears at the end of the report. Any other information, such as book titles, publication journal, and so on, is redundant here and serves only to distract. In multiple citations, reference your sources in alphabetical order. In the (relatively) rare case in which more than one article has been published by a single author in the same year, and you wish to cite all, or some of this work, such publications are distinguished using the letters a,b,c, etc. after the citation. (Eysenck (1989a); Eysenck (1989b) etc.). The identifiers (a,b,c) are used in the order in which you cite the work in the text, and not in the order in which they were published in the particular year in question. And of course, the identifiers accompany the full reference at the end of the report. (This last point might come as something of a surprise to some students who, in reproducing references from other sources, include the alphabetic identifiers without knowing why.)

Box 7.14   References and citations

1. Journal articles

Archer, J. (1991). The influence of testosterone on human aggression. *British Journal of Psychology*, 82, 1–28.

Johnson, M.H., Karmiloff-Smith, A., and Patry, J.-L. (1992). Can neural selectionism be applied to cognitive development and its disorders? *New Ideas in Psychology*, 10, 35–46.

Note that: (a) capital letters are not used in the titles of the articles except at the beginning of the title (or when proper names are used); (b) inverted commas are not used; (c) journal names are given in full; (d) journal names and volume numbers are italicised (or underlined, if you are not using a word-processor).

2. Books and chapters in books

Berkowitz, L. (1993). *Aggression: Its causes, consequences, and control.* New York: McGraw-Hill.

Moreland, R.L. (1987). The formation of small groups. In C. Hendrick (ed.), *Group processes* (pp. 80–110). Newbury Park, CA: Sage Publications.

Note that: (a) capitals are not used in the titles except at the beginning of the title (b) inverted commas are not used; (c) book titles are italicised (but not chapter titles); (d) page numbers are given.

3. Citations in the text

In the text itself, sources are cited by surnames and date only. Citation can be direct or indirect:

Direct:
Archer (1991) found higher testosterone levels in the more aggressive group.

Indirect:
Higher testosterone levels were found in the more aggressive group (Archer, 1991).

Quotations are best avoided unless the full quotation given is of direct relevance to your own work. If you do quote verbatim from an author, give the page number as well, e.g., 'Comparisons . . . revealed higher testosterone levels in the more aggressive group' (Archer, 1991, p. 21). If there are two authors, give both surnames using 'and' for direct citation and '&' for indirect, e.g.,

| **Direct:** | Barry and Bateman (1992) |
| **Indirect:** | (Barry & Bateman, 1992) |

If there are more than two authors, give all the names the first time the source is cited (e.g., Johnson, Karmiloff-Smith, and Patry, 1992). For subsequent mentions, use 'et al.' (e.g., Johnson et al., 1992).

7.7 Appendices

These should include the details of statistical calculation, and all test materials and examples of any stimuli used in the study. Note that most tutors and examiners will not welcome reams of computer output, even in an appendix, and raw data are certainly not welcomed (although there is an understanding that this could be made available for inspection should it be required). Again, if in doubt, you need merely consult the typical format used in a standard journal.

7.8 Presentation and style

Remember that presentation is important. Try to ensure that your work is free from spelling and grammatical errors. Check your work for errors before you hand it in. The style of writing should be plain and relatively formal, and as a rule you should use the past tense throughout and write in the third person; many novice researchers frequently use 'I' and 'we' in their writing ('we felt repeated measures were more appropriate'), but this tends to create an impression of informality, lack of scientific rigour or subjectivity. And, whether accurate or not, impressions do count. It is much better to place some distance between yourself and the report, as in: 'It was found that/observed/noted', etc.

7.9 Presenting a report

7.9.1 Oral presentation

There is an increasingly common expectation – if not a requirement – that undergraduates offer an oral presentation of their work to staff and fellow students at some stage during the conduct of a project. Timings vary, with some colleges and universities scheduling presentations at some point before data collection begins, while others wait until the entire project has been completed. Either way, presentations are now a familiar part of undergraduate life and they serve a variety of functions. At the most obvious level they provide the student with an opportunity to show off as it were – after all, a great deal of reading has probably gone into the development of a research project, only a fraction of which is ultimately used in the study proper. How satisfying to be able to demonstrate to your tutors that you have actually put considerable effort into your work (especially useful in those cases where presentations comprise an assessable component of a research methods module). Presentations also demonstrate the depth of your familiarity with a topic and tutors will often ask probing questions about issues which, even if they did not form a part of your study, you might be expected to know something about if your reading really was comprehensive.

If presentations occur at an intermediate stage then they serve the extremely useful function of generating constructive feedback, with an audience being given the chance to offer advice ('you need a larger sample for this type of analysis', or 'have you read . . ?'). And of course finally, having to prepare and give a presentation can now be regarded as an important element of general research methods training – anyone hoping to pursue a career in the field will find that giving conference presentations and research papers is a major method of contemporary information dissemination. Consequently, a few guidelines on presentation techniques might come in useful.

The aim of a presentation is to describe, in the course of a 10-minute talk (sometimes longer, but not much) the study which you have carried out. During the presentation you must identify the research issue you have explored, outline the research background to the issue and provide a rationale for what you have done. The actual study must be described in sufficient detail that an audience can follow your design and procedure, and results should be offered in a format which describes the outcome without confusion. Finally, you should be able to present your view of the implications of the study, and all in a manner which is interesting, informative and accurate. All in all, a pretty terrifying prospect!

In structure a presentation should be like a trimmed-down version of a standard research report, comprising more or less the same major sections and subdivisions. It will have a title, much like the report title, followed by a brief statement of what the study was about. This is not quite like an abstract since data and findings would not be offered at this stage, but more like an expanded explanation of the title, highlighting the general research area and stating the hypotheses which were being tested. ('an observational study in the area of . . . and exploring the specific issue of . . .').

A review of the background to the research is important, and this will take the form of a summarised version of the literature review found in the written report. Naturally, key studies would have to be mentioned, with their findings, along with any research which provides a rationale for the study, ending with a statement of the hypotheses to be explored.

An outline of the procedure followed would be offered next, with illustrations provided of questionnaires or stimuli. The data collected should be described in descriptive terms, followed by precise details of results. While most of the other sections would tend to be presented in general terms, this, the results section, should be full and precise. It remains only to make concluding comments about the conduct of the study, how the findings relate to the research issue in general and the hypotheses in particular.

7.9.2 | *Practicalities: giving a presentation*

The previous section outlined the content of a typical presentation, but said little about how this material might be presented. This section attempts to offer some practical advice.

A key point, when preparing for a presentation, is that an oral exposition of a piece of work differs from a text version. In the write-up you have ample opportunity to explain in detail the conduct of previous research in your field, to include the results of complex statistical analyses and to discuss at length your findings. In a presentation this is not possible to anything like the same extent. For one thing, there are time constraints in a presentation and, contrary to popular undergraduate belief, 10 minutes is not really that long; what you say has to be a much condensed version of your study, but one which nevertheless contains the essence of what you did. For another, while a reviewer or assessor can reread the contents of a report, or follow up material in appendices, a presentation is a 'one-shot' affair – you have a single opportunity to say what you want, to make your points and show that you have done a good job. So how do you do this?

The starting point is your written report – if this is complete before presentations are given (as is the norm) then you already have all the information necessary for an oral version. You actually have too much information, so the report should be read carefully and important information extracted. Box 7.15 offers a summary of what is required.

The next stage is to decide how best to present the information gleaned from the full report: some undergraduates will simply write a summary, based

Box 7.15 Talking it through

The following is a suggested listing – with comments – of the major elements which should comprise an oral presentation. They appear in the typical order in which they would be introduced to an audience. They also represent the likely content of a series of slides or overheads which would be used as a basis for a presentation.

1. A title for the presentation, which will be based on the title of the study itself. Accompanying notes would expand on this title, identifying the research area in which your study was based, and outlining the research questions posed.

2. An outline of key research in the area. An overhead would display the authors of research, the date of the published work and the research findings – these might be in terms of mean scores for different groups, or a description of factors identified in the research. Accompanying notes would expand on the studies cited, explaining the findings in more detail and demonstrating how they formed a basis for your work.

3. A statement of the aim of the study, in general terms, and statements of the hypotheses being tested. Notes would expand on the aim, reminding the audience of how the stated aim has developed from previous research (or whatever), and each hypothesis would be explained in turn: what was the basis for each hypothesised prediction and what the expected outcomes are.

4. A description of procedural elements, such as the sample characteristics (where relevant to the conduct and findings of the study), details of any apparatus used, including questionnaires and standardised test instruments. In the case of tests or questionnaires, examples of items, coding and scoring systems can be displayed. Full copies might also be distributed among the audience. Notes here would provide descriptive details of how samples were drawn, why certain characteristics were controlled for (e.g., extraneous variables) and how subjects were assigned to groups, if appropriate, and whether or not the design was within- or between-groups. Details would also be given on questionnaires, including pilot study data if appropriate. An explanation of the development of items would be given and the role and composition of subscales discussed.

(Note: a lot of information is covered in this section and this might be represented in several overheads – e.g., one might deal with subject characteristics, there might be two or more giving examples of test items and there might be an additional slide reviewing the findings of a pilot study.)

5. A summary statement identifying independent and dependent variables and noting any extraneous factors. Notes would briefly review the procedure, reminding how independent variables were manipulated and explaining how outcome measures were taken.

6. Presentation of results. Key findings would be illustrated, first in the form of summary statistics, and then in terms of analysis. These would include means, t-values, F-ratios and correlation coefficients, for example. Probability values would also be shown. Notes would indicate how the statistics were derived and what tests were carried out and any significant effects highlighted.

7. More results. If additional analysis were carried out further to explore a finding, or you wish to highlight some unusual or worthy finding this should be presented next. Graphs of various types are useful here. Notes would explain why additional analysis was necessary (e.g., 'it was noted that mean scores for males in the sample were larger than previous reported norms'), and any figures would be discussed.

8. Hypotheses would be restated and upheld or rejected in light of the results. Notes would expand upon the relationship between the findings and the predicted outcomes. Explanation would then extend to re-considering the entire research issue in view of the study just outlined. The presentation at this point is likely to return to the kind of general discussion of issues introduced at the very beginning.

on their notes, and the presentation comprises a rather tedious reading aloud of this summary. This is not a particularly effective method of giving a presentation – it tends to be dull, it doesn't allow the audience to focus on key elements and it can also be intimidating for the speaker; with no other source of stimulation the audience's entire attention is focused on the oral presentation itself.

A far better solution is to make use of some form of visual aid: overheads, slides and computer-generated screen graphics are all ideal and most departments will happily make facilities available for students. The advantages of this approach are considerable:

1. Key points of a study can be put on an overhead or slide allowing you to emphasise to your audience the important elements of the study – for instance you might display the hypotheses being tested as you explain procedural matters, making it easier for your audience to appreciate why you carried out your study *this* way, as opposed to *that* way.
2. Complex information can be presented more effectively in this format than by verbal explanation – just imagine trying to explain the results of a multiple group comparison analysis verbally. A table or a graph projected onto a screen will describe at a glance what might take you several minutes to explain.

3. A series of overheads tends to impose its own structure on a presentation, covering, as they usually do, the logical sequence of activities which comprised the study (e.g., you will probably have, in order, overheads displaying the title of the study, examples of previous work, statement of hypotheses, procedural matters, results, etc.). They also serve as *aides mémoire*, reminders of what you need to talk about next, or which part of your notes to consult. Relying totally on notes, without this kind of external structure, can lead to confusion and loss of place, especially if the notes are extensive.

4. Using visual displays takes pressure off the presenter, especially useful for the nervous undergraduate who can panic quite freely in a corner while everyone's attention is focused on a projected image somewhere else.

Clearly there are advantages in using presentation aids of this type, but there are certain cautions which should be made. First, the temptation to cover your slides with everything you want to say should be avoided at all costs. The purpose of these aids is to present key points and illustrations – any more than this and it would be as easy to provide each audience member with a text version of your talk. Legibility is another issue – if you've never used overheads before it's important to find out how big writing or font sizes need to be so that an audience can read them. And thirdly, organisation is important. There is nothing guaranteed better to destroy a nervous presenter's confidence than to discover their slides are in the wrong order, or that one is missing.

Material in support of overheads has to be considered. Previously it has been suggested that a slide can act as an *aide mémoire*, triggering recall in the mind of the presenter and reminding them of what to say next. In fact, only skilled presenters and lecturers are likely to be able to do this well and, unless a talk is well-rehearsed, students are advised to use notes to accompany each overhead. Even experienced lecturers are often caught out by an overhead whose existence, never mind content, comes as a complete surprise to them, recognisable when a staff member is caught staring blankly at a screen, for some time.

Examples of test materials can also be made available to an audience, especially if a questionnaire has been custom-designed for a study. Even copies of standardised tests might be distributed if an audience comprises largely fellow students who might not be familiar with specialised instruments.

To conclude this section on presentations, it is worth noting that giving a presentation is a skilled activity, and therefore requires practice to develop. Few undergraduates are going to be superb at this task but, with a bit of organisation and a lot of preparation, presentations can be made competent and interesting.

7.10 Review

Any study, no matter how elaborate and irrespective of its contribution to the fount of human knowledge, will ultimately be judged on the written exposition of the background, design, conduct and findings of the research. This is true whether the report is based on an undergraduate project, represents a submission to a periodical editor or is a published article in an international journal. In every case, a reader, tutor or reviewer is looking for the same kind of thing – evidence that the study has been well carried out, the data competently analysed and the research issue fully explored. A judgement here can only be based on the written report or article and, while your own research might not necessarily set the world of academia alight, if you have followed all the guidelines in this chapter, you will at least guarantee yourself a fair and objective hearing. Box 7.16 is the concluding illustration in Chapter 7 and offers a summary of the main points a reviewer or tutor will be looking for in a written report. It will be in the interests of all readers to study this summary carefully!

It only remains to offer once again the advice that, if anyone is still unclear about any element of report writing, the flowchart at the beginning of this chapter should guide them to the appropriate section. We wish you luck.

Box 7.16 Some typical assessment criteria for project reports

Originality

To what extent is the choice of research area, and the general orientation of the study your own? Does the work show some originality in design or approach?

Initiative

Have you shown initiative in collecting data or in preparing test materials?

Introduction

How well have the research issues been identified and explained? Is the review of the literature relevant and thorough? Has the scope of the project been clearly presented? Are the hypotheses unambiguously stated, and is it clear how they relate to previous work?

Design

Is the design of the project appropriate for the research question? Have issues concerning sampling and control been addressed? Have independent and dependent variables been correctly identified? Has this section been expressed in the appropriate language of design?

Procedure

Is it possible to understand exactly what procedures were followed in collecting data? Are these procedures appropriate? Could the study be replicated on the information provided?

Results
> Are the results clearly presented? Is the analysis appropriate for the level of data? Does the analysis actually address the hypotheses or research questions under test?

Discussion
> Are the results discussed with reference to the issues raised in the introduction? Are the results discussed with reference to previous findings and relevant theory? Are any problems or limitations of the study fully understood and discussed?

References
> Are all references given in full? Are they presented in a standard format?

Presentation
> Is the project well presented? Is it free from spelling errors? Is it well written? Are arguments clearly and carefully presented?

(Note: the sections on initiative and originality, while relevant for any piece of research, are likely to be particular issues for undergraduate studies)

7.11 Recommended reading

Coolican, H. (1996). *Introduction to Research Methods and Statistics in Psychology.* London: Hodder & Stoughton.

Day, R.A. (1989). *How to Write and Publish a Scientific Paper,* 3rd edition. Cambridge: Cambridge University Press.

Howard, K., and Sharp. J.A. (1983). *The Management of a Student Research Project.* Aldershot: Gower.

Kantowitz, B.H., Roediger III, H.L., Elmes, D.G. (1994). *Experimental Psychology: Understanding Psychological Research.* 5th edition. St Paul, MN: West.

Sternberg, R.J. (1988). *The Psychologist's Companion: A Guide to Scientific Writing for Students and Researchers.* Cambridge: Cambridge University Press.

Index